THE EUROPEAN UNION AND NATIONAL MACROECONOMIC POLICY

Edited by James Forder and Anand Menon

London and New York

First published 1998
by Routledge
11 New Fetter Lane, London, EC4P 4EE

Simultaneously published in USA and Canada
by Routledge
29 West 35th Street, New York, NY 10001

Typeset in Baskerville by Routledge
Printed and bound in Great Britain by Creative Print and Design
(Wales), Ebbw Vale

British Library Cataloguing in Publication Data
A catalogue record for this book is available from the British Library

Library of Congress Cataloguing in Publication Data
Forder, James
The European Union and national macroeconomic policy / James Forder
& Anand Menon.
(State and the European Union series)
Includes bibliographical references and index.
1. European Union countries–Economic policy. I. Menon, Anand, 1965– .
II. Title. III. Series.
HC240.F587 1998
339.5'094–dc21   97-30746
                                                                      CIP

ISBN 0–415–14196–6 (hbk)
ISBN 0–415–14197–4 (pbk)

CONTENTS

ILLUSTRATIONS

FIGURES

TABLES

CONTRIBUTORS

Christopher Allsopp is Fellow and Tutor in Economics at New College, Oxford, and is a member of the Court of the Bank of England.

M. J. Artis is Professor of Economics at the European University Institute, Florence.

Andrea Boltho is Fellow and Tutor in Economics at Magdalen College, Oxford.

James Forder is Fellow and Tutor in Economics at Balliol College, Oxford.

Mary Gregory is Fellow and Tutor in Economics at St Hilda's College, Oxford.

Jeffrey Harrop is Lecturer in Economics in the Department of European Studies at the University of Bradford.

Anand Menon is University Lecturer in European Politics and Fellow of St Antony's College, Oxford.

Peter M. Oppenheimer is 'Student' (i.e. Tutor) in Economics at Christ Church College, Oxford.

Jacques Reland is Senior Lecturer at the London Guildhall University.

Ingeborg Schroeder is a researcher at the Stiftung Wissenschaft und Politik, Research Institute for International Affairs.

Elke Thiel is a Senior Research Associate at the Stiftung Wissenschaft und Politik, Research Institute for International Affairs, and Professor of European Politics, University of Bamburg.

Giacomo Vaciago is Professor of Economics at the Catholic University, Milan.

Daniel Weiserbs is Professor of Economics at Université Catholique de Louvain, Louvain-la-Neuve, Belgium.

PREFACE

This volume is based on a series of ESRC-funded research seminars entitled 'State Autonomy in the European Community', held in Oxford in the academic year 1993–4. The seminars examined the impact of EC action on the content of national policy and on the relationships between actors at the national level, with the aim of assessing the implications of EC policy for the member states and the extent to which their autonomy has been affected. The seminars, which were interdisciplinary, addressed developments in the following areas: industrial, financial and service sectors; social policy, environmental protection and consumer policy; macroeconomic policy and defence policy. The impact of EU membership on national administrative systems was also the subject of a seminar.

Neither the research seminar series nor this book would have been possible without the support of ESRC Award no. A 451 264 400 248.

ACKNOWLEDGEMENTS

We would like to acknowledge the efforts of David Hine and William Wallace, who made this project possible, and to express our thanks to two of the series editors, Hussein Kassim and David Hine, for their support, help and encouragement throughout the preparation of this volume. We are grateful to the Warden and Fellows of Nuffield College who allowed us to stage the seminar on which this volume is based in the College. Finally, we should like to thank all the participants at the seminar for making it a stimulating and successful event. Our greatest debts are to the contributors to this volume, for their patience in coping with the two editors, and to Jane Wyatt for her professionalism in editing the texts.

1

INTRODUCTION

James Forder and Anand Menon

The study of both national macroeconomic policy and the economics of the European Union have attracted great academic attention. The whole corpus of international economic theory might of course be applicable to Europe, and some aspects, such as the theory of optimal currency zones derived from Mundell (1961) and McKinnon (1963) are particularly relevant. It is also arguable that the policy coordination literature derived from Hamada (1976) has a particular application to Europe, but here there has perhaps been little policy progress and hence little study of it. In addition there are studies of trade flows and exchange rate stability such as El-Agraa (1990) for the former and Giavazzi and Giovannini (1989) and Haldane and Hall (1991) for the latter.

A neglected area, however, is the effect of European integration on national policy. Many economists' working assumptions are based on Giavazzi and Pagano's (1988) account of the possibility that joining the EMS, and thereby pegging to the deutschmark, improves the credibility of policy. But detailed accounts of how such an effect – if it exists – or any other effects have actually changed policy or policy making are harder to find. This book seeks to fill that gap.

It is the third in a series of volumes which seeks to examine the impact exerted by the European Union on the policies and policy-making processes of its member states. The earlier books – Kassim and Menon 1996; Howorth and Menon 1997 – found the whole area of the impact of the EC/EU on member states to be a surprisingly under-studied aspect of European integration. Where there are studies of this area, they tend to be extremely broad in scope and often somewhat abstract. There is thus a dearth of detailed, empirical investigations of the relationship between European integration and national policy in the member states. This is surprising, not only because of the importance of the effects of integration on the member states in the public debate – witness debates during the 1997 French legislative election campaign concerning the effects of the Maastricht convergence criteria on French economic performance – but also because, as Moravcsik (1993: 479) has argued, the fact that substantive policy adjustment results from EU action is one of the central aspects of the integration process.

The relative absence of such studies is all the more surprising when the policy sector in question is macroeconomic policy. There is a commonly held opinion that the impact of integration on the member states has been, and will continue to be, greater in this sphere than in any other. As the *Economist* put it in 1989: 'More than any other great issue the European Community has faced, economic and monetary union raises questions of national sovereignty – real and imagined . . . [it] calls for a transfer of national power to the Community that goes beyond anything the EEC has known' (*Economist*, 22 April 1989: 45).

The study of the impact of the EU on the member states is also closely related to a central theoretical debate which has exercised political scientists: are the institutions of integration simply tools of the nation states, as Moravcsik (1993, 1994) and Milward (1992) suggest – that is to say, are they mere reducers of transaction costs intended to promote the interests of those states in areas where collective action produces more benefits than the individual actions? Or do they, in certain circumstances, actually constrain states, imposing policy choices at variance with national preferences and limiting national freedom of manoeuvre?

The answer we receive may not be a clear or consistent one. That is to say, we ought to be sensitive to the fact that EU impact may vary not only between countries but also between sectors. The series aims, by means of a comparison of several different sectors (industrial, services, financial, defence, social, environmental, consumer and macroeconomic) based on studies of the four large EU member states (France, Germany, Italy and the United Kingdom) to determine the nature and scope of the impact of the EU across countries and policy sectors.

COMPETING PRESSURES ON STATE AUTONOMY

In this series, we have deliberately avoided utilising the notion of 'sovereignty' as a guide. This is because sovereignty, whilst an important politico-legal notion, fails to capture the practical ability of the state to achieve its objectives. It is in certain respects too broad, and in others too narrow a concept for our purposes. Too broad, first, because apparent losses of sovereignty may not have an impact on policy. Under the terms of the Treaty of Rome, for instance, the European Commission enjoyed wide powers over competition policy. But the powers were not fully employed for many years. On the other hand, even in the absence of a surrender of sovereignty, the ability of national governments to pursue policies of their own choosing can be severely circumscribed – as Howarth and Menon (1997) show to be the case with defence policy.

The conceptual tool we have used to structure our investigations has been that of 'autonomy', but this requires careful handling. According to Nordlinger (1981: 19), the most thorough examination of the term autonomy is the ability of the state to translate its preferences into authoritative actions. In other words, the impact of the EU on state autonomy can be ascertained by examining the extent to which EU action has affected this ability of the state to formulate and implement policies based on its preferences.

Nordlinger defines autonomy simply in relation to societal pressures on the state. These can affect policy in numerous ways, either through more – or less – institutionalised forms of lobbying behaviour or, less frequently, through the ballot box. Hence, farmers in France, backbench Conservative MPs in Britain and public opinion in all countries (especially immediately prior to elections or in referenda) have played a role in shaping and constraining national policy.

Nordlinger's conception of autonomy is based on a simplification of the notion of state preferences in that he assumes that these can, for analytical purposes, and whatever the differences of opinion that exist within the state machinery, be taken as coherent. However, it is worth noting the possibility that divisions can appear and persist within the state machinery itself. On the one hand, this clearly affects the freedom of manoeuvre of the national executive concerned – as increasingly occurs, for instance, when politicians come into conflict with independent central bankers. Moreover, a state which is internally divided is more susceptible to external influence, particularly if actors outside the state machinery can ally themselves with elements of the bureaucracy or political class.

More importantly, Nordlinger's account of autonomy is inadequate, since it disregards any potential constraint exerted by international pressures in general, and most importantly in this case, by the EU.[1] It is thus necessary to expand the concept of autonomy in order to encompass both internal and external pressures. Since the 1960s, scholars, following the seminal work of Cooper (1968) have pointed to the fact that international economic interdependence constrains national autonomy, especially as far as macroeconomic policy is concerned. More recently, theorists of the phenomenon that has come to be known as globalisation have reasserted, and in some cases strengthened, these claims. Thus Garrett and Lange (1991) posited that the workings of the international economic system preclude national autonomy over fiscal and monetary policy. Ohmae (1994) goes rather further, suggesting that the creation of a truly global economy has entailed the undermining of the autonomy of the state as free trade, the rise of transnational corporations and increasing flows of capital across the globe have liberated firms, allowing them to escape from the confines of the territorial state and relocate to wherever conditions suit them best. As a result, monetary and fiscal policies are not defined according to the ideological or any other preferences of national political authorities, but rather in an effort to attract such footloose firms.

In itself this change of circumstance has brought a reorientation of the way in which policy is made. Consequently one side-effect of globalisation is the increased negotiating power enjoyed by foreign firms in obtaining various kinds of concession as a condition of investment in a country. The other side of this coin is that policy actors who previously concentrated their efforts at the national level may well begin to transfer their activities (and their business) outside the home state. One consequence of this, as Crouch and Menon (1997) have claimed, is that globalisation will undermine the position of organised labour, reducing its influence at the national level. Milner and Keohane (1996: 3) put the point forcibly: 'we can no longer understand politics within countries – what we still conventionally call "domestic" politics – without comprehending the nature of the linkages between national economies and the world economy and the changes in such linkages'.

The pressure with which we are primarily concerned is that from the European Union. There are of course a variety of ways in which EU action might influence the autonomy of the state. Certain kinds of policy are determined at the European level and cannot be evaded. This would obviously be the position of monetary policy in a full monetary union. Another possibility is that EU action may alter established national patterns of policy making, which in turn affect state autonomy by preventing the formulation or implementation of certain policies. Many claim, for example, that independent central banks (in many cases granted this independence as a result of a desire to fulfil the Maastricht criteria) will limit the policy options of Governments. Another indirect form of EU impact concerns cases where activity by the EU in one policy sector affects national policy in another. As other volumes in this series have shown, the Maastricht convergence criteria have had an effect on many other policy sectors by restricting public spending.

THE EUROPEAN UNION, MACROECONOMIC POLICY AND THE STATE

Multifarious pressures, therefore, have the potential to affect state autonomy. The existence of these pressures points to two factors of direct concern in the analysis of EU impact. First, the simple fact that national policies appear to be shifting in the direction of policy at the European level does not imply proof that the EU has brought about such shifts. In some cases, other pressures provide more convincing explanations of national policy and policy change. Hence one advantage of the use of autonomy as opposed to the concept of sovereignty is that it forces us to examine the practical impact of EU measures as opposed to their implications for legal sovereignty.

Second, the domestic and international constraints facing the state raise possibilities for the EU to enhance national autonomy. This is potentially the case in several respects. For one thing, it may be that collective action within the EU, for instance by means of the creation of a single currency, will allow the European states better to resist the pressures imposed by the international economy in general. It may, for example, benefit the European states by diminishing the special advantages and status conferred on the United States by the dollar as the international reserve currency. Internally, many observers have pointed to the fact that integration can reduce pressures on the state from societal interests. Moravcsik (1994) is prominent amongst such writers, claiming that integration serves as a way for national executives to 'internationalise' domestic policy issues and hence limit the constraints imposed by other domestic actors. We should therefore be prepared to discover a complex reality of EU impact varying between states, between sectors and between types of impact: direct and indirect, enhancing autonomy or reducing it.

A related possibility is that the EU may be found to facilitate achieving the benefits of international policy coordination as they have been analysed by economists, following the general spirit, although not the details, and much less the conclusions, of Hamada (1976). That analysis pointed to there being benefits (in certain circumstances) of collective action by nations. In the early days of this kind of analysis, high on the list of likely benefits was surer and quicker ends to worldwide recession through collective action. Since then a bewildering array of other possibilities has been considered, a sample of which is explained in Forder's chapter. Although at the worldwide level, little explicit policy coordination has been attempted, it was at one time very much on the European agenda. Its aspiration of promoting such policy at least in Europe is one of the aspects of the creation of the EMS that leads Oppenheimer in this volume to approve of its common sense, sandwiched between the Werner and Delors Reports. The same themes, although striking a different note for a later plan, are the subject of Allsopp's contribution.

These considerations already point to another aspect of the notion of 'autonomy'. It is not the implication of Hamada or those following him that 'autonomy' should be sacrificed, although this would, in principal, be one of the ways of achieving the benefits of coordination. What Hamada considers is the possibility of mutual gain from a group of countries agreeing to act in a coordinated way. There is no implication that they should give up the power to act differently, only that if they choose to act together, there are – strictly economic – benefits to be had.

STRUCTURE OF THE BOOK

This book is divided into three sections. In the first, four chapters consider the broadest issues. Harrop gives a picture of EU involvement with macroeconomic policy and its relationship to the policies pursued at national level, charting the increasingly wide and ambitious scope of EU macroeconomic initiatives. One of the editors offers an account of how economists have considered issues of state autonomy in international economics. Oppenheimer considers the reasons for which states have chosen to join the exchange rate mechanism and hence potentially sacrifice a degree of autonomy. Gregory and Weiserbs put all this analysis into the context of changing national strategies since the 1950s, painting a historical picture of the changing relationships between policy objectives at the national and European levels.

In the second section, policy in the four larger member states – France, Germany, Italy, United Kingdom is considered. Whilst Reland gives a rich political economy analysis of the various rationales behind French macroeconomic policy since the mid 1980s, both Vaciago and Artis provide more technical accounts of the pressures impinging on the autonomy of the Italian and British states respectively. In contrast, Thiel and Schroeder place German monetary policy within the context of European monetary arrangements, illustrating how the impact of these structures on German autonomy differed from that on Germany's partners. Taken together, whilst representing different kinds of approach to the question of state autonomy, these country studies provide a firm basis for a comparative investigation of EU impact across the member states.

The third and final section looks at specific issues of central importance to macroeconomic policy in Europe. Both Boltho and Allsopp consider the merits or otherwise of the convergence criteria set for monetary union and the possible future effects of these criteria on the member states, though from different perspectives. Whilst Boltho investigates the necessity of unemployment levels to be taken into consideration in order to arrive at 'real' convergence, Allsopp concentrates on the question of whether fiscal policy has been accorded adequate attention (and in the right way) by the architects of the institutional structures that will govern EMU. Whilst presenting a useful critique of current EU policies, these chapters also lay the basis for educated hypotheses concerning the future impact of the EU on national policy.

Clearly, this volume does not pretend to provide definite answers to the question of the degree of impact exerted by the EU on national policy. What it does seek to do, however, is to give a broad sense of the nature and variety of that impact. This it does by adopting an interdisciplinary approach to the question. Most of the contributors to the volume are economists. They have endeavoured, however, to produce chapters that are easily accessible to non-economists. It is only through such interdisciplinary work that complex questions spanning the boundary between politics and economics – such as those posed in these pages – can satisfactorily be addressed.

NOTES

1   It should be noted that certain of those writers who have attempted to claim that integration strengthens the state have approached this question simply from the perspective of domestic constraints (see notably Milward 1992 and Moravcsik 1994). This clearly represents incomplete analysis, as the constraints imposed by the EU itself are hence completely ignored.

BIBLIOGRAPHY

Cooper, R. N. (1968) *The Economics of Interdependence: Economic Policy in the Atlantic Community*, New York: Council on Foreign Relations/McGraw-Hill.

Crouch, C. and Menon, A. (1997) 'Organised interests and the state', in M. Rhodes, P. Heywood and V. Wright (eds) *Developments in West European Politics*, London: Macmillan.

El-Agraa, A. M. (1990) *Economics of the European Community*, London: Philip Allen.

Garrett, G. and Lange, P. (1991) 'Political responses to interdependence: what's "left" for the left?', *International Organisation*, 45, 4, autumn, 539–64.

Giavazzi, F. and Giovannini, A. (1989) *Limiting Exchange Rate Flexibility: The European Monetary System*, Cambridge MA: MIT Press.

Giavazzi, F. and Pagano, M. (1988) 'The advantages of tying one's hands: EMS discipline and central bank credibility', *European Economic Review*, 32: 1055–82.

Haldane, A. G. and Hall, S. G. (1991) 'Sterling's relationship with the dollar and the deutschmark, 1976–89', *Economic Journal*, 10: 436–43.

Hamada, K. (1976) 'A strategic analysis of monetary interdependence', *Journal of Political Economy*, 84: 677–700.

Howorth, J. and Menon, A. (1997) *The European Union and National Defence Policy*, London: Routledge.

Kassim, H. and Menon, A. (1996) *The European Union and National Industrial Policy*, London: Routledge.

McKinnon, R. (1963) 'Optimum currency areas', *American Economic Review*, 53: 717–25.

Milner, H. and Keohane, R. (1996) 'Internationalisation and domestic politics: an introduction', in R. Keohane and H. Milner (eds) *Internationalisation and Domestic Politics*, Cambridge: Cambridge University Press.

Milward, A. (1992) *The European Rescue of the Nation State*, London: Routledge.

Moravcsik, A. (1994) *How the European Community Strengthens the State: Domestic Politics and International Cooperation*, Boston MA: Harvard University Center for European Studies Working Paper, Series 52.

——(1993) 'Preferences and power in the European Community: a liberal intergovernmentalist approach', *Journal of Common Market Studies*, 33: 4 December.

Mundell, R. A. (1961) 'A theory of optimum currency areas', *American Economic Review*, 51: 657–65.

Nordlinger, E. (1981) *On the Autonomy of the Democratic State*, Cambridge MA: Harvard University Press.

Ohmae, K. (1994) *The Borderless World: Power and Strategy in the Interlinked Economy*, London: Harper Collins.

Part I

BROAD ISSUES

2

THE EU AND NATIONAL MACROECONOMIC POLICY†

An empirical overview

Jeffrey Harrop

INTRODUCTION

Macroeconomic policy, the legacy of Keynes, is concerned with the use of a range of policy instruments, such as fiscal, monetary and exchange rate policies. These impact upon output, unemployment, inflation and the balance of payments. As the process of integration evolves, countries are becoming increasingly interdependent and particularly dependent upon the German economy. To maintain successful macroeconomic outcomes, EC countries have consulted together and established policy coordination. They are moving towards more centralised decision-making competence which can produce overall macroeconomic outcomes superior to those achievable when each country conducts its own separate policy. However, this has involved modifying wholly nationally-determined preferences and moving closer to German preferences; it also assumes that countries are affected in the same way by major external changes and this is not always the case, as shown by German unification.

Before examining trade, budgetary and monetary policies, three preliminary points are worth making. The first is to distinguish between fundamental changes in the EU which are constraining national policy makers and those artificially contrived but represented as EU constraints by policy makers. In Italy in recent years, governments have lacked stability and have responded by claiming that unpopular macroeconomic policies have been imposed by the EU. Since Italy has taken quite a federalist position, it has used the EU to underpin its own

† For much of the chapter the term EC is used when speaking of the past and the term EU refers to the post-Maastricht situation. Reference to a Union reflects the progress from microeconomic to macroeconomic policy making. However, economic union is not an end in itself, but a vehicle for the achievement of political union.

legitimacy, whereas in reality the EU may not have been so constraining, leaving governments scope for independent action.

Second, EU policies, though affecting all members, do not do so equally. For example, smaller economies – Benelux and Ireland – clearly enjoy less autonomy than the larger member states. For example, Germany has the most powerful role, which has been further enhanced through the way it has dominated the ERM. Unfortunately, from the viewpoint of the real economy, this has resulted in deflationary policies and rising unemployment. Partly because of this, the UK has adopted a more independent stance not just in its monetary policy, but also in relation to steering inward investment towards it, especially from Japan.

Third, the loss of policy autonomy varies not just between countries but also between policy areas. This reflects the evolution of policies, with the greatest loss in the most established spheres, such as trade. In the future there will be a significant loss of monetary and exchange rate policy when the Maastricht Treaty provisions are finally realised. This will leave significant national control only for fiscal and budgetary matters, though even here some marginal erosion of national control will continue to occur.

THE MARKET

Trade

Integration was concerned first and foremost with removing barriers to trade between member states: this was the customs union phase. The EC, unlike EFTA, opted for a common external tariff (CET) to cover both industrial and agricultural trade. In trade policy, therefore, there has been almost a complete loss of national autonomy over trade with other member states, and also a significant loss of independent action in relation to trade with the outside world. Within the EU there has been a tremendous amount of trade creation, and much of the new trade has been intra- rather than inter-industry. Hence, generally, whole industries have not been wiped out and firms have been able to specialise in parts of industries. The growth of free trade within the EU is recognised to be highly desirable in stimulating economic growth, even by those who have reservations about worldwide free trade (Goldsmith 1995).

Whilst the main focus of this section is on internal free trade, it is worthwhile to begin by looking at the common trade policy. This has inevitably resulted in some sacrifice in national freedom of action for member states (Hine 1985: 74). There were wide differences in national protection before the EC was formed, and after the imposition of the CET the higher level of protectionism practised in France and Italy had to be brought down towards the more liberal approach of Germany and the Netherlands. Within the EU the effects of national protectionist lobbies have been significantly diluted. The common commercial policy of the EU has been necessary to prevent national subsidies adversely affecting the competitive position of other countries. The CET has also strengthened the EU's bargaining power and has not created significant trade diversion, apart from that in agricultural products, as a result of various tariff-cutting rounds in GATT. In GATT (now renamed the World Trade Organisation) the Commission negotiates instead of the member states, though the latter decide policy through their membership of the Council of Ministers.

The low level of the CET now prevailing conceals protectionist measures to defend European industry against unfair practices. EU trade agreements have increasingly taken over from national agreements, though there are some areas where member states were for many years loath to relinquish all their remaining powers, as in relation to the quantitative control by the Italian car industry on imports from Japan. However, there is now a common EU Voluntary Export Restraint (VER) limiting Japanese exports of cars into the EU up to 1999 (to 1.23 million). There have been understandings between several member states and Japan relating to products such as cars, televisions and VCRs. The French in particular favour relatively extensive use of VERs, and their pressure has resulted in more EU-wide VERs being introduced. This common position has been consolidated further since the creation of the Single Market. The EU has considered it necessary to safeguard particular industries against outside competition to prevent serious injury to domestic producers, such as that caused through dumping. There has been concern not just about unemployment in sunset industries but also about offering infant industry protection to some sunrise industries. At national level, the main measures available to member states are to take their own action against counterfeit goods and to undertake surveillance of damaging imports, though it is mainly at the EU level where action is taken through the application of anti-dumping duties, countervailing duties (against subsidised imported goods) and safeguard measures (through quantitative restrictions such as VERs).

One consequence of the expansion of trade is that EU economies have become far more open to outside influences and much more interdependent. For instance, EU exports and imports as a percentage of GDP were 28.7 per cent and 27.9 per cent respectively in 1990. For the smaller economies, trade is even more significant. Belgian exports represented 75.3 per cent of GDP and imports 73.1 per cent (Neilsen *et al.* 1991: 225); its intra-EU trade in 1990 for exports was 63.1 per cent and for imports 59.5 per cent. The consequence of this growing interdependence is that macroeconomic policy is less effective since expansionist measures to reduce unemployment spill over to other economies. Furthermore, countries cannot resort to overt national protectionism and common action has to be taken at the EU level against outsiders. How protectionist this is depends upon whether there are sufficient countries of a like mind, and on the power the EU enjoys in its trading policy relative to the rest of the world. Whilst in the Uruguay round France sought to constrain the more liberal role of Leon Brittan in bargaining with outsiders such as the US, at the end of the day it was recognised that steps to further free trade would be beneficial internationally.

The phase of negative integration – removing barriers to trade between member states – was easier to agree on initially than more positive policies. This is partly why it was revived again as part of the Single Market Programme after 1985. Even the UK could accept this, since it assumed the EU was embracing its own national liberal economic policies and applying them throughout the market: this offered benefits in sectors where the UK enjoyed a comparative advantage, especially in the service sector. Building from microeconomic foundations, major macroeconomic benefits were predicted from the SEM (Cecchini 1988). Unfortunately the early 1990s saw a return to recession and higher unemployment, which in turn led to the need for the EU to devise new unemployment initiatives and to take further measures to improve competitiveness (Commission of the EC 1994). This is partly because, within the Single Market, national measures to assist particular sectors are more and more constrained by EU competition policy, and preferential national procurement policies are also outlawed under the Single Market Programme.

The removal of barriers to trade, particularly quotas and tariffs, in the context of a customs union, was followed by the emphasis on removing remaining non-tariff barriers (NTBs) as part of the Single Market Programme. Whenever national controls are removed as part of EU developments, there is invariably a search for and a growth in alternative measures by member states. These are exemplified in particular by extensive national aids both to industry and agriculture. The latter was also assisted by the use of Monetary Compensatory Amounts to insulate farming from the consequences of exchange rate changes. The EU has been permanently on the alert to root out such practices, since its main purpose is to ensure fair trade. As a common market it has also gone further than this, being characterised by free movement not just of goods and services, but also of labour and capital. Labour migration is important in redirecting unemployed workers to areas of labour shortage in expanding regions, providing crucial adjustment. However, given the great economic imbalance with the outside world, most of the migration has consisted of extra-EU immigration rather than intra-EU migration. Ultimately, if the EU is to evolve towards the model of the USA and national macroeconomic policy instruments are to be lost, then it will be necessary to try to create the much greater degree of labour mobility which is characteristic of the American labour market.

Taxation in the Single Market

In relation to taxation, the EU has not forwarded proposals to harmonise direct taxes on labour income. These will remain under national control and continue to be a major instrument of national fiscal policy. The EU has also made only limited progress on company taxation; for example, by removing double taxation on companies and reducing the range of corporation taxes. These are needed to prevent capital movements and companies' product prices from being too distorted. The greatest impact of the EU has been on indirect taxation.

14

The EU has been concerned not just with free competition but with fair competition. This has necessitated the harmonisation of policies in many fields, including indirect taxation. Before the Community was formed, countries had different systems of indirect taxation. It was argued that indirect taxes constituted a non-tariff barrier. Moreover, where countries used different sales taxes, these distorted competition and adversely affected trade. Thus the Treaty of Rome (Article 99) specified in particular that indirect taxes should be harmonised and approximated. Progress has been greater on harmonisation of the indirect tax structure than on approximation of tax rates (Hitiris 1988: 106).

VAT

The fifteen EU countries vary in their dependence on different types of taxes. The UK traditionally used to rely more on direct taxes because of the greater ease of collection (through PAYE) compared to several continental countries which found direct taxes being avoided and evaded more easily than sales taxes. However, the EC has moved all member states on to using the French system of VAT. An important motivation for this was that it reduced the distorting effect on production, since under VAT companies had no incentive to seek to avoid tax through vertical integration. Nevertheless, the Richardson Committee had concluded that retention of the British system of purchase tax would be preferable, but this was not permitted under the terms of the Treaty of Rome.

The share of VAT in total government receipts still varies widely. Indirect taxes were 11.3 per cent of EC GDP in 1987. This varied from 9.6 per cent in Italy and 10 per cent in Spain to 17.6 per cent in Denmark and 18.3 per cent in Greece. The weight of both indirect and direct taxation is heaviest in Denmark. In other countries the higher level of indirect taxation tends to compensate for relatively low direct taxes on income and profits. For example, direct taxes as a percentage of GDP range from 6.4 per cent in Greece and 6.9 per cent in Portugal to 28.4 per cent in Denmark.

The rates of VAT have varied quite widely, but the Single Market led to the introduction, from 1 January 1993, of a minimum rate of 15 per cent (and subsequently proposals for a maximum rate). Germany moved up to the minimum rate and France moved down towards it. Also, those countries operating three different rates of VAT which included an increased rate on so-called 'luxury goods' – Belgium, Greece, Spain, Portugal, France and Italy – agreed to conform to the Cockfield two-band system. The lower rate is not to be below 5 per cent, though zero rating may be retained for a transitional period.

Excise duties

These are important sources of government revenue since they are raised on products with a fairly inelastic demand. They constitute a significant proportion of the price of three main product groups: oils, tobacco and alcoholic drinks.

The greatest harmonisation has been on cigarettes, but for other products there has been wide variation on levels of excise duties. For example, excise duties on beer, wine and spirits have been high in Denmark, Ireland and the UK. Yet wine has had no excise duty levied on it in Spain, Portugal, Greece and Italy. The Court of Justice has ruled against member states whose excises are seen to discriminate against imports. Also, the EC is seeking some convergence of excise duties, but has made less progress than with VAT. Although many minor excise duties have been abolished on products such as tea, coffee and salt, there has been more resistance, justified in terms of national policies on health, to greater harmonisation of the major excise duties.

As part of the Single Market measures from 1 January 1993, the EU adopted minimum excise duties. One example of this relates to mineral oils and these have been set (per 1000 litres) for leaded petrol at ECU 337, unleaded petrol ECU 287, road diesel oil ECU 245, heavy fuel oil ECU 245 and zero for heating oil. Furthermore, the aim of these excise duties is to move to target convergence over time.

To conclude, the Market has focused on harmonising and approximating taxes to deal with the most mobile elements, in particular relating to goods.

THE ROLE OF THE BUDGET IN THE EUROPEAN COMMUNITY

Since 1970 the Community has been given its own resources, including customs duties and agricultural levies. In addition, the EC receives a significant proportion of VAT receipts plus a GNP-based contribution. The latter covers the difference between EU spending and revenue raised from other sources. Both VAT and the GNP-based component may be considered as national components. The composition of revenue sources in 1993 was customs duties 20 per cent, agricultural and sugar levies 3.4 per cent, VAT 54.5 per cent and the GNP-based contribution 21.4 per cent (plus a miscellaneous 0.7 per cent). The budget constituted 1.20 per cent of EU GNP in 1993.

The regressiveness of the revenue side of the budget, which led to acrimony over Britain's contribution, has been largely alleviated by giving back to the UK two-thirds of the difference between its VAT contribution and the EC's budgetary expenditure in the UK. This has been reconfirmed since the Edinburgh Agreement in December 1992, where it was decided also to reduce the share of VAT in the budget to 34.38 per cent and raise the GNP share to 47.90 per cent by the late 1990s. This will be achieved as the maximum rate on the harmonised VAT base is lowered in equal steps from 1.4 per cent down to 1 per cent by 1999.

In relation to assigning taxes to different levels of government, one finds that customs duties are nearly always the exclusive competence of the federal level, as in the EU. At the other end of the spectrum, wealth and property taxes tend to be applied exclusively at the lower state or provincial level (Commission of the EC 1993a: 184). Other taxes are split between the different levels. In relation to the EU being assigned new taxes in the future, these could comprise a tax on central bank profits and a new environmental tax on pollution to curb the emission of carbon dioxide.

National budgetary expenditure

Before examining budgetary expenditure at the level of the EU it is necessary to provide some coverage of national budgets. This will show the role of national budgets, the extent to which such expenditure is constrained by EU policy, and finally will provide a measure of comparison with the Community budget itself.

There has been an inexorable growth of public expenditure in EU member states to provide more public or social collective goods (for example, defence, law and order) and to stop 'free riders'. Politicians, driven by short-term electoral pressures, tend to reinforce increased governmental spending. In addition, following the oil price shock in 1973, budget deficits increased to tackle rising unemployment. Macroeconomic stabilisation policy has been applied by governments to reduce deviations of actual output from full employment output. This has been done by influencing variables such as consumption and private investment by adjusting taxes and in particular by altering government spending. However, the effectiveness of stabilisation is limited by lags in obtaining and interpreting statistical data, lags before action is taken and lags before policy takes effect. Although the second oil price shock at the end of the 1970s created further macroeconomic problems, EC policy was better coordinated.

In conformity with the requirements of the Council's convergence decision (February 1974), the Commission has examined the economic situation of the Community and especially the budgetary policies of the member states. During the 1980s the rate of growth of governmental expenditure decreased, with some improvement in the budgetary situation. This has led to a growing consensus on basic budgetary principles. These are that there should be non-monetary financing of public deficits. The result would be that governments would have no automatic access to central bank financing. There would also be no compulsion on commercial banks to invest in government securities. But by December 1990 much monetary financing still occurred in Belgium, Greece, Spain, Italy, Ireland and Portugal. However, such facilities were being curtailed in Belgium, Spain and Portugal (Commission of the EC 1990: 173). It is no coincidence that excessive budgetary deficits have tended to exist in most of these countries.

EU member states have come to recognise, somewhat belatedly, the need to constrain the growth of public expenditure since too much concern with equity through the redistribution of income conflicts at the margin with wealth creation; government spending may also tend to crowd out the private sector. Furthermore, increasing taxes and social security contributions add to inflationary wage pressure, reducing business profits and investment. It has been decided that excessive budgetary debts of any member state will not be bailed out by the EU. The aim is to ensure that budgetary expenditure rises more slowly than GNP. Countries are being forced to take steps to tackle their debt by raising tax revenue and/or reducing budgetary expenditure. This is leading to painful consequences since the main brunt is borne by public expenditure cutbacks, yet in many instances demographic factors such as an ageing population are dictating the need for higher expenditure on sectors such as healthcare. Hence there is a growing recognition that some services may merit greater private provision.

The main reason for pursuing greater prudence and budgetary discipline is to fulfil the new Maastricht budgetary limits. The main changes (compared with the 1974 Council decision) were that in embarking on stage 1 of EMU from 1 July 1990 there would be a focus not only on convergence of economic policies but also of economic performance. Member states are engaged in coordination of policies in the framework of multilateral surveillance, with greater emphasis on ex-ante surveillance (Wildavsky and Zapico-Goñi 1993). Countries have to submit their convergence programmes to the Ecofin Council.

During stage 2 of EMU there is to be further multilateral surveillance and member states are obliged to avoid excessive budgetary deficits. To pass to stage 3 of EMU, various criteria have to be met, including binding measures to avoid excessive budgetary deficits. The first condition to be met is that the ratio of planned or actual government deficit to GDP is not to exceed 3 per cent, though the Commission may be tolerant provided the ratio has declined and is close to this, or alternatively if it is just over 3 per cent, but this is exceptional and temporary. The second condition is that the ratio of government debt to GDP is not to exceed 60 per cent, though again the Commission may be tolerant provided that the ratio is dropping sufficiently and approaching the 60 per cent limit at a satisfactory pace (Wildavsky and Zapico-Goñi 1993:74). The Commission reports on the budgetary situation, and after the Monetary Committee has given a view, if an excessive deficit is considered to exist, the Commission addresses an opinion to the Council.

In 1992 there were only four EC countries (Denmark, France, Ireland and Luxembourg) which had a budgetary deficit below 3 per cent, though Germany and the Netherlands could be considered borderline cases. Also, in 1992 only five member states (Germany, Spain, France, Luxembourg and the UK) had a gross debt-to-GDP ratio less than 60 per cent. The growing recession and high unemployment have worsened the budgetary situation and hence, on a strict interpretation, only France and Luxembourg were achieving the two criteria. Therefore much hinges on economic recovery and the continued commitment of member states to accepting a further tightening of their national budgetary situation. For example, the UK, despite its medium-term financial strategy committing it to balancing the budget, has generally run a budget deficit. The latter has on occasion necessitated significant and unpopular tax increases. Whilst the Maastricht budgetary conditions do not impose automatic national expenditure cutbacks, with some leniency in times of slump, they do narrow even further the room for national manoeuvre. They represent a further move away from Keynesian contra-cyclical stabilisation policies. Nevertheless, in terms of budgetary policy most of this is still to be conducted nationally rather than at the level of the Community.

Community budgetary expenditure

The EU budget has two distinctive features. The first is that it is very small, currently just over 1 per cent of Community GDP, compared with an average of around 50 per cent of GDP for national spending. EU budgetary expenditure is similar to that of the UK education budget or German spending on the eastern Länder, and less than 10 per cent of what the US spends on defence. Although EU fiscal federalism is not a precondition for EMU since, for example, common currencies were created without fiscal federalism in both the USA and Canada, nevertheless an enhanced budget would greatly facilitate EMU (Eichengreen 1992: 152).

The second feature of the community budget is that it is an accounting budget, and according to the Treaty, revenue has to balance expenditure. In contrast, national budgets have been functional, based on automatic stabilisers, and unbalanced. Following the legacy of the Keynesian revolution, there have often been budgetary deficits as government expenditure exceeded the tax intake, increasing demand to reduce unemployment. In contrast, the EU cannot run budget deficits in times of slump to stabilise the EU economy. Indeed, such a role could engender conflict between member states, as some, such as Germany, have traditionally been more concerned about inflation and balanced budgets. The Community budget does not play a stabilisation role and lacks flexibility as a result of its multi-annual programming. If anything, it could be said to be pro-cyclical since its spending ceiling is expressed as a percentage of Community GDP (Commission of the EC 1993a: 23). Clearly, some additional measure of Community stabilisation would be helpful. Italianer and Van Heukelen (1993) proposed a reserve to operate outside the general budget which would be transferred in the form of an outright grant to economies suffering an exogenous shock which raised their unemployment rate significantly above the EC average. It would probably account for about 0.22 per cent of EU GDP.

However, one should remember that the EU does undertake loans, especially via the European Investment Bank; moreover, the New Community Instrument (Ortoli Facility), created in 1973, was conceived of as an anticyclical weapon mainly to stimulate investment. Furthermore, the EU also offers conditional loans to member states with balance of payments difficulties, though this function will disappear in stage 3 of EMU in a currency union. In addition, the EIB has been given the power to create the European Investment Fund, initially of ECU 2 billion, to boost investment. This will be injected mainly into trans-European networks (TENs) and small- and medium-sized enterprises (SMEs), including loan guarantees and also through equity participation.

The degree to which the EU budget can grow in the future depends upon a variety of circumstances and issues. These include the extent to which member states are prepared to see some switch of spending upwards to the Community level. For example, unlike other federations which are responsible for defence, the EC, having rejected a European defence community in 1954, has had no defence component. Such a component, however, would generate further economies of scale, with common procurement policies providing an additional stimulus to high-tech EU industries.

The EU assigns most of its expenditure to areas other than those – social welfare and defence – central to federal political systems. EU budgetary expenditure has revolved around agriculture. If the EU is fully to reflect European citizenship, one could foresee it taking on additional welfare tasks.

In 1977 the MacDougall Report recommended that the EC budget increase to a minimum of 2–2.5 per cent of GDP and, for successful monetary union, to be raised to 5–7 per cent of EC GDP. Whilst the budget could evolve in this way under pressure for common defence and social responsibilities, there are also competing elements at work restricting the growth of a central EU budget. These include a desire to decentralise and operate subsidiarity as enshrined in the Maastricht Treaty. There is also worry about greater waste and lack of democratic accountability in a centralised budget. Moreover, many member states are questioning the role even of the state (let alone the EU) in providing public goods and particularly merit goods. Privatisation is reining back the public sector and has spread from Britain to other member states on the grounds of both microeconomic efficiency and macroeconomic benefits (reducing government borrowing by selling off loss-making state activities and turning round their economic performance).

An influential report by an independent group of economists believes that a small budget of around 2 per cent of Community GDP could be sufficient to sustain an effective EMU (Commission of the EC 1993a). An increase in the budget to this level is likely to occur where there are common benefits to be reaped by an EU level of provision. For example, the EU role in R&D activities was 3.3 per cent of the budget in 1993 and has potential to grow further. Similarly, the EU provides external aid to the rest of the world (which reached 4.6 per cent of EU budgetary expenditure in 1993). In addition, one also needs to add ECU 1.5 billion provided by the European Development Fund (which is kept outside the general budget because of its different financing). If the EU were given greater power in external relations, this would enable countries to purchase from the cheapest EU supplier, making the value of the aid go further. EU aid to less developed countries (LDCs) in 1993 was 0.48 per cent of GDP compared with the UN norm of 0.7 per cent of donors' GDP. National aid by the member states is far in excess of that given by the EU, especially to LDCs, though the EU does handle about a third of the aid given to eastern Europe. Some would like to see an enhanced development effort by the EU for eastern Europe along the lines of the Marshall Plan and on the same scale.

EU budgetary expenditure could also rise with further EU enlargement. The inclusion of EFTA countries such as Sweden, Finland and Austria from 1 January 1995 has added significantly to EU revenue. Future enlargement to embrace eastern European countries will create major pressures on budgetary expenditure. For example, enlargement to include eastern Europe would require additional expenditure mainly to finance the large agricultural sectors there and peripheral backward regions. The Visegrad 4 plus the Balkan and Baltic Republics would require an additional 0.85 per cent of EU GDP by 1999. If the former republics of the USSR were included it would rise by a further 1.3 per cent of EU GDP – an amount similar to the total budget for the EC(12) in 1993 (Commission of the EC 1993a: 114).

Redistribution through the budget

The main elements of redistribution have occurred through spending on regional and social policies, and through the more recently established Cohesion Fund which redistributes a relatively small amount of funding to countries with less than 90 per cent of the EU average income per capita. The Cohesion Fund is not unconditional, but is dependent on poorer member states pursuing a programme of economic convergence to prepare them for EMU, thus providing another means for the EU to influence macroeconomic policies.

However, it is the European Agricultural Guidance and Guarantee Fund (EAGGF) which has tended to dominate budgetary expenditure. Since this has been concerned mainly with price guarantee rather than agricultural restructuring, it has meant larger producers have tended to benefit most. A more selective system of targeted direct income transfers would provide a more suitable approach to income redistribution. Since the effect of the Single Market is likely to exacerbate regional inequalities as competition leads to the closure of less efficient firms, the EU has recognised the need for regional expenditure to rise. Furthermore, EMU prevents lower exchange rates making such firms competitive.

The unemployment rate in the EU is higher than that of either Japan or the USA. Despite the creation of new jobs, with over nine million created between 1985 and 1991, unemployment fell by only three million (Commission of the EC 1993b: 17). Many of the new workers who came into employment, such as married women, returned from households rather than unemployment registers. In depressed and more peripheral regions, job opportunities were lower and regional unemployment consequently higher. A Commission White Paper on Growth, Competitiveness and Employment diagnosed the unemployment problem in the 1990s, setting the target of creating fifteen million new jobs by the year 2000. It recognised the need to support key growth industries, improve infrastructure and pursue measures to encourage firms to take on more labour. However, the EU is constrained by the different viewpoints of member states as well as the need to limit national budgetary deficits and to maintain EU budgetary balance.

The EU has concentrated its increased structural funding on five Objectives. Objective 1 regions, whose GDP is less than 75 per cent of the EU average, accounted for 63 per cent of EU structural expenditure 1989–93, and this is set to rise to 68 per cent of EU structural funding 1994–99. Objective 1 regions include the whole of Greece, Portugal, Ireland, southern Italy and most of Spain, plus several new areas, for example, the five new Länder in eastern Germany and east Berlin (Commission of the EC 1993c: 12).

Other areas, especially the declining industrial areas of Britain, have bene-fited from Objective 2 status. Objective 3 is now defined to include both the young and the old who are unemployed and all those groups socially excluded. Objective 4 is defined as helping those who are in employment but are threat-ened by industrial change. Objective 5 relates to agriculture.

The ESF has moved, since 1958, from emphasising labour mobility in a high-employment labour market to vocational training for the unemployed since the 1970s, particularly helping to tackle high youth unemployment. The ESF has also concentrated on those unemployed in depressed regions and in those sectors facing rapid decline, such as textiles. The adoption of appropriate supply-side improvements and skills is helpful, particularly in weaker economies where skill levels have tended to be poor compared with competitors such as Germany. However, harmonisation in labour market measures relating to social costs and minimum wage legislation causes greater inflexibility in the labour market, adding to the difficulties of creating jobs.

The EU in its expenditure policies is of growing importance not so much in an absolute sense, but mainly in relation to particular areas of expenditure. For example, through its structural funds, local beneficiaries have started to look more to Brussels than to national capitals. In other words, a local cadre exists, committed to an EU of the regions. For those fortunate enough to receive EU funds, they are having a significant impact. However, additionality is not easy to establish when the money is transferred to member states, but they are expected to maintain their macroeconomic spending at least at its level in the previous programming period. The new Cohesion Fund accounting for 7 per cent of total structural expenditure in 1993 is subject to macroeconomic conditions. Transfers cease if the member state has an excessive budgetary deficit and has taken insuf-ficient measures to eliminate it (Commission of the EC 1993a: 63).

Redistribution within the EC is of a different order from that within the nation state. In the latter, citizenship is conferred by certain common rights, including entitlement to welfare benefits. Income nationally is redistributed between people both from the side of ability to pay, with progressive tax ensuring the rich pay most, and from the side of benefits, with the poor getting most subsidies. Occasionally national policy may be criticised for entailing high marginal tax rates for the relatively low paid and indiscriminate subsidies to all groups, not just the poor. Income redistribution within the EU has been much weaker and essentially between regions. Although there is considerable overlap between poor people and poor regions, one still has some poor people in rich regions subsidising some rich people in poor regions. Furthermore, EU citizenship, despite the Maastricht Treaty, is insufficiently developed to tolerate further income transfers. This has been apparent in German unification and applies even more at an EU level where income transfers are seen to be given to the poor who are unenterprising and workshy. Hence cohesion in the EU will continue to reflect more the aim of equality of opportunity with structural improvements to hard infrastructure such as transport, and soft infrastructure such as human capital, to raise regional potential.

ECONOMIC AND MONETARY UNION

In the interests of conciseness, this section merely sketches the background of EMU. Apart from touching on some of the key developments, most attention is given to the current Maastricht conditions for EMU.

The Treaty of Rome was more concerned with the Common Market and microeconomic issues than with macroeconomic integration. Only the rudimentary aspects of monetary integration were considered, such as stabilisation of exchange rates, help in the case of balance of payments difficulties and some coordination of national policies (Molle 1990: 390). The institutional framework has involved various monetary, budgetary and economic committees to coordinate policies and to promote greater convergence.

When the EC was first established, it was able to rely on the successful Bretton Woods fixed exchange rate system, and European economies enjoyed good growth rates with high employment. This can be looked back upon as a golden age marked by a high degree of real convergence in per capita GDP, with nominal convergence internally on low costs and prices and externally in exchange rate stability. However, the breakdown of the fixed exchange rate system in the late 1960s, with the devaluation of sterling and the French franc and the revaluation of the D-mark, created problems; for example, in the operation of the CAP.

In 1969 at the Hague Summit, there was an agreement to create economic and monetary union: a blueprint for this was drawn up by P. Werner. This established a stage-by-stage plan to achieve EMU by 1980 through narrowing exchange rate margins, integrating capital markets and finally establishing a common currency and a single central bank. In 1972 came the formation of the European currency band, the so-called 'snake'. This pegged EC currencies, with fluctuations in a band of up to ±2.25 per cent between member currencies. The currencies experienced repeated speculative pressure and the UK, Italy and France all dropped out of the system, so that by 1978 it was mainly a D-mark area. This comprised Germany, the Netherlands, Belgium, Luxembourg and Denmark (which rejoined), plus Norway; Austria was an informal associate member. The root of the problem lay in discordant economic and monetary policies, partly arising from different reactions to the oil price increase.

The creation of the European Monetary System, 1979

In 1978 the President of the EC Commission, Roy Jenkins, proposed a new leap forward to EMU, arguing that this was crucial to lower the rate of inflation. Germany was concerned about the adverse effects of a rise in the value of the D-mark on German trade and business profits, and recognised the need to take a monetary initiative and establish a new European Monetary System (EMS). For France it offered a chance to return to a close monetary partnership with Germany and to stiffen their own anti-inflationary policy. This was also true of Italy which secured additional financial assistance.

The EMS was relatively successful in reducing exchange rate variability and there were fewer exchange rate realignments by the late 1980s. The UK finally decided that the time was ripe to join in 1990. This led to plans being drawn up for a complete EMU. Unfortunately, no sooner was the new blueprint produced than a speculative crisis created currency turmoil in September 1992 and July 1993. There was political uncertainty related to ratifying the Maastricht Agreement. In addition, the resources needed for successful German unification drove up interest rates. Eventually the ERM collapsed in the cataclysm of widening bands to ±15 per cent (apart from Germany and the Netherlands).

Countries hoping to participate in EMU have to modify their national macroeconomic preferences, reaching either some common preference, or following the preference of a dominant economy, such as Germany. The consequence for weaker economies in trying to attain a lower rate of inflation is a much higher level of unemployment. However, given the monetarist perspective that no long-term tradeoff between unemployment and inflation exists, then countries were prepared to converge towards the lower German inflation level. Unfortunately the short-term consequence of this has been heavy unemployment, necessitating even more transfers via the structural funds than when more exchange rate flexibility exists. Pressure to alleviate unemployment, especially via an expansionist fiscal policy, is placed on politicians who are reluctant to persevere with continued deflation when they see more readily effective measures being available in the short run.

Maastricht

Only with economic convergence via economic union is a durable EMU feasible. Otherwise there is always some credibility doubt, even in the case of strong economies such as the Netherlands, since their devaluation of the guilder has meant that interest rates there have had to be slightly above those in Germany. The economic perspective emphasising convergence is recognised strongly in the Maastricht Treaty. Stage 1 was launched under existing EU powers from 1 July 1990, with action taken to improve economic and monetary coordination between member states and to extend the work of the Committee of Central

Bank Governors. Stages 2 and 3 necessitate changes in the Treaty since they involve setting up new institutions. These include in stage 2 (from 1 January 1994) the establishment of a European Monetary Institute to strengthen cooperation between national central banks and to coordinate monetary policies.

Four convergence criteria have been established and one of these – no excessive budgetary deficits – has already been referred to above. Failure of the member states to coordinate economic policy and maintain budgetary discipline could trigger further action, such as the EIB reconsidering its lending policy to that country, a requirement to make an interest-free deposit with the Community, or imposition of fines.

Not only are most countries failing on the budgetary criterion, but some of the other criteria are creating problems, in particular the criterion concerning the maintenance of normal exchange rate bands of ±2.25 per cent. The normal fluctuation margins of the ERM should have been respected for two years without severe tensions and without a devaluation on the member state's own initiative. However, with the severe tensions since September 1992, are we to take the bands as ±2.25 per cent, or ±15 per cent? It is now clear that in practice the answer will be the latter.

An additional convergence criterion is that long-term interest rates are to be within 2 per cent of the average of the three lowest rates. Finally, inflation is not to be more than 1.5 per cent more than that of the average of the three best-performing states. In 1992 these were Belgium, Denmark and France, whose rates ranged from 2.1 per cent to 2.8 per cent, hence the reference value for inflation ranged from 3.6 per cent to 4.3 per cent. Five other member states satisfied this criterion, the exceptions being Greece, Portugal, Italy and Spain.

Stage 2 of EMU is intended to run until 1 January 1999. We will then have in stage 3 a European Central Bank (ECB) with a single monetary policy. All national bank governors are part of the ECB, plus some independent members. The Bank's aim is to pursue price stability and it is based in Frankfurt, giving some reward to Germany for giving up the D-mark for the ECU. As national central banks become more independent of government, only with reluctance will they surrender some of their new-found powers to the ECB. Furthermore, the UK and Denmark have an opt-out of stage 3 of the Maastricht Treaty. If the UK does not join stage 3 it retains all its powers for monetary and exchange rate policy and will not be subject to EC disciplines, apart from its commitment not to run excessive budgetary deficits.

CONCLUSION

Member states are increasingly interdependent and therefore completely independent national macroeconomic policies are being surrendered within the EU. This has gone furthest in trade policy, with the removal of trade barriers between member states and a common commercial policy to outsiders. Only a few policies, such as VERs and national aid, can be resorted to, to protect national industries, though countries are increasingly ingenious in creating new support measures to replace the ones which have had to be abandoned in market integration.

Most flexibility to member states exists in fiscal policy, though even here there are limits, affecting, for example, policies on indirect taxation. There are limits to the variation in VAT rates and though there continue to be much higher rates of excise duty in the UK on beer, wine and spirits, one wonders how long these can continue, as consumers bring in cheaper supplies for their own consumption through cross-border shopping. In budgetary expenditure there is a case for more spending to be switched towards the central EU level to stabilise and redistribute income. The Community impact is of growing significance, especially in regional and social policy expenditure. However, EU budgetary expenditure is still likely to remain too small and most expenditure will continue to be at national level, though this enables countries with different economic structures to respond to differential external shocks. One worrying feature of EU fiscal ambitions is that the Maastricht conditions are tending to reinforce a deflationary economic stance.

Finally, EMU involves the surrender of the potent exchange rate instrument, monetary policy becoming more centralised in a new ECB and eventually a new single currency. The levers of national economic management are being weakened and will be shared increasingly with the EU. The pace at which this occurs will be determined by the size of the EU and with variable geometry a multi-tiered Europe offers greater discretion to national policy makers in the 'outer core', whilst a multi-speed Europe would simply provide more time for all member states to reach the common goals. Whilst Maastricht has set important monetary and budgetary goals, it has also enshrined the concept of subsidiarity. This principle will be invoked by those who feel that further EU encroachment is not warranted when actions can be carried out better at a lower level. Given that member states are still insufficiently integrated, for example in terms of labour mobility in practice, there is need for greater EU budgetary redistribution than currently seems to exist, otherwise EMU will be an extremely painful process.

BIBLIOGRAPHY

Cecchini, P. (1988) *The European Challenge 1992: The Benefit of a Single Market*, Aldershot: Wildwood House, Gower.

Commission of the EC (1989) DG for Economic and Financial Affairs, 'Economic convergence in the Community', *European Economy*, 41 (July).

——(1990) DG for Economic and Financial Affairs, 'Annual Economic Report 1990–1', *European Economy*, 46 (December).

——(1993a) DG for Economic and Financial Affairs, 'Stable money – sound finances', *European Economy*, 53.

——(1993b) *European Social Policy*, 551, Green Paper.

——(1993c) *Community Structural Funds, 1994–9 – Revised Regulations and Comments* (August).

——(1994) 'Growth, competitiveness, employment', White Paper.

Eichengreen, B. (1992) 'Is Europe an optimum currency area?', in S. Borner and H. Grubel, *The European Community after 1992*, London: Macmillan.

El-Agraa, A. (ed.) (1985) *The Economics of the European Community*, Oxford: Philip Allan, 2nd ed.

Goldsmith, J. (1995) *The Response*, London: Macmillan.

Gros, D. and Thygesen, N. (1992) *European Monetary Integration*, London: Longman.

Guerrieri, P. and Padoan, P. C. (eds) (1989) *The Political Economy of European Integration*, Hemel Hempstead: Harvester Wheatsheaf.

Harrop, J. (1992) *The Political Economy of Integration in the European Community*, 2nd ed., Aldershot: Edward Elgar.

Hine, R. C. (1985) *The Political Economy of European Trade*, Brighton: Wheatsheaf.

Hitiris, T. (1988) *European Community Economics*, Hemel Hempstead: Harvester Wheatsheaf.

Italianer, A. and Van Heukelen, M. (1993) 'Proposals for Community stabilisation mechanisms: some historical applications', in 'The economics of Community public finance', *European Economy*, 5.

MacDougall, D. *et al.* (1977) *Report of the Study Group on the Role of Public Finance in European Integration*, Luxembourg: Office for Official Publication of the European Communities.

Molle, W. (1990) *The Economics of European Integration*, Aldershot: Dartmouth.

Neilsen, J. U-M., Heinrich, H. and Hansen, J. D. (1991) *An Economic Analysis of the EC*, Maidenhead: McGraw Hill.

Nevin, E. (1990) *The Economics of Europe*, London: Macmillan.

Stewart, M. (1983) *Controlling the Economic Future*, Hemel Hempstead: Harvester Wheatsheaf.

Thompson, G. F. (1993) *The Economic Emergence of a New Europe*, Aldershot: Edward Elgar.

Wildavsky, A. and Zapico-Goñi, E. (eds) (1993) *National Budgeting for Economic and Monetary Union*, Netherlands: Martinus Nijhoff.

3

'NATIONAL AUTONOMY'

Some economic approaches[1]

James Forder

If the notion of 'autonomy' concerns a nation's ability to achieve its policy goals, then most if not all macroeconomics concerns the analysis of autonomy. Whether it be to delimit the boundaries of the possibilities of a state achieving its aims, or the analysis of the best way of going about pursuing them, economics has always been concerned with analysing such possibilities – why else is Adam Smith's second great work an enquiry into 'the nature and causes of the wealth of nations'?

Since Smith, it has become both increasingly true and increasingly recognised that the economic opportunities open to a nation are substantially affected by the international sphere. To match domestic constraints of resource endowments, technological knowledge, political stability, under-investing firms, over-ambitious trade unions and many other things, they face constraints imposed by economic outcomes in the rest of the world – how much can we export? Can domestic firms compete with imports from abroad? Will international capital markets supply credit and if so on what terms?

More recently still, these interdependencies have been seen specifically as creating issues which may require policy coordination. In the pure form, these arise from a recognition, first, that if our policies affect outcomes in other countries, others react to our policies with a change in their own policy; and second, that this factor must be considered in determining what is our optimal policy: what appears optimal on the basis of other countries' current policy may not in fact be so when it is recognised that our policy change changes their policy preference.[2]

This attitude contrasts sharply with another that our optimal policy can be determined without reference to others. For example, there is a widely held – indeed orthodox – view that free trade is optimal for a small country irrespective of the trade policy of other countries. Consequently, there would be no sense in 'retaliating' against protectionism, even if others' protectionism does indeed harm us.[3] Famously advocated by Ricardo and his followers, this view is sometimes summed up with the question 'if others put rocks in their harbours, should we put rocks in ours?'.[4] In this case, although our welfare is ultimately determined by others' actions, and theirs by ours – so there is interdependence – there is no true role for policy coordination. Our best action is independent of their actual action, and vice versa.

In other areas – most notably macroeconomic management – it has been argued that the interdependencies between countries' policies are such that there is a potential benefit in explicit policy coordination. It is said that circumstances arise where both[5] countries can benefit from a joint change of policy that neither is willing to undertake individually. Such cases have been extensively studied by economists, with, for example, Hamada (1976) usually credited with first drawing explicit attention to such possibilities in macroeconomic policy. This is known as the 'policy coordination' literature.

The literature on these things is immense, with much of it showing all that is best and worst in contemporary economics – technical skill, rigorous analysis and a challenge to see how it might apply to the world we inhabit. Consequently, the whole area cannot be considered here. But in this volume we are concerned with macroeconomic policy making in Europe, and in this area certain aspects of the literature, and certain arguments, can be identified as having been particularly influential in policy making at various times. Therefore the objectives of this contribution are to give a flavour of the way that economists have discussed these issues; to indicate the variety of conclusions that can be drawn and the difficulty – in most cases – of achieving a reliable determination of which of them is correct; but most importantly, to indicate the lines of thought that have been influential in European developments, and how economic analysis has rationalised them.

The intended audience is that part of the readership of this book which, having not previously been exposed to the economic theory of international macroeconomic interdependence, would appreciate the politics of European economic policy making being discussed in the light of economists' thinking on these things. No one, therefore, will mistake this piece for an attempt to offer a complete survey of the economics literature on international policy coordination, and certainly not on international economic interdependence.[6] And nor, be it added, should anyone mistake it for a piece which accidentally achieves that laudable aim.

EARLY THINKING ABOUT MACROECONOMIC POLICY COORDINATION IN EUROPE

The Werner Committee's report is described, for example by Tsoukalis (1977), as having achieved a compromise between 'economists' and 'monetarists'. The former felt that the creation of a monetary union required a prior convergence of inflation rates; the latter that the creation of the union would bring such convergence about. Each, therefore, understood the basic relationship between fixed exchange rates and inflation: if two countries' exchange rate is to be fixed, inflation rates must, within fairly narrow limits, be the same in both. One cannot imagine a permanent and large deviation of one country's prices or price movements from those of another. As a consequence of this, one is led to conclude that within a monetary union or fixed exchange rate area, both the price level and the rate of inflation must be broadly similar throughout. There is no sense in which a country has 'autonomy' in the choice of its own price level once it is part of a monetary union.[7] One can immediately see the sense in the Irish attitude to the EMS discussed by Oppenheimer in this volume: seeking to peg their currency to the pound had resulted in British levels of inflation in Ireland; pegging it to the D-mark would result in German levels.

Thinking of the consequences of this for international cooperation, the fact that fixed exchange rates require broadly common inflation rates is at the heart of the parallel that is sometimes drawn between the relationship between the United Kingdom and the Gold Standard, the United States and the Bretton Woods System and Germany and the European Monetary System. In each case, the most powerful country was presumed to have stable prices, and fixed exchange rates were therefore supposed to be consistent with price stability throughout the system. Some of the literature gives the 'central' country a special role in 'enforcement' of the 'rules of the game'. But it can be difficult to identify the enforcing. Rather, the other countries tend to perceive membership of the system as in their interests.[8]

Of course, the characteristic of fixed exchange rates – that inflation rates must be almost the same – has also been seen as an argument for floating exchange rates. Friedman (1953) famously contended that for the Europeans to abandon the Bretton Woods System and float their currencies with respect to the dollar would allow them to determine their own rate of inflation, rather than in effect being compelled to adopt that of the United States. Theoretically persuasive, and certainly prescient considering it was long before American inflation became widely recognised as a problem in the rest of the world, his argument nevertheless had more force in countries where domestic inflation tended to be lower than American inflation – Germany for example – than in those, like Britain, where it tended to be higher. Emminger (1977) is a now little read, but insightful account from inside the Bundesbank of how the fixed parity gradually came to be perceived as an inflationary menace both by the Bundesbank and the German government. Ultimately, of course, they took Friedman's advice, albeit twenty years after it was offered, and then only after the United States had abandoned the gold convertibility of the dollar. Other countries – notably Britain – foresaw a different benefit of floating. Their perception was that deteriorations in the current account constrained policy and that floating the pound would allow the exchange rate to equilibrate the current account, leaving policy free to pursue other objectives – high employment, specifically.

However, each of these views treats the achievement of domestic goals very largely as a matter of domestic policy. They see external commitments like

Bretton Woods as constraints which prevent the achievement of their goals. The essence of the policy coordination literature is to recognise that interdependence of countries' policies and goals is fundamental, rather than treat it as characteristic of a particular regime.

Explicit attention had been given to these things by the time of the creation of the EMS in 1978. Consideration of macroeconomic interdependence had been advanced by the Bonn Summit and by Hamada (1976). These developments were based on the idea that there may be significant ways in which unemployment, as well as inflation, is to some extent internationally determined. Any event which causes the rest of the world's demand for the home country's products to fall will cause unemployment.[9] These events can be categorised into three types. One is a switch of demand to other products, perhaps caused by changes in tastes; another is a switch in demand to other suppliers of the same product, due perhaps to the opening of trade with another country; and third, there may be a general fall in demand in the rest of the world, perhaps because of a recession. Thus a recession in American may lead to a fall in demand for European products; if this causes a recession in Europe then that may also lead to a fall in demand for American products, worsening the recession there. Thus the process is in some measure cumulative.

What is less clear, and depends on one's general view of economic management, is the extent to which there is any role for policy in rectifying such problems. On the view that, for example, the labour market is pretty good at sorting these things out and that workers will soon price themselves back into jobs by accepting lower wages so that any such problems will be temporary, the role of policy, internationally coordinated or otherwise, is likely to be minimal.

Taking the alternative view that there is a worthwhile role for active policy, Hamada identified the possibility that the whole world could benefit from an agreement to undertake counter-recessionary policies, for example, a joint fiscal expansion. The argument is that extra government expenditure financed by borrowing will raise demand and therefore employment. From the point of view of an individual country, some of that extra demand will be demand for imports and therefore the extra employment will be foreign. The consequence of this will be that each country will expand 'too little' from the point of view of the world as a whole, although it expands just enough from its own, selfish point of view.

The reason for this is that whilst only some of the benefits of expansion accrue to the expanding country, it bears all of the costs. For example, we might suppose that the policy which raises demand increases imports and causes a deterioration of the current account of the balance of payments. In this case the benefit of lower unemployment comes at the expense of a worsened current account.[10] For each country the optimal degree of expansion balances the deterioration of the current account against the increase in its own employment. What does not feature in the calculation is the extra benefit accruing to the world as a whole in the form of an increase in employment in other countries.

Those other countries are of course themselves limiting their expansion for the same reason. Consequently the world as a whole under-expands.

Looked at this way, there is an opportunity for collective gain in an agreement to expand more than each country would wish to alone. The effect of a joint expansion is that each country's expansion, by raising the others' exports, protects their balance of payments. The whole world reaches a position of acceptable balance of payments and higher employment than they would have achieved when acting alone.

This argument offers an understanding of the depth of recession after the oil shock of 1973–4. Faced with an increased oil bill, the developed countries as a group faced a deterioration of their balance of payments. Each one acting alone could, and some would say did, seek to maintain an approximation to equilibrium by reducing domestic consumption and thereby imports. Such action worsened the payments position of the other developed countries since they experienced a fall in their exports. Thus for the group, the policy resulted in deeper recession and a smaller improvement of the balance of payments than any one would have anticipated viewing their policy change in isolation. It is arguable – and this is the broad direction in which thinking along the lines of the Hamada points – that the group as a whole would have been better served by accepting some deterioration in its payments position with the oil exporters whilst seeking a greater degree of employment stabilisation. This conclusion was explicitly drawn by Bruno and Sachs (1985). Given the policy responses of others, attempting to correct the balance of payments would in any case be substantially ineffective, but suitable coordination might succeed in maintaining employment.

The Bonn summit and the creation of the EMS both show signs of having been influenced by this line of thinking. At the Bonn summit, West Germany and Japan both agreed to undertake a fiscal stimulus which, it was clearly recognised, would have some beneficial effect on employment in the rest of the world.[11] This became known as the 'locomotive' approach, since these countries were supposed to pull the rest of the world out of recession. Similarly, had the EMS evolved as a truly 'symmetric' system, it could be construed as promoting policy coordination. If the consequence of 'symmetry' is that all countries seek to keep a current account equilibrium[12] so that countries in surplus would feel obliged to expand demand, any initial expansion by one country, by increasing the exports of another, could lead to expansionary policy in that country too.[13]

In the event, the fashionability of this view was short-lived. The Bonn summit was followed by the second oil shock and thereafter any attempt at coordination of that kind – notwithstanding the benefits its advocates adduced – ended. Many German policy makers even formed the view that coordination was responsible for the increase in inflation which followed, and therefore harmed them. Holtham (1989) has disputed this, but still the advocacy of coordination suffers, particularly in Germany. In a sense the unhappy shadow of coordinated policy can be seen in the failure of French policy before 1983. An attempt to run an expansionary policy in France in the face of contractionary ('non-coordinated') policy in most other countries resulted in inflation, balance of payments crises, a collapse in the value of the franc and little, if any, perceptible benefit in terms of employment or growth – all of which was followed by, of course, the abandonment of the policy. The advocates of coordination would see in this failure of unilateral policy evidence of the need for coordination. The idea that coordinated policy would have worked better is of course far from substantiated by the fact that uncoordinated policy failed, yet nor can it be said that coordination, of the kind envisaged by Hamada, was ever given a run.

THEORETICAL AND PRACTICAL DOUBTS ABOUT COORDINATION

Since Hamada's contribution, many objections to coordination have been raised. The first and perhaps most obvious being the fear of 'free-riding'. That is to say, when there is an agreement to undertake a coordinated expansion, an individual country has an incentive not to participate. It will still benefit from the expansion of others, but without bearing the costs. In an extreme case, such a country might agree to the coordinated policy, but do nothing. The same argument of course applies to all the countries and thus, in the absence of a way of enforcing the agreement, attempts at coordination might come to nothing. Putnam and Bayne (1987) and Putnam and Henning (1989) undertook detailed studies of international negotiations and found no tendency to enter into this kind of deception. Nevertheless, it is reasonable to suppose that there have been occasions – such as after the second oil shock – when coordination has not been attempted as a result of an acknowledgement that certain countries, particularly concerned about inflation, would not cooperate and that without them it was difficult for the smaller countries to achieve significant policy improvements.

Other difficulties soon became apparent. It was pointed out that policy makers might not have the objectives Hamada supposed. Indeed, once emphasis shifted to the control of inflation, it became apparent that coordination problems exist here, just as they did with Hamada's earlier concern about unemployment. If one considers the case of two countries facing a common inflation-generating shock in a regime of floating exchange rates, the implications of interdependence are rather different from those suggested by Hamada. One might suppose that in a closed economy either fiscal or monetary contraction would be effective in eliminating the inflation, and some optimal balance between the two can be achieved. In an open economy, with uncoordinated policy, both countries would seek to raise the value of their currency since this brings an anti-inflationary benefit in the form of lower import prices and competitive pressure on the prices of close substitutes for imports produced domestically. The means of seeking to appreciate the currency is a monetary tightening, since higher interest rates attract capital, bidding up the value of the currency. However, since both countries are trying to appreciate their currencies in the same way, both fail. At the same time, the consequence is that monetary policy, in the form of high interest rates, is bearing too much of the burden of fighting inflation relative to fiscal policy, in the form of tight control of government deficits. All in all both countries end up with interest rates which are 'too high' and budget deficits 'too large' relative to the ideal. The consequence of either of these factors is likely to be that investment falls below the level it would otherwise reach. In contrast, a coordinated policy would see both countries agree to an appropriate increase in interest rates with no attempt to 'outbid' the other to appreciate their currency, and together they could then pursue the optimal disinflation strategy.

Clearly this argument has much in common with Hamada's. In both cases it is recognised that each country's autonomy is restricted by the international environment and the other country's actions. In both cases these considerations give rise to an opportunity to improve the outcome for all by agreeing to set policy jointly. Thus Hamada's most fundamental insights are supported by this argument. The difficulty is, of course, that the form of coordination which brings the benefit has changed as the immediate objective of policy makers changed.

The problem is hardly fatal, however. Once it is understood, an appropriate agreement can be reached. Even if it should happen that different countries have different objectives at a particular time it is still possible to construct an appropriate agreement. A more serious problem comes with the observation that the understanding of just how the international economy works is rather more difficult than it seems. Hamada's story about the international propagation of unemployment is entirely plausible, but it can hardly be said to be self-evidently correct, and other stories have challenged it. For example, Canzoneri and Gray (1985) showed that it is possible to develop models where uncoordinated policy is overexpansionary, not overcontractionary as Hamada suggests. When different countries face different shocks, there are even more possibilities, as shown by Canzoneri and Henderson (1991).

This raises the issue of the nature of the international transmission of policy from one country to another. Is the transmission of fiscal policy from the United States to Europe positive, meaning that an American fiscal expansion raises European employment as Hamada's line of thinking suggests, or is it negative, leading to an increase in interest rates throughout the world and thereby reducing output in Europe? Similar questions can be raised about almost any policy tool that one might contemplate coordinating. Fundamentally the difficulty is that, whilst we can say that if the nature of economic cause and effect is such and such then there is a benefit to policy makers agreeing to pursue one policy rather than another, we are woefully short of a clear view of the structure of the economy. In a sense, this problem reflects disputes about domestic policy. If we have little agreement as to when interest rates or government borrowing should rise or fall to manage the domestic economy, it is hardly surprising that there is a substantial problem about coordinating their rises and falls with other countries.

Although sufficient to engender a good deal of scepticism about the feasibility of policy coordination itself, this problem has been thrown sharply into focus by two later contributions. McKibbin and Sachs (1991), whilst certainly well disposed towards the ultimate feasibility of improved worldwide economic performance, particularly through fiscal policy coordination, make clear the number of issues that must be resolved. In addition to the obvious question as to whether we are dealing with fixed or floating exchange rates, they point to the issues of the degree of capital mobility, the way in which expectations about asset prices are formed, asset holders' attitudes to the riskiness of assets denominated in different currencies and the way in which wages are set. Resolving all the empirical issues that are involved for each country (not just two!) clearly exceeds most people's expectations of the capabilities of governments and of the economics profession. Yet the issue is central to effective policy coordination. Considering just wage setting, McKibbin and Sachs make the extent of the difficulties clear:

> Consider the effect of a US monetary expansion on the rest of the world. If nominal wages are assumed to be fully fixed, this effect is positive under fixed exchange rates and negative under flexible exchange rates. Under flexible rates, the negative transmission effect becomes positive if the foreign country has a high degree of wage indexation! Clearly, the institutional setting matters greatly.
>
> (McKibbin and Sachs 1991: 20)

A consequence of this which is immediately obvious is that efficacious agreements on coordination must await resolution of the issue of the nature of the international transmission of policy effects from one country to another. In practice, the problem presents itself in the form of disagreement between different policy makers as to the appropriate policy for each to follow.

A related point is exploited by Frenkel and Rockett (1988) in an impressively destructive contribution. They showed that the benefits of coordination all but disappear once reasonable degrees of uncertainty are introduced into policy makers' understanding of the structure of the world economy. There is nothing about such a disagreement which makes coordination of policy theoretically impossible: so long as policy makers understand each other's view, it is possible to reach an agreement which leaves each believing they are better off.[14]

However, Frenkel and Rockett assessed the probability of actually achieving benefits from coordination by taking ten well respected macroeconomic models and supposing one of them to be 'believed' by the United States, one by the rest of the world, and one to be the true model. This gave a thousand combinations of truth and belief. They then supposed that the US and the rest of the world reach an agreement that both parties believe leaves them better off, and tested whether in fact it would, given the model assumed to be true. Barely more than half the time was the US better off, and the same applied to the rest of the world, although in the nature of the simulation, both parties always believed they were better off.

In addition to these problems of agreeing on the appropriate model and priorities, one must acknowledge that lack of perfect foresight makes coordination more difficult. This was amply illustrated by the Bonn summit where an agreement to expand demand was reached just before an oil shock. There can be little doubt that, as a general rule, policy which has to be internationally agreed will be even slower to react to developments than domestically determined policy.

Thus one is driven towards a sceptical conclusion very much in the tradition of that brand of *laissez-faire* economics which argues against governmental intervention not on grounds of markets providing ideal outcomes, but merely because, all things considered, the likelihood of attempts to improve on them doing any good is small.

VIEWS OF ECONOMIC INTERDEPENDENCE IN THE 1980s

With the movement towards prioritising the control of inflation that emerged in the 1980s came different attitudes to international economic interdependence. In Europe, attention became progressively focused on the idea that 'policy credibility' could be improved by following the policy of the Bundesbank. Globally, the analysis of the causes and consequences of the prolonged rise of the dollar between 1980 and 1985 provoked great controversy amongst both academics and policy makers.

As for policy credibility, the story is that it is easier to reduce inflation or keep it low if private agents expect that it will in fact be kept low, because, for example, such a belief results in lower wage settlements. However, the benefit of allowing it to rise is also greater when they have this belief, because given the low wage settlements, a rise in inflation will temporarily encourage firms to hire more labour as the wage is fixed in the short term, but inflation is raising their product price, leading them to make and sell more. On this basis, anything which has the effect of promoting expectations of low inflation is useful, whether or not the expectations ultimately turn out to be justified.[15] The story that became fashionable is that committing to maintaining a fixed exchange rate with the D-mark was the most convenient means of controlling expectations. This view is based on the supposition that such a commitment is costly to break – presumably because the political costs of devaluing are substantial – and that it will be necessary to break it if inflation is allowed to rise. Thus the government is understood to have painted itself into a corner where it must keep inflation down. The resultant low wage settlements mean that this can be done with a minimum loss of employment.

Clearly this argument is not really a matter of policy coordination. It makes the assumption that the central country (Germany) reliably has low inflation. Its

role is to continue to pursue this policy. The others also pursue a se..
policy, not basing their action on any agreement. In the technical ecoı..
sense this behaviour is uncoordinated: everyone does what seems best on the
assumption that others' behaviour cannot be changed. There is no attempt to
reach an agreement for all to behave in some way different from this.[16] Nor can
it be said to be very fully worked out: for example, there is the seldom acknowledged implication of Rogoff (1985) that the credibility of German policy should
be worsened by others' practice of pegging to the D-mark since any 'surprise'
inflation adopted by Germany will be copied by the others and therefore be all
the more effective in increasing German output as their exports rise. In addition,
hard evidence that credibility benefits of this kind exist is extraordinarily difficult
to come by. The mere fact that inflation fell in many countries hardly qualifies,
since the credibility benefit is not a fall in inflation, but a fall in the costs of
reducing inflation. Several of the disinflating countries suffered and continue to
suffer greatly in terms of high unemployment.

The rise of the dollar ultimately gave rise to a temporary reinvigoration of
the idea of policy coordination at the Plaza Agreement of 1985, where the
major states agreed a programme of joint intervention designed to lower its
value. Again, this does not directly fit the pattern of coordination described
above since all countries had the same objective – a lower dollar – and each
could presumably achieve it to some degree acting alone. Nevertheless, the
public agreement to pursue it may have some effect as well as legitimising a
degree of intervention in the foreign exchange market that might otherwise have
been controversial. In addition, financial markets may respond to the agreement
as distinct from the action. The Louvre Accord of 1987 was a similar agreement
to stabilise the dollar. Since then however, macroeconomic policy coordination of
any kind has largely disappeared from the international (as distinct from
European) agenda.

The experience of the dollar led to more analysis of international economic
interdependence, however. A large part of this is concerned with seeking to
explain the course of the dollar and is really a matter of the theory of exchange
rate determination rather than international interdependence. Frenkel and
Razin (1987, 1992) supply an advanced analysis of theoretical developments in
interdependent aspects of fiscal policy, much of it inspired by the experience of
Reaganomics. Arguing in a more applied vein, Sachs (1985) suggested that had it
somehow been possible for the United States to reduce inflation without the
dollar rising, this would place an undue burden on the part of the American
economy which is not externally exposed, whereas to achieve it with an appreciation forced some of the burden onto the international sector in the form of a
loss of competitiveness. Correspondingly, from the point of view of the rest of
the world, they could be protected from the effects of the recession in the United
States by an improvement in their competitiveness. Thus US disinflation by
appreciation might suit everyone.

Of course the Europeans were also seeking to disinflate at the same time. To

ion of their currencies made this harder and caused
, more than they otherwise would have, we have a case
cy leading to excessively high interest rates all round the
manifested itself at the time in the origin of European
e the United States to reduce its budget deficit. The percep-
 much borrowing by the United States government was both
dollar by attracting capital from the rest of the world and raising
st rates, because a high proportion of world savings were finding
to the United States, making life hard for other borrowers. The US
gove ment for its part tended to argue that the Europeans and Japan should
seek to expand their economies, rather than leave the 'locomotive' role to the
US, and that their failure to do so left the US with an excessive deficit on its
current account. We have here a good case of the Frenkel and Rockett dilemma
of policy makers broadly agreeing on the problem, but having different understandings of how to solve it. The most striking case of an attitude making
coordination difficult is perhaps the 'theoretical' view of the first Reagan administration, that the rise of the dollar was merely an outcome of American
'strength', and did not call for a policy response at all.

In the latter part of the 1980s the European Union became focused on the
completion of the internal market; although that certainly involves many aspects
of policy coordination, including fiscal coordination in the sense of being
concerned with tax harmonisation, the emphasis moved away from macroeconomic policy, which is the concern of this book. It was not until the issue of
monetary union moved to the fore right at the end of the decade that macroeconomic interdependence once again became a prominent issue in European
debates. But this time the understanding was far removed from that of Hamada.

FISCAL COORDINATION AND MONETARY UNION

Monetary union has itself been presented as a means of solving a coordination
problem: that is, the problem of avoiding 'competitive devaluations'. It has been
argued, for example, by Padoa-Schioppa (1994) that in the absence of any other
barrier to trade, we should be wary of governments seeking to protect domestic
industry by occasional devaluations which will increase their market share at the
expense of other countries and might therefore be said to 'export unemployment'. Since the policy works only at the expense of imposing costs on others, it
is to be expected that they will retaliate by a similar devaluation. The net effect
will be much turmoil but no substantial benefit to anyone, so the total effect on
welfare is presumably negative. Padoa-Schioppa has even gone so far as to argue
that such retaliatory actions might escalate into the imposition of conventional
trade barriers, thereby undoing the movement to free trade which Europe has
enjoyed.[17] That such a danger is real is said to be a lesson of the interwar period.

free trade could be lost

From a certain perspective the appropriate solution is for the countries concerned to reach an agreement that they will not indulge in such devaluations; but if they cannot be trusted to keep such an agreement, the creation of a monetary union might be the solution. This view supposes that the likelihood of circumstances arising where realignment is warranted by a genuine change in the economic circumstances of the members is small. It must also be said that there is a certain tension between Padoa-Schioppa's view and that which claims that the benefits of monetary union arising from a saving of transactions costs outweigh the costs due to the loss of the ability to realign.

The savings in transactions costs, although quite clear, are fairly small on any estimate. To justify monetary union, that small benefit might be expected to outweigh the costs of the loss of a policy tool – devaluation. So that loss must be small and consequently the benefit of devaluation, even when such a policy is warranted, is small. But then the difficulty is to understand why countries would be tempted to pursue a policy of which the benefit is small and might – following Padoa-Schioppa – lead down the path to the dissolution of the European Union.

As to fiscal policy, since the Delors Report, European discussions have revolved primarily around the adverse international consequences of a country borrowing too much, either in terms of its current borrowing or in terms of its accumulated debt. In this regard, the terms of the Maastricht fiscal convergence criteria and of the 'Stability Pact' can be thought of as emanating from a common set of presumptions. Various rationalisations drawing principally on the consequences for interdependent countries might be given, but there are two which stand out in the European case.

One is the view that 'excessive' borrowing by one state raises the interest rate faced by others, imposing costs on them not of their own making and therefore justifying regulation. Popular as this view is, it leaves open two questions. One is why it should be thought specific to a monetary union. To the extent that capital is internationally mobile, it is a problem which exists in any case. Indeed, the raising of world interest rates was a criticism levelled at the United States for much of the 1980s. Yet the Europeans showed little sign of wishing to regulate each others' borrowing prior to the adoption of the monetary union plan. Further, if this were to be the rationale of the fiscal rules, one would want to limit the larger countries to lower borrowing than the smaller ones: a 3 per cent deficit in Germany has a much larger impact on the world market than a 3 per cent deficit in Luxembourg. The second question is why this problem would be thought to apply specifically to debt: if one country consumes 'too much' of anything, it raises the price faced by others.

Perhaps a better approach is to think in terms of the solvency of governments. Developed sovereign states borrow overwhelmingly in their own currency. This makes them all but immune to the danger of a formal default since they have the power, literally if necessary, to print money with which to pay their debts. This is no longer true in a monetary union since the member states are not able to repay debt in this way. So do we need rules to prevent a default? This pessimistic view rests on two further assumptions. One is that governments of member states cannot be trusted to ensure that they do not borrow too much themselves. The second is that neither can the financial markets be relied upon to refrain from lending them too much. Whilst the irresponsibility of elected governments is coming close to being conventional wisdom in neoclassical economics, the incompetence of financial markets is less commonly assumed. Evidence presented by Goldstein and Woglam (1992) suggests that financial markets do rate the solvency of US states with those borrowing large amounts consequently paying higher rates of interest.

An argument advanced by Emerson *et al.* (1992) is that the creation of a monetary union in itself makes problems of excess borrowing more likely since it will increase the perceived likelihood of a 'bail-out'. Such a 'bail-out' could mean that one government takes responsibility for paying another's debts. Ultimately this means that citizens of one member state would be taxed to pay the debts of the government of another. Alternatively, the bail-out could come in the form of an inflation throughout the monetary union which would reduce the real value of the debt.[18]

It is then argued that insofar as it is governments who perceive this, they will presumably be inclined to borrow more to ensure being on the receiving end rather than the paying end; insofar as it is the capital markets, they will be less inclined to monitor the solvency of the states and will therefore allow them to borrow more. Whether even this makes either a default likely, or fiscal rules the appropriate way to prevent one, remains largely an open question.

Another and rather different strand of thinking about fiscal problems in a monetary union concerns the issue of how to secure effective management of the economy in addition to the 'good housekeeping' concerns about debt sustainability. Allsopp *et al.* (1995) adopt the basic outlook of Hamada. The danger is, they suggest, that faced with high unemployment throughout Europe, each country has an incentive to refrain from bearing the costs of a fiscal expansion, the benefits of which will accrue substantially to others. To the extent that monetary union and other aspects of integration have increased the substitutability of imports for domestically produced goods, the benefit to others will be a greater share of the total than would have been the case at the time of Hamada's analysis. Thus the danger is that governments will borrow too little, not too much.

Their view, which is also developed by Allsopp in the present volume, nonetheless denies the need for 'fiscal federalism' – that is, the creation of a large central budget. This was influentially advocated by Sala-i-Martin and Sachs (1992) who suggested that the success of the American monetary union was attributable to the substantial fiscal transfers which stabilise regional income in the presence of economic disturbance. Creating a central authority for fiscal policy, as they suggest, is an institutional way of achieving a policy equivalent to a high degree of 'coordination'. Allsopp claims that a coordinated policy would be preferable; but if it is not feasible, perhaps because of the difficulties in achieving agreement between policy makers, a centralised policy is preferable to nothing.

The view that the principal problem in the design of macroeconomic rules is the controlling of otherwise irresponsible governments can be seen rather clearly in the 'Stability Pact' agreement to subject to fines those members of a monetary union who continue to borrow excessively. The proposal has been criticised for imposing an extra fiscal burden on those, perhaps temporarily, worst equipped to meet it. Whilst this observation is accurate, it is still easy to imagine that the problem it creates is one of 'discipline' and that all that is required is for the government to be sufficiently firm in controlling its expenditures and levying the necessary taxes. This is a mistake, for a reason identified by Keynes (1929) in discussing the feasibility of Germany meeting war reparations payments – a theoretical equivalent of stability pact fines.

The fundamental problem is that a fined country must pay the fine in Euros rather than its domestic currency, which will of course no longer exist. While it may appear that the government can raise the required number of Euros by appropriate taxation, to imagine that this ends the problem is incorrect. The country as a whole acquires Euros from selling exports and spends them buying imports. The payment of a fine requires that the value of exports exceed that of imports by the amount of the fine. To achieve such a payments surplus starting from equilibrium, the country must sell extra exports or import less. Whilst the increase in tax will result in some fall of imports, there is no reason to think it would be sufficient.[19] To export more, an improvement in competitiveness is required. In the short term this requires a fall in cost which is unlikely to be achieved in any way other than a fall in wages relative to wages in other countries. In the context of very low inflation, this may require a fall in nominal wages. The fined country's households must then accept both higher taxes and a fall in relative wages. To the extent that this fall does not come about, the exports cannot be sold and the government therefore does not raise the tax it anticipated. The fundamental problem in paying the fine is therefore that of inducing a sufficient improvement in competitiveness of firms, not of discipline or firmness on the part of the government.

CONCLUSION

Unsurprisingly, attitudes to interdependence have been moulded by the environment in which policy is being formed. Economic ideas rationalised the Bonn summit and the EMS; a changed perception, particularly of the importance of inflation control, went hand-in-hand with the evolution of the EMS towards a system centred on the Bundesbank, and the drafting of the Maastricht Treaty was clearly influenced by similar ideas. Whilst 'economic interdependence' at the level of macroeconomic policy was briefly seen as motivating active management of the economy at an international level, most recently the emphasis in both theory and policy has been on limiting the freedom of action of countries for fear that their policy will exploit its interdependence with the rest of the world. Consequently, we move towards attempts to limit the independence of members of the European Union, and to require them to relinquish autonomy over policy. The rest of this book will explore the empirical picture of how state autonomy has in fact been affected.

NOTES

1 Peter Oppenheimer gave helpful comments on an earlier draft.
2 If our country is small enough, it may not have this kind of effect on others. Still, a group of small countries collectively may have such an effect.
3 In the theoretical presentation, it is still possible that our retaliation, or threat thereof, pushes the other country into a free trade policy. In that case, there is a different kind of interdependence relating to how the policies get made. On a purely economic level, however, our optimal policy is independent of their actual one.
4 It is not suggested that this was the extent of the arguments of the free-traders of the last century.
5 The 'economic both' stands for any number greater than one.
6 Which might be sought in several of the contributions to Jones and Kenen (1985).
7 Two things it does have are some influence over the price level of the whole area and probably some possibility of a slightly different price level or temporarily different inflation rate. No one is surprised to find prices higher in London than elsewhere in the British monetary union, but it would be surprising to find the price of transportable goods (not real estate) say ten times higher. The prices are basically anchored to being about the same. And all the while the price levels have to be about the same, so in the long run do inflation rates, although again it is no surprise to find quite substantial, but temporary, deviations.
8 If required to find an example of enforcement of the rules of the game by the central country, my choice would be the Athenian monetary union of the fifth century BC, but to my limited knowledge this has escaped the attention of international relations theorists.
9 There is the theoretical limiting case where the fall in demand results in immediate changes in the home country: either a fall in the wage or a reallocation of the labour force to other activities. Realistically, although in some cases these changes may be swift, they are rarely fast enough to prevent unemployment increasing. Indeed, they are largely brought about by the increase in unemployment.
10 The exact nature of the cost of expansion is not too important. It could be that expansion causes a deterioration of the terms of trade – by increasing our demand for imports, we raise their price – and this factor is clearly welfare-harming. Or it could simply be that we take on an increased debt burden which will impose costs on taxpayers in the future.
11 Putnam and Bayne (1987) consider the details.
12 The European Council resolution establishing the EMS states 'We are firmly resolved to ensure the lasting success of the EMS by policies conducive to greater stability at home and abroad for both deficit and surplus countries'.
13 This is obviously an imperfect mechanism for achieving policy coordination, but here is not the place to debate the details of the objectives of the EMS.

14 Of course one or both will be disappointed, either receiving less benefit from the coordination than they anticipate or being harmed by it, but given their beliefs, that does not make it an unreasonable agreement to reach. It might also be objected that in practice when policy makers disagree in this way it is rarely within the realm of practical politics to reach an agreement at all. The Frenkel and Rockett argument has a power which goes beyond that point however.

15 Low wage settlements make it possible to reduce inflation at lesser cost in unemployment. On the other hand, if inflation is not reduced, the lower wage settlements mean an increase in employment.

16 Indeed, as told, this account does not even give the central country any benefit from the arrangement. It is sometimes said that the benefit is that the whole arrangement keeps other country's currencies from depreciating, thereby damaging the central country's competitiveness. There is a peculiarity about this, since it suggests that such depreciation would bring a material benefit to the other countries, but the main story seems to suppress that.

17 Implying a curious view, to say the least, of the successive Treaty obligations furthering the creation of a unified market.

18 So long as the debt is nominally denominated in Euros, not foreign currency. The debt is a fixed number of Euros, but inflation, by raising wages and prices, other things being equal, raises the government's revenue and hence its ability to pay.

19 Households spend less because of higher taxes, but the reduction is divided between imports and domestic production.

BIBLIOGRAPHY

Allsopp, C., Davies, G. and Vines, D. (1995) 'Regional macroeconomic policy, fiscal federalism, and European integration', *Oxford Review of Economic Policy*, 11, 126–44.

Bruno, M. and Sachs, J. (1985) *Economics of Worldwide Stagflation*, Cambridge MA: Harvard University Press.

Canzoneri, M and Gray, J. (1985) 'Monetary policy games and the consequences of non-cooperative behavior', *International Economic Review*, 26: 547–64.

Canzoneri, M., Grilli, V. and Masson, P. (eds) (1992) *Establishing a Central Bank: Issues in Europe and Lessons from the US*, Cambridge: Cambridge University Press and CEPR.

Canzoneri, M. and Henderson, D. W. (1991) *Monetary Policy in Interdependent Economies: A Game Theoretic Approach*, Cambridge MA: MIT.

Emerson, M., Gros, D., Italianer, A., Pisani-Ferry, J. and Reichenbach, H. (1992) *One Market, One Money*, Oxford: Oxford University Press.

Emminger, O. (1977) 'The DM in the conflict between internal and external equilibrium, 1948–75', *Princeton Essays in International Finance*, no. 122, Princeton NJ: Princeton University Press.

Frenkel, J. and Razin, A. (1987) *Fiscal Policies and the World Economy*, Cambridge MA: MIT.
——(1992) *Fiscal Policies and the World Economy*, 2nd ed., Cambridge MA: MIT.

Frenkel, J. and Rockett, K. (1988) 'International macroeconomic policy coordination when policy makers do not agree on the true model', *American Economic Review*, 78: 318–40.

Friedman, M. (1953) 'The case for flexible exchange rates', in M. Friedman (ed.) *Essays on Positive Economics*, Chicago IL: University of Chicago Press.

Goldstein, M. and Woglam, G. (1992) 'Market-based fiscal discipline in monetary unions: evidence from the US municipal bond market', in M. Canzoneri, V. Grilli and

P. Masson (eds) *Establishing a Central Bank: Issues in Europe and Lessons from the US*, Cambridge: Cambridge University Press and CEPR.

Hamada, K. (1976) 'A strategic analysis of monetary interdependence', *Journal of Political Economy*, 84: 677–700.

Holtham, G. (1989) 'German Macroeconomic Policy and the 1978 Bonn Summit' in Putnam, R. and Henning, C. R. (eds) *Can Nations Agree?*, Washington DC: Brookings.

Jones, R. and Kenen, P. (eds) (1985) *Handbook of International Economics*, Amsterdam: North Holland.

Keynes, J. M. (1929) 'The German transfer problem', *Economic Journal*, 39: 1–7.

McKibbin, W. and Sachs, J. (1991) *Global Linkages*, Washington DC: Brookings.

Padoa-Schioppa, T. (1994) *The Road to Monetary Union*, Oxford: Oxford University Press.

Putnam, R. and Bayne, N. (1987) *Hanging Together*, London: Sage.

Putnam, R. and Henning, C. R. (eds) (1989) *Can Nations Agree?*, Washington DC: Brookings.

Rogoff, K. (1985) 'Can international policy coordination be counter productive?', *Journal of International Economics*, 18, 199–217.

Sachs, J. D. (1985) 'The dollar and the policy mix: 1985', *Brookings Papers on Economic Activity*, 1: 117–85.

Sala-i-Martin, X. and Sachs, J. (1992) 'Fiscal federalism and optimum currency areas: evidence for Europe from the United States' in M. Canzoneri, V. Grilli and P. Masson (eds) *Establishing a Central Bank: Issues in Europe and Lessons from the US*, Cambridge: Cambridge University Press and CEPR.

Smith, Adam (1976) (first published 1776) *An Enquiry into the Nature and Causes of the Wealth of Nations*, Oxford: Oxford University Press.

Tsoukalis, L. (1976) *The Politics and Economics of European Monetary Integration*, London: Philip Allan.

4

CHANGING OBJECTIVES IN NATIONAL POLICY MAKING

Mary Gregory and Daniel Weiserbs

The loss of momentum in the 1990s in the movement towards European integration, centring particularly on monetary integration, has reopened wider questions of the role and direction of macroeconomic policies within the EU. The four decades since the Treaty of Rome have already spanned two major eras in terms of the role of macroeconomic policies in member states. In each of these previous eras the focus of macroeconomic policy was clear. The 1950s and 1960s were the heyday of the commitment to full employment, the welfare state and Keynesian demand management. The priority attached to full employment was unquestioned, both as an end in itself and as the means of spreading prosperity widely through the population. The welfare state was the social adjunct of this economic approach, its universal safety-net ensuring that no groups were excluded from the growing prosperity. Keynesian demand management, in practice fiscal policy, supplied the necessary toolkit, adjusting levels of public expenditure and taxation to maintain overall demand at the full employment level. The 1970s saw this comfortable world shattered. Full employment as the objective and demand management as the mechanism were both discarded as governments sought to adjust to a world in which double-digit inflation became a regular feature, output fell in many cases for the first time since the postwar recovery, and growth projections were revised heavily downwards under the threat of energy shortages. Particularly following the second oil-price increase of 1979, curbing inflation became not only the dominant objective of macroeconomic policy, but frequently its only objective. Throughout the 1980s demand management gave way to monetary policy focused narrowly on the rate of inflation. Full employment disappeared from the political vocabulary and employment policy became a minor category of supply-side policies.

The 1990s have seen the start of a third and more uncertain phase. This has been marked firstly by the emergence of conflicting policy stances among member states, and increasingly by uncertainties in policy direction at national level. Following the reunification of Germany the economic boom there, requiring restrictive measures, coincided with recession elsewhere in the EU.

This conflict of policy stances, centring on interest rates, culminated in the crises of 1992–3 when suspensions of ERM participation, forced realignments of exchange rates, and widening of parity bands abruptly ended the narrow-bands glide path to monetary union. Since then, disagreements about the appropriate timing and form, and to some extent even the desirability, of monetary union have become more frequent and prominent. Behind these conflicts at the level of the EU lie uncertainties in macroeconomic orientation within individual member states. With inflation reduced almost to its levels of the 1960s, but with over twenty million workers unemployed throughout the EU, the issue of unemployment is forcing its way back onto the political agenda. While there is concern at the level of the EU as a whole, it takes a sharper form in individual member countries. Will further moves towards economic and monetary union 'lock in' existing levels of unemployment, or worse, exacerbate them? Might the price of further integration be too high? The worries about social cohesion which prompt this renewed concern with unemployment are reinforced by the pressure on government budgets from the rising costs of welfare provisions. When the population of working age has to support increasing numbers of the elderly, the 10 per cent who are unemployed, contributing nothing to national output and with a claim on welfare support, are a significant further burden. The directions which policy should take are, however, less clear. How far should the level of employment be a government responsibility? To the extent that it is, what policies are appropriate? How far should welfare provision be a public responsibility? What are the tradeoffs between public expenditure, taxation and competitiveness, as well as between unemployment and inflation?

This chapter looks at the evolution of national priorities in macroeconomic policy, and the ways in which these changing national priorities have interacted with the development of institutions and policies within the EU. Our view of this process of evolution suggests that, while the development of the EC in earlier decades for the most part supported or reinforced national policy orientations, the continuation of this mutual interest remains in question. Further tensions among the policy requirements of individual members, of the sort which brought the disruptions of 1992–3, remain a possibility. The process of closer integration will involve the further transfer of economic policy-making powers and instruments to the level of the EU. There is a significant danger that this will leave member countries insufficiently equipped to protect or pursue national interests, without providing the EU itself with adequate instruments to replace these on a collective or coordinated basis. In this event the cohesion of the earlier years will become harder to sustain.

THE COMMON MARKET YEARS

Although macroeconomic policy was not at centre stage in the early development of the Common Market, the context which it provided was extremely important. Member countries shared the same macroeconomic agenda: full employment and expanding prosperity. Within the Common Market area the 1950s and 1960s – the great economic boom, or the golden years, as economic historians are increasingly describing them – were a time of rising prosperity, widely shared, and rapid structural change. New products were finding mass consumer markets, changing the patterns of both production and consumption. Large numbers of workers were moving from agriculture, particularly its more traditional forms, into industrial jobs in the towns. The growth of manufacturing was being accelerated by the activities of multinational corporations, mainly, but not exclusively, American. Although changes were rapid and widespread, it was also an era of financial stability, with exchange rates pegged to the dollar and the US, the hegemon of the Bretton Woods System, setting a low inflation environment.

This shared view of the macroeconomic agenda was given formal expression in Article 1 of the Treaty of Rome with its explicit commitment to enhancing the prosperity of member states. The two main EC policies, the Common Agricultural Policy and tariff reductions on manufactures, worked with the grain of these developments. The CAP, by supporting agricultural incomes, redistributed part of the new prosperity to the agricultural sector. Whatever its microeconomic inefficiencies, particularly subsequently, at that stage it provided the agricultural and rural sectors with a buoyancy which tempered the shift in working population into manufacturing and urban areas. The reduction in internal tariffs and in barriers to trade among member states gave the stimulus of expanded markets, dovetailing with the rapid changes in industrial structure. Trade became a major engine of growth, with trade volumes throughout western Europe expanding twice as rapidly as national output. Again, the full employment environment facilitated the structural changes, new job opportunities being available to absorb those displaced by the decline of traditional industries and the changing patterns of production and trade.

The macroeconomic context set by the individual states in the 1950s and 1960s and the thrust of specific Common Market policies thus worked in tandem to promote the Treaty's goal of increased prosperity. Full employment, as the common objective among member states, and the extended prosperity which accompanied it, provided a highly favourable context for the first steps towards economic and political integration.

CURBING INFLATION

The upsurge of inflation in the 1970s changed the macroeconomic perspective in fundamental ways. The control of inflation progressively displaced full employment as the dominant objective of macroeconomic policy. While this applied throughout the advanced industrialised world, the issue of inflation control became particularly acute within the EC. The inflation rate for the EC as a whole was high relative to international levels, notably those of the US and Japan. Moreover, within the EC the low rate achieved by Germany was perceived by the other members as placing them under intense and sustained competitive pressure. Not entirely inconsistently, the Germans for their part were concerned that the periodic devaluations undertaken by the other member states, as a consequence of their higher rates of inflation, in turn placed Germany at a competitive disadvantage. As a macroeconomic environment inflation is disliked by business, while the uncertainty which high and variable inflation generates inhibits investment and new project development, particularly across national borders. High and variable inflation rates were therefore seen as a major obstacle to the process of further European integration.

For all the EC members, with the exception of the UK, the chosen means of inflation control, particularly following the second massive oil-price increase in 1979, was the acceptance of the commitment to fixed exchange rate parities within the EMS, including the commitment to eventual progression to monetary union. This applied in the case of the original eight (full) participants at the formation of the EMS in 1979, and the three subsequent new members, Spain, Portugal and Greece, also willingly adopted the framework. The motivation was partly a cooperative one, to establish a 'zone of monetary stability' as in the Bretton Woods era. A further powerful influence on the choice was the difficulty of implementing the CAP under the floating exchange rates which prevailed intermittently through the 1970s. For the UK government, on the other hand, the strategy of inflation control adopted at that time was based on the Monetarist prescription of tight domestic monetary policy. Since an active monetary policy requires a floating exchange rate, for the UK government the adoption of a fixed exchange rate was incompatible with their fundamental macroeconomic strategy, regardless of their wider views on European economic integration. While membership of the EMS was possible, participation in the ERM, its system of managing the fixed exchange rates among its members, was not.

During the first half of the 1980s the average inflation rate among members of the ERM was reduced by half, from over 10 per cent in 1979 to 5.5 per cent in 1985. Although a comparable reduction in the average level and dispersion of inflation rates among non-EC members can be claimed, this reduction in infla-tion is widely acknowledged as a major achievement of the ERM in this phase of its development. Parity realignments were agreed at relatively frequent intervals, as was required to maintain the international competitiveness of the economies with higher inflation rates. However, the devaluations were geared to providing incomplete compensation for inflation differentials, so maintaining pressure towards sustained disinflation in the higher-inflation countries. The successful disinflation in member countries achieved during this first phase can be attributed to two factors. From an economic perspective, the ERM provided a favourable framework. By fixing their exchange rate parities to trading partners with lower inflation rates, notably Germany, those countries with higher inflation were able to import lower inflation rates through the prices of their imports. By making realignments a relatively frequent and low-profile matter, adjustments could be based on technical rather than political considerations. The realignments were typically well judged, striking an effective balance between the need to restore competitiveness and the pressure for further disinflation. But the political dimension was also deployed to good effect. The formal commitment to fixed parities and eventual monetary union had several advantages. The public nature of the commitment served to stiffen the resolve of governments in pursuing disinflation, while making it easier for them to pass off unpopular policies at home. And, to the extent that successful control of inflation came to be anticipated, the credibility which was gained in turn enhanced the effectiveness of further anti-inflation measures – the advantages of 'tying one's hands' in the phrase of Giavazzi and Pagano (1988). The most striking example of this was Italy, the most inflation-prone member of the EC. There the commitment to the ERM allowed the government eventually to eliminate the wage indexation guaranteed through the *scala mobile*, thereby removing a powerful part of the inflation mechanism and undermining the expectations of continuing inflation.

The effectiveness of the ERM route to inflation control appeared to gain its final accolade with the decision by the UK government in 1990 to join, after policies of monetary targeting in a sequence of forms had failed to consolidate the successful initial disinflation. The low inflation and EC-wide boom of the end of the 1980s seemed to be confirmation of the success of this strategy, prompting the elaboration in the Delors Plan of the detailed timetable for the achievement of monetary union.

The eager adoption of the ERM by its members as the vehicle for disinflation had, however, a major unplanned consequence: the nature of the ERM itself was radically altered. At its inception the system had been designed explicitly with a view to overcoming the perceived deficiencies of the Bretton Woods regime of fixed exchange rates. In particular, it was to be a balanced system without a 'hegemon' or anchor currency. The new common currency, the ECU, was a basket currency, made up proportionately from all the individual member currencies. Parities, expressed through the grid, were set on a multilateral basis, with realignments by agreement of all participants. The divergence indicator was calculated against all other currencies, with each central bank then under the obligation to work towards maintaining any currency within its bands, as it approached either the top or the bottom. But in practice the dominance of the counterinflation strategy meant that the target became matching the German rate of inflation. With the D-mark consistently the strongest currency within the ERM and the German inflation rate setting the standard, the ERM quickly lost its balanced, multilateral character. Germany became the hegemon and the D-mark the anchor currency of the ERM.

THE CHANGING POLICY PERSPECTIVE

In earlier years the adoption of a rigorous anti-inflation policy would have been tempered by fears of its cost in terms of unemployment. The progressive acceptance through the 1970s that there was no long-run tradeoff between inflation and unemployment came to be seen by policy makers as releasing them from this constraint. Moreover, the renewed emphasis on the efficacy of market forces seemed to provide an assurance that the appropriate level of employment would be generated, and more soundly based, through market-driven decisions than through government manipulation. Although 'squeezing inflation out of the system' would involve some increase in unemployment, this would be limited in extent and short-lived. So while the control of inflation replaced full employment as the prime objective of macroeconomic policy, disinflation was not seen as inconsistent with, let alone designed to be an attack on, full employment. By controlling inflation and minimising distortionary interventions the government would provide the stable macroeconomic background and the enabling environment which would encourage well founded employment decisions. Employment could, and should, be dropped from the macroeconomic policy agenda. Demand management to influence employment was no longer accepted, or even acceptable.

This new orientation of economic policy towards market forces and deregulation emerged first and most sharply in the UK but gained ground progressively throughout the EU in the course of the 1980s. Although the UK led the way, the most dramatic instance of this policy shift occurred in France with the *tournant de la rigueur* in 1983. The confrontation between Germany and the Mitterrand government in France made it explicit that the overriding priority was to be the control of inflation and the fixity of exchange rate parities as the approach route to monetary union. Since that date macroeconomic policy in France has adhered so staunchly to these priorities that it has become the *cause célèbre* of disinflation through the EMS.[1]

Although neither the scale nor the duration of the rise in unemployment experienced throughout the EC over the first half of the 1980s were intended, or even foreseen, their effect has been profound. Unemployment throughout the EC rose from 5.7 per cent in 1979 to 10.9 per cent in 1985, and has subsequently remained more frequently above 10 per cent than below it, and well above its levels in the US and Japan. 'Eurosclerosis' has come to be widely seen as a macroeconomic disease. The need to respond to this disease, already perceived as early as the mid-1980s, was a major impetus to the renewed initiative of the Single Market Programme and in turn to the enhanced emphasis on the movement towards economic and monetary union (Commission of the EC 1990).

A further consequence of the priority given to the control of inflation and the repudiation of demand management was that monetary policy assumed primacy over fiscal policy. Again this was most explicitly articulated in UK through the Medium Term Financial Strategy. The main role of fiscal stance came to be set, via the financing implications of the government's borrowing requirement, in terms of its potential monetary implications. Particularly strikingly, in the smaller countries at the heart of the emergent monetary union – Belgium, the Netherlands and Luxembourg – fiscal policy became essentially identified with curbing the budget deficit.

These developments in macroeconomic perspectives through the 1980s have shaped the strategy towards monetary union incorporated in the Maastricht Treaty. The qualifying criteria are based first and foremost on the successful control of inflation, as measured through the rate of inflation itself, exchange rate stability and the level of nominal interest rates. In terms of explicit policy approaches, the enthronement of monetary policy and the accompanying downgrading of fiscal policy is directly reflected in the provisions of the programme. The ultimate requirement for fiscal stance is now to deliver a deficit and debt position in each member state which will pose no threat to the smooth progression towards monetary union. On the other hand, the Treaty is strikingly silent on issues relating to the 'real' economy, particularly levels of output and employment.

MACROECONOMIC POLICY WITHIN THE MAASTRICHT FRAMEWORK

Since membership of a monetary union implies the loss of monetary policy in addition to the exchange rate as instruments of national macroeconomic policy, the potential role of fiscal policy assumes greater importance (Goodhart 1990). It becomes one of the very few remaining means through which individual countries within the Union can influence their own macroeconomic situation and respond to country-specific developments.

The early years of the EMS provide some striking examples of the use of national discretion in fiscal policy to compensate for the lack of alternative instruments. In 1981 Belgium, in what has come to be known as the 'Maribel operation', sought to circumvent the fixity of the exchange rate by using the fiscal policy to 'mimic' a devaluation. The government reduced employers' social security contributions for blue-collar workers, who made up a larger fraction of the workforce in traded goods and construction than in the sheltered sectors, combined with an increase in VAT on durable goods, which were mostly imported. Simultaneously they persuaded firms and unions in the 'interprofessional agreement' to accept a lower level of real wage growth. In this way fiscal policy was used to engineer a relative price adjustment aimed at inducing a switching of expenditure in favour of home-produced goods, increasing the profitability of firms in the 'open' sector of the economy. The creative use of fiscal policy in this way is however restricted; for member states of the EU VAT rates must be kept within the predefined bands and not be product-specific.

It is clear that the Maastricht framework envisages substantial national control continuing within the fiscal area. The financial resources to be deployed by the central authorities within the EU are, and are to remain, only a small fraction of those in national budgets. At present only between one and two per cent of the combined GDPs of member states passes through the EU budget; while an increase in this is being sought, the proportion will remain extremely low. This contrasts with an average of between 40 and 50 per cent of GDP passing through the national budget within the member states, and around 30 per cent in federal states such as the US and Australia. Fiscal federalism within the EU is still very much in its infancy – particularly in view of the high proportion of the EU budget absorbed by the CAP. However, even without the new provisions in the Maastricht Treaty, the degree of national discretion in fiscal policy within the EU should not be exaggerated. Given the high level of intra-trade among member states, the imperative of controlling inflation in order to maintain competitiveness is an ongoing constraint. Market integration, even without formal moves to tax harmonisation, limits the degree of local discretion in choice of tax rates, as goods move ever more cheaply across borders and the location of production is increasingly determined on an international basis.

The provisions of the Treaty place strict limits to the overall outcomes from any exercise of national fiscal autonomy, imposing ceilings on permitted budget deficits at 3 per cent of GDP and on the outstanding debt stock at 60 per cent of annual GDP. The basis for these restrictions is the perceived risk of over-borrowing by countries with high deficits as the integration of capital markets expands borrowing opportunities and the fixity of exchange rates brings a single European interest rate close. Their cogency in this context has been robustly challenged (Buiter *et al.* 1993; Boltho 1997). Notwithstanding these criticisms, they have, in one important respect, been of assistance to member countries. In much of the EU in the 1990s budget deficits had become structural; given prevailing levels of taxation and public expenditure, the government budget had become persistently in deficit even at high levels of economic activity. This situation, arising from the combined effects of rising social security expenditure and pressures towards tax cuts, required correction. As with deflation a decade earlier, the EU, through the Maastricht criteria, has administered a timely push, stiffening the resolve of national governments in cutting welfare provisions and social expenditure, while giving them the opportunity to deflect part of the resulting unpopularity.

Our focus, however, is on the implications for national macroeconomic policy, and particularly the potential deflationary bias which the Maastricht criteria are likely to impose throughout the EU. Discretionary fiscal adjustment is the appropriate response to a country-specific change in demand. A striking example was the domestic economic boom in Germany following reunification, brought about by the launching of the reconstruction of the economies of the former GDR states. This required a tightening of fiscal stance in order to release the resources being committed to these states. A more typical instance would be recession in a major export market. In this case, on the assumption that prices and wages are less than perfectly flexible instantaneously, domestic income will contract. The budget deficit increases as revenues decline and transfer payments rise. Under the EMU rules, if the country has already reached its ceiling in terms of the permitted deficit ratio it must then take corrective fiscal action, in the form of reduced expenditure or increased taxation. This will exacerbate the income reduction. If it has not reached its borrowing ceiling, financing the deficit by way of borrowing on EU capital markets will put upward pressure on the European interest rate.[2] The consequent rise in the European interest rate will raise debt servicing outlays throughout the EU, forcing members on the average closer to the deficit ceiling. The more closely the constraint binds elsewhere, the greater the likelihood of further contractionary responses, i.e. the greater the consequent negative externality to other members of the EU from the deficit ceiling. With either scenario, therefore, whether or not the country initially affected is debt-constrained, the new EMU rules imply a bias towards deflation. In the event of an adverse demand shock affecting a single member state, countries throughout the EU may be required to tighten their fiscal stance, accentuating the initial recessionary impact.

A further aspect of this can be developed in terms of the role of automatic stabilisers. Their normal effect is to reduce the impact on national income of an exogenous demand change. Given sticky prices, the size of the multiplier depends inversely on the propensities to save and to import, and traditionally also negatively on the tax rate. The higher the tax rate, the lower the multiplier, and therefore the impact of the exogenous shock. But under the new EMU ceilings this effect can be reversed. In the case of a country with a fiscal position which just stabilises its debt-to-GDP ratio, when this debt ratio is at the maximum permitted level the multiplier becomes a positive function of the tax rate. The reason is straightforward: the higher the tax rate, the greater the government's loss of revenue and the consequential reduction in public expenditure which it must make as unemployment rises. The role of taxation as an automatic stabiliser is reversed.

In addition to the general deflationary bias introduced by the deficit and debt ceilings, which threatens to make the EU as a whole prone to more severe recessions, a further effect is likely to be the increasingly unequal incidence of recessions between regions. The deficit and debt ceilings will bind differentially, even outside the country experiencing the initial adverse shock. Those countries at the ceiling will be required to take more systematic deflationary action than those below. The deficit and debt rules will operate as a transmission mechanism, focusing deflation on countries at the ceilings. This is certainly counter to the objective of Article 1 of the Treaty of Rome, which aimed at the levelling-up of living standards throughout the Community.

The source of the deflationary bias lies in the inherent asymmetry of the deficit rule (Bean 1992; De Grauwe 1992; Gros and Thygesen 1992). Countries experiencing a negative shock when at or close to their deficit ceiling must take contractionary action, but there is no corresponding obligation to undertake

expansionary action at any other point in the system. By focusing the requirement to adjust exclusively on the deficit country, the Maastricht provisions
impart the same deflationary bias as was implicit in the case of external deficits
under the Bretton Woods System.

Although significant asymmetric demand shocks, impacting on individual
countries, may seem unlikely, the possibility should not be dismissed lightly. The
disruption to the development of the EMS following the reunification of
Germany has already shown the powerful effects of a country-specific demand
shock. Since virtually all the members of the EU in the mid-1990s are over, or
close to, the deficit and/or debt ceilings, enforced deflation is not a remote
scenario. And further, the impact of deflation on unemployment is potentially
extremely serious. European experience since the mid-1980s gives strong
evidence of hysteresis in unemployment, where the level of unemployment is
heavily influenced by its past history. Any substantial increase in unemployment
leads to longer unemployment durations and a higher proportion of long-term
unemployed. Since these workers search less actively for jobs, and/or are
perceived by employers to be less employable, they exert less downward pressure
on wage inflation. Higher unemployment becomes an equilibrium at the existing
rate of wage inflation, with a higher level of unemployment then required to
achieve further disinflation. The implication of this process is that once unemployment has become high it tends to remain high until a favourable demand
shock occurs.[3] This evidence of the intractability of unemployment following a
contraction in demand warns against a regime involving any persistent
deflationary bias.

Within the Maastricht framework a country at its deficit and debt ceilings
faces severely limited policy options to counter a negative demand shock. The
modification of relative prices through the adjustment of indirect taxes and the
use of direct subsidies (as in the Belgian instance above) is ruled out. Fiscal
adjustment may even have to be perverse. The only remaining option is the
'classical' one of the change in relative prices through downward adjustment of
domestic wages and prices. Achieving this is likely to be a protracted and painful
process. More importantly, it is the appropriate response to a different problem.
Adverse 'supply' developments, such as lagging productivity, require changing
relative prices. Demand shocks are appropriately countered by demand adjustments; general wage and price deflation is an inefficient response to these.
Moreover, since a major effect of price deflation is on trade, forcing individual
counties to counter a demand shock by wage and price adjustment is tanta-
mount to requiring it to export its unemployment. Applied in an inappropriate
situation, wage and price deflation are just as much a competitive 'beggar-
thy-neighbour' strategy as devaluations and trade restrictions. The risk of a
competitive deflationary spiral as member states attempt to cope with their individual macroeconomic problems within the Maastricht framework provides an
ominous parallel with the competitive devaluations and restrictions on trade of
the 1930s.

SOME FUTURE PROSPECTS

The influence of the EU on policy making in member states has increased and is set to increase further.[4] However, the loss of national policy instruments has not yet been adequately offset by the development of EU-wide instruments.

A crucial missing link is the automatic stabilisation which the central government budget provides to lower units within a federation and to regions within a unitary framework. Analysis of US experience suggests that 30–40 per cent of an income contraction in an individual state is automatically offset by lower tax payments to the federal budget and higher receipts from it (MacDougall *et al.* 1977; Eichengreen 1990). The minuscule size of the EU budget, its very limited basis in economic activity (1 per cent of VAT revenues, nothing from income or corporate taxes) and the discretionary nature of its major disbursements, such as through the Regional and Social Funds, are inadequate to provide any significant automatic stabilisation. The need for a fiscal policy designed at the European level seems unquestionable, to provide a shock-absorber mechanism particularly for the structurally weaker economies through automatic rather than discretionary transfers.

For individual countries, membership of the EMS and the move to EU-wide decision making involves giving up some independent decision-making powers in return for more powerful common decisions. These common decisions will only be frictionless if no conflicts of interest are involved. More generally, explicit coordination and conflict resolution will be necessary. At a minimum these will require suitable mechanisms and policy instruments. The path will be smoother if resources are available to support and compensate losers. The moves towards a European Central Bank have begun the formal transfer of monetary policy to the EU level. But, as at the level of the nation state, monetary policy has its inflexibilities, and a monetary stance which is too lax for one region may be too tight for another. This gives fiscal mechanisms an important role to play. Moreover, again as within nation states, monetary policy may work with or against fiscal policy. To allow the effective coordination of the fiscal-monetary policy mix at European level, some comparable coordination, if not centralisation, of fiscal stances is required (Drèze *et al.* 1987; van der Ploeg 1991). Further rebalancing of the roles of fiscal and monetary policy at the European level, and a framework for their coordination, is imperative.

The ultimate objective is the realisation of the EU as an 'optimum currency area', as analysed by Mundell (1961). The issue of an optimum currency area brings to the fore the tradeoff between microeconomic efficiency and macroeconomic stability. Microeconomic efficiency requires the integration of goods and factor markets. Given sticky prices locally, this tends to be at the expense of macroeconomic stability. For example, world recession will redistribute economic activity within the Union if different members have different degrees of exposure and sensitivity to world developments; that is, external events are likely have an asymmetric impact, causing internal tensions. The solutions are greater price and labour market flexibility, now being addressed by initiatives on competitiveness and unemployment in the EU, involving the medium-run, supply-side policies of deregulation and increased flexibility. For the shorter run, demand-side policy instruments superseded at the national level need to be replaced at the level of the EU if tensions are not to prevent further progress towards integration.

NOTES

1 A vivid account of the decision by the Mitterrand government to give priority to disinflation within the ERM is given in Giesbert (1990). For analyses of the subsequent French experience, see Sachs and Wyplosz (1986) and Fitoussi *et al.* (1993).
2 This assumes that national borrowing is not carried out at a national interest rate, where a multiple-rate structure would reflect the differing credit risks attaching to individual countries.
3 For further discussion of hysteresis in European unemployment see Blanchard and Summers (1986), Blanchard (1990) and Bean (1994).
    In many countries the credit boom brought about by financial liberalisation in the later 1980s provided just such a shock, but one which soon required sharply contractionary measures.
4 An interesting earlier view on macroeconomic policy within the EMS is given in Melitz (1988).

BIBLIOGRAPHY

Bean, C. (1992) 'Economic and monetary union in Europe', *Journal of Economic Perspectives*, 6, 4: 31–52.
——(1994) 'European unemployment: a survey', *Journal of Economic Literature*, 32, 2: 573–619.
Blanchard, O. (1990) 'Getting the questions right – and some the answers', in C. Bean and J. Dreze (eds) *Europe's Unemployment Problem*, Cambridge MA: MIT Press.
Blanchard, O. and Summers, L. (1986) 'Hysteresis and the European unemployment problem', in S. Fischer (ed.) *NBER Macroeconomics Annual*, 1, Cambridge MA: MIT Press.
Boltho, A. (1997) 'Should unemployment convergence precede monetary union?', in J. Forder and A. Menon (eds) *The European Union and National Macroeconomic Policy*, London: Routledge.
Buiter, W., Corsetti, G. and Roubini, N. (1993) 'Excessive deficits: sense and nonsense in the Treaty of Maastricht', *Economic Policy*, 16: 57–100.
Commission of the European Communities (1990) 'One market, one money', *European Economy*, 44.
De Grauwe, P. (1992) *The Economics of Monetary Integration*, Oxford: Oxford University Press.
Drèze, J., Wyplosz, C., Bean, C., Giavazzi, F. and Giersch, H. (1987) 'The two-handed growth strategy for Europe: autonomy through flexible cooperation', Centre for European Policy Studies, Brussels, *Paper* 34.
Eichengreen, B. (1990) 'One money for Europe? Lessons from the US currency union', *Economic Policy*, 10: 117–88.

Fitoussi, J-P., Atkinson, A. B., Blanchard, O. E., Flemming, J. S., Malinvaud, E., Phelps, E. S. and Solow, R. M. (1993) *Competitive Disinflation: The Mark and Budgetary Politics in Europe*, Oxford: Oxford University Press.

Giavazzi, F. and Pagano, M. (1988) 'The advantages of tying one's hands: EMS discipline and central bank credibility', *European Economic Review*, 32: 1055–82.

Giesbert, F-O. (1990) *Le Président*, Paris: Editions du Seuil.

Goodhart, C. (1990) 'Fiscal policy and the EMU', in K. O. Puhl *et al.* (eds) *Britain and EMU*, London: Centre for Economic Performance/London School of Economics.

Gros, D. and Thygesen, N. (1992) *European Monetary Integration*, London: Longman.

MacDougall D., Biche, D., Brown, A., Forte, F., Fréville, Y., O'Donoghue, M. and Peeters, T. (1977) *Public Finance in European Integration*, Brussels: Commission of the European Communities.

Melitz, J. (1988) 'Monetary discipline and cooperation in the European Monetary System: a synthesis', in F. Giavazzi, S. Micossi and M. Miller (eds) *The European Monetary System*, Cambridge: Cambridge University Press.

Mundell, R. (1961) 'A theory of optimum currency areas', *American Economic Review*, 51: 657–65.

Sachs, J. and Wyplosz, C. (1986) 'The economic consequences of President Mitterrand', *Economic Policy*, 2: 261–305.

Van der Ploeg, F. (1991) 'Macroeconomic policy coordination issues during the various phases of economic and monetary integration in Europe', *European Economy*, special issue: 136–64.

Wyplosz, C. (1991) 'Monetary union and fiscal policy discipline', *European Economy*, special issue: 165–84.

5

MOTIVATIONS FOR PARTICIPATING IN THE EMS[1]

Peter M. Oppenheimer

INTRODUCTION

Exchange rate policy has necessarily both a political and an economic dimension. Decisions regarding the identity of a state's currency and its mode of exchange with other currencies are part of the exercise of sovereignty or autonomy by a political authority. At the same time, these decisions are liable to affect a state's economic welfare and performance in important ways, notably regarding the stability of the currency's purchasing power and the level of economic activity.

In the case of the European Monetary System in the decade-and-a-half after 1978, and more particularly its exchange rate mechanism (ERM), the story is more complicated. Both the political and the economic objectives of participating European states were multiple in character. Moreover, the priorities attached to the different objectives varied over time and between countries. It is therefore necessary to give some degree of chronological treatment to the subject, as well as distinguishing the attitudes of various national governments.

THE BACKGROUND

The main features of the EMS were agreed by the European Council in the second half of 1978, principally at meetings in Bremen on 6–7 July and in Brussels on 4–5 December.[2] It is crucial to appreciate the background to the negotiations stemming from, on the one hand, macroeconomic management issues, and on the other hand, efforts towards European integration.

By late 1978 the world economy, including the western industrial countries, had lived for five years in the turbulence dating from the collapse of the Bretton Woods System, the commodity price boom of 1972–3 and the 1973–4 oil shock. In that time annual world inflation rates had averaged nearly 10 per cent, with widening disparities among countries. Realisation was strengthening that macroeconomic policy in the industrial states would have to focus increasingly on the restoration of price stability, and leave employment and growth to market forces. But a full consensus on the point had not yet been established. Governments were worried by unemployment levels not experienced since the 1930s and were conscious also that the accumulation of unspent oil revenues by low-absorbing OPEC countries had imposed a significant measure of demand restraint (initially 2 per cent of OECD countries' GNP) upon the global economy.

The United States authorities were among those which sought to encourage a renewed upswing in economic activity. Their main instrument for doing so, however, was relaxation of monetary policy. The shift to floating exchange rates following the collapse of Bretton Woods appeared to facilitate this. But it also radically altered the *modus operandi* of monetary policy. The exchange rate now became a major short-run transmission mechanism. Easier money brought depreciation of the currency and so enhanced competitiveness of the home country's tradeable goods. By the same token, however, with a country as large as the United States, its competitors experienced a perceptible loss of competitiveness and a corresponding threat to output and employment levels. The expansionary impetus in the US economy, far from clearly spreading to other countries, was achieved in part at their expense, subjecting them to an additional element of deflation (so-called negative transmission) (Oppenheimer 1989). This element was unevenly spread, falling disproportionately on countries whose currencies were viewed as the preferred short-term investment alternative to the dollar: the D-mark in particular, and also the Swiss franc.[3]

Meanwhile, within the European Community, membership had increased from six to nine with the accession in 1973 of Denmark, Ireland and the United Kingdom. But efforts to deepen the integration process had lost power. Following earlier debates among the six, the Werner Report in 1970 had envisaged a three-stage progress to monetary union (a virtual common currency) by 1980. The first stage was to involve narrowing the margins of fluctuation among Community currencies relative to the margins practised by all countries in general under the Bretton Woods System ('the snake in the tunnel').[4] The Werner Report had made light of technical and political obstacles to the establishment of monetary union. But in any event its proposed timetable would not have survived the economic upheavals of the early 1970s. Even before the dollar was finally allowed to float in March 1973, the attempt to preserve 'the snake' as a system of pegged exchange rates among EC countries had begun to crumble. Speculative pressure forced sterling out of the snake in June 1972. The Danish krone also exited a little later, but rejoined after an interval. The Italian lira followed early in 1973, while the French franc offered a double act, leaving the snake in January 1974 and making a repeat appearance from July 1975 to March 1976. What remained was a D-mark mini-bloc with the Benelux countries and Denmark. The search for new ways forward resulted in two further noble-sounding reports in 1975, on European Union (the Tindemans Report) and on monetary integration (the Marjolin Report). It was Tindemans who first adumbrated the notion – not in a monetary context – of a two-speed or two-tier Europe. Another two years on, in October 1977, Commission President Roy Jenkins gave a widely cited speech advocating once again, more in pleading than in expectation, a revival of plans for monetary union.

THE FEDERAL REPUBLIC

In these circumstances the German Federal Chancellor Helmut Schmidt saw the reconstruction of Europe's exchange rate arrangements in 1978 as a means of both resuming progress in European integration and – more immediately important – facilitating some expansionary adjustment in Germany's macroeconomic policies.

Besides being himself sympathetic to a measure of fiscal reflation on Germany's part, Schmidt was under partially conflicting pressure from several sources. German industry was lobbying against the strength of the D-mark and the consequent profit squeeze. The United States authorities, themselves facing international demands to counter the excessive weakness of the dollar, were urging Germany to take a larger share of responsibility for global anti-recessionary measures (the 'locomotive' model of world economic recovery, sometimes modified to a 'convoy' model, with a larger number of economies brought into the discussion). The American view enjoyed muted support from other OECD countries. The strength of Germany's trade balance in the mid-1970s almost resembled that of a low-absorbing OPEC state: in the aftermath of the 1973–4 jump in oil prices, the German current payments surplus, far from turning into a deficit, actually doubled in size.

On the other side was the Bundesbank, already at loggerheads for some years with economic policy makers in the German government and hostile to any return to Bretton-Woods-style pegged exchange rates, which might again oblige it to lend support to more inflation-prone currencies and obstruct the pursuit of price stability in Germany.

Between the Bremen and Brussels meetings of the European Council which set up the EMS occurred the Bonn economic summit of the Group of Seven, a uniquely wide-ranging attempt at international policy coordination, at which the German government agreed to undertake a modicum of fiscal reflation. The creation of the EMS needs to be viewed in relation to this. While partially going along with American demands for German reflation, Schmidt also sought to emphasise the stronger partnership between Germany and France, to reflect a degree of dissatisfaction with America's geopolitical leadership.[5] Surprisingly, commentators have tended to keep the Bonn summit and the EMS in separate compartments, even while giving them the same political interpretation – namely that they represented a defeat for the Bundesbank and a victory both for the German industrial lobby and for the cause of European integration.[6]

The extent of the Bundesbank's defeat must not, however, be exaggerated. The resolution of the European Council in December 1978 and the agreement of the participating central banks in March 1979 'serve only as a framework and do not prescribe the actual operation of the system in detail' (Ungerer *et al.* 1986: 1). Moves towards centralisation of EC countries' exchange reserves and creation of a European currency support mechanism (see below) were embryonic. There was no suggestion that parity changes should be only a last-resort measure. Indeed, one reason for endowing the grid of bilateral exchange rates with relatively generous margins of fluctuation (2.25 per cent on either side of any bilateral parity) was to permit small but perceptible parity changes which would retain an existing market rate within the newly announced range of fluctuation. The practical functioning of the system remained to be determined; and there was no indication that Chancellor Schmidt was likely to achieve his objective of dampening upvaluations of the D-mark in the face of a weak dollar.

FRANCE (I)

The fact that France had joined and abandoned the 'snake' not once but twice between 1972 and 1976 left it with a certain credibility problem on rejoining the pegged-rate club yet again. Its wish to do so rested on several interlinked motivations.

A long-standing *dirigiste* preference for fixed exchange rates was reinforced by the wish to secure the future of the EC's Common Agricultural Policy. France still saw its farmers as principal beneficiaries of the CAP, even though their share of Europe's agricultural output had not risen as originally expected. (The negotiated price levels gave too much protection to other countries' farmers.)

Exchange rate changes, and especially floating exchange rates, were an embarrassment, because they were judged to be reconcilable with the CAP only by 'temporary' application of complex border taxes and subsidies, the so-called Monetary Compensation Amounts or MCAs. These gave added protection to farmers in strong (revalued) currency countries and penalised those with weak (devalued) currencies. The principle in either case was that MCAs on farm exports and imports bridged the gap between the actual market rate of exchange and what came to be known as the Green Rate, the agreed conversion factor for translating European-unit-of-account prices of agricultural items into national currency prices.

Border taxes and subsidies might be thought incompatible with the concept of a unified market, but were not necessarily any more so than differentiated national rates of VAT or excise duty. The true inconsistency, or illogicality, was the dependence of the whole mechanism on *nominal rather than real exchange rates.* Faster overall inflation in France than in Germany, with the nominal exchange rate fixed, means a real appreciation of the franc relative to the D-mark. With agricultural prices uniform, MCAs ought to be brought into operation forthwith so as to prevent French farming from becoming relatively less profitable, and German relatively more profitable, than was intended at the outset. When the nominal exchange rate is adjusted to restore the real rate to (approximately) its initial position, the MCAs should then be removed. Granted this more logical arrangement, the French predilection for fixed nominal exchange rates might have been overturned rather than reinforced by concern for the farming interest.

In any event there were other factors impelling the French to seek a new monetary link with Germany in particular. First, in the matter of economic management, President Giscard d'Estaing and his Prime Minister Raymond Barre wished to give priority to monetary stabilisation and considered that this would be aided by pegging the franc to the D-mark. They hoped indeed that in the longer run this strategy would enable France to emulate Germany's economic performance. Restrictive financial policies in Germany for most of the 1970s contrasted with the wavering and relatively expansionary line followed in France. The outcome was that Germany achieved not only much lower inflation (averaging under 6 per cent a year, compared with about 9 per cent in France) and a strong balance of payments, but also less unemployment (4.5 as against 6 per cent). In the initial phase of the new EMS, France's unemployment might now have to rise further, but a major parliamentary election victory in March 1978 for the right-wing group of parties had given the government an appropriate mandate.

Second, the French authorities strongly supported the objective of a united European presence in world affairs, so as to lessen the dominance of the United States and of the dollar.

On the other hand the French were always in two (or more) minds as to the route by which this objective should be pursued. In a word, what they wanted was a Europe dominated by France rather than by Germany. This gave an added spur to their desire to match Germany's economic status not merely in the financial sphere but in industry and technology. In a celebrated TV interview in October 1978, Giscard d'Estaing presented France as the world's third military power but only its fifth economic power (after the US, USSR, Japan and Germany), and urged the promotion of French high-technology exports in order to forestall German dominance.[7] As regards European integration, French governments were regularly searching for ways of subordinating Germany to European institutions in the hope that this need not involve subordinating France.[8]

ITALY

Italy has always viewed the EC/EU as a bulwark of democracy and as a kind of guarantee against surrender to domestic political disorder and extremism. The Foreign Ministry in particular has been keen to emphasise the country's

European commitment. Big business has taken a similar line on the importance of Europe for Italy's industrial growth and prosperity. In the late 1970s this included the need to confront the excessive wage demands of the trade union movement.

On the other hand, the country's financial problems – high inflation (averaging 13 per cent a year in the 1970s), big budget deficits and intermittent balance-of-payments weakness – rendered problematic its capacity to rejoin an enlarged 'snake' arrangement like the EMS. The Bank of Italy in particular was sceptical, arguing that to seek monetary stabilisation by joining a semi-fixed exchange rate system was to put the cart before the horse, and that another failed attempt at membership would be worse than staying out in the first place (Bank of Italy, *Annual Report*, 1978. See also Spaventa 1980). The Bank's opposition would have been quelled if Britain had agreed to participate. In the event, the Bank had to content itself with securing a low initial parity for the lira, together with a wider band of fluctuation (6 per cent on either side) than other member currencies.

The decision to join was essentially political, taken by Prime Minister Giulio Andreotti at the head of a factious and quarrelsome five-party coalition government (Christian Democrats, Communists, Socialists, Social Democrats and Republicans). The Communists in the end opposed entry, thereby strengthening the determination to join of the right-wing parties. In the admirable phrase of Marcello de Cecco (in Guerrieri and Padoan 1989), EMS entry 'became one of those *scelte di civiltà* which have often been made in postwar Italy'. In other words, to vote for the EMS was to vote for freedom and the democratic order.

IRELAND

More than that of any other country, Ireland's initial approach to the EMS anticipated what was later to become the main proclaimed achievement or rationale of the system, namely the curbing of inflation. This was, of course, because Ireland was already (and had been since 1921, or rather since 1826) the small component of a two-state monetary union, and was all too conscious of the severe inflation which this caused it to share with the United Kingdom in the 1970s. Membership of a larger and less inflationary currency association would (almost) automatically bring greater stability to the Irish price level. It would also give the Irish a voice in joint policy making which they did not have in the monetary union with Britain alone.

These advantages would accrue in some measure whether or not Britain itself joined the new system. If Britain did not join, the prospects for early importation of price stability from Germany should be strengthened. Furthermore, separating the Irish punt from sterling would be a strong proclamation of the autonomy of Ireland's economic policy making.

Admittedly Britain remained Ireland's most important trading partner, but much less so than formerly. In the twenty years up to 1978 the UK's share of Irish trade had fallen from 78 per cent to 47 per cent, while that of the other seven EC countries had risen from 5 per cent to 30 per cent (Ludlow 1982: 184). Shifting from a sterling to a D-mark link could be presented as a forward-looking move, not least from the point of view of encouraging greater investment flows into Ireland's economy from the European continent.

Moreover, Irish opinion generally favoured stronger links with the European Community as enhancing the republic's independence and widening its political horizon – a revealing and very understandable contrast with Britain's chronic anxiety about losing independence or sovereignty.

At the same time, whether from political opportunism or from genuine anxiety about the burden of adjustments likely to fall on the Irish economy, the government sought a substantial increase in resource transfers from the rest of the Community as a *quid pro quo* for immediate entry to the ERM. The amount requested was £650 million (10 per cent of Irish GNP) over five years, i.e. 2 per cent of GNP per year.[9] The response – at the December 1978 European Council meeting – was an offer of subsidised fifteen-year loans whose benefit element was calculated by the Irish Government at about one-third of what they had asked for. At the last moment they managed to extract a further £50 million over two years in the form of bilateral packages. Given that they had effectively declared their intention of entering the ERM in any event, they had no reason to be dissatisfied with the outcome.[10]

UNITED KINGDOM (I)

The United Kingdom declined at the outset to participate in the Exchange Rate Mechanism of the EMS, though as a matter of constitutional formality it was admitted to the System itself.

Unlike the authorities in Ireland and in Germany's continental partners, British governments in the late 1970s and early 1980s saw little merit in an exchange rate peg to the D-mark as a stabilisation device. After dropping out of the 'snake' in mid-1972, the country had indeed landed itself with inflation rates far above the world average and also with labour market unrest, culminating in the disruption of fuel supplies and the industrial three-day week at the start of 1974. Moreover, the Labour government which took office thereafter required another two years and a traumatic encounter with the IMF to bring the situation clearly under control.[11] But then, from 1976 to 1978, by a mixture of financial restraint and direct wage regulation (incomes policy), inflation was lowered from around 20 per cent to under 10 per cent per annum without adding greatly to unemployment. The country thus passed through a significant crisis of its political and industrial system, and there was no perception that the whole episode could have been avoided or softened by giving a different priority to exchange rate relations with Europe.

In fact, some clash of interest with Germany emerged in the later stages. The recovery of sterling after 1976 was magnified by the weakness of the dollar noted above; and Britain felt – like Germany but perhaps with more reason – its industrial competitiveness to be under threat. The British Government had no interest in promoting a scheme intended to inhibit appreciation of the D-mark and/or encourage appreciation of sterling.

In addition, Britain did not view global economic policy making in the same European perspective as its continental partners. It was inclined to support the American line in favour of German reflation (and in other areas). It laid more stress on global monetary institutions such as the IMF than on regional structures. And it had no great wish to push ahead with the deeper integration of the European Community. A substantial (albeit declining) share of UK trade was, after all, still with non-European countries.

The other factor cited both at the time and subsequently as militating against UK membership of the ERM was sterling's status as a petro-currency. Britain was about to become an oil exporter, and this also affected global demand for sterling assets. The point, however, was a convenient excuse rather than a genuine argument. If the British authorities had taken it seriously, they would at least have considered the scenario that a D-mark peg would in some circumstances hold sterling lower than otherwise, rather than higher; in which case ERM membership would be good for industrial competitiveness rather than bad.

In May 1979, two months after the EMS began operating, a general election brought Mrs Thatcher to power at the head of a Conservative government. The previous decision to remain outside the ERM was unaltered. It corresponded to Mrs Thatcher's political inclination. It also reflected the Conservatives' initial conviction that the way to cure inflation was by monetary targeting – in the context of a medium-term financial strategy firmly proclaimed – and that this would be hampered rather than facilitated by a pegged exchange rate.

EVOLUTION OF THE SYSTEM

The creators of the EMS were keen to endow the system with specific institutional features beyond the mere regional affiliation of its membership. The European Currency Unit (ECU) was chosen as the numéraire and unit of account of the system. This was a currency basket comprising prescribed amounts of each EC currency (whether participating in the ERM or not) and subject to five-yearly revision. Revisions were made in September 1984 (partly to incorporate the Greek drachma) and in September 1989 (mainly to incorporate the peseta and the Portuguese escudo). The Treaty of Maastricht (1991) ruled out any further revisions with effect from 1993.

The ECU was used to define central exchange rates and hence the grid of bilateral ERM parities. Central rates were to be changed only by common agreement. There was also a notion that the ECU would be increasingly used as the denominator of central bank interventions in defence of exchange rates, and hence also as the means of settlement among the central banks. This would have the important merit of sharing the exchange risk between debtor and creditor country – albeit unevenly, since the weighting of the ECU carried a bias in favour of traditionally strong currencies, chiefly the D-mark.

To facilitate such development, the European Monetary Cooperation Fund (EMCF) was established, which issued participating central banks with ECUs on a three-month revolving swap basis against the deposit of 20 per cent of their gold and dollar reserves. When currencies reached the boundary of their permitted margins of fluctuation and were consequently entitled to unlimited official support, participating central banks could grant each other unlimited very short-term credit through the EMCF, in order to allow intervention in EC currencies rather than in dollars. This was an addition to other, more conventional short- and medium-term facilities, partly inherited from the former 'snake'. Authorities were of course free to intervene in the exchange markets without waiting for the grid boundaries to be reached.

Besides the ECU and the EMCF, the system incorporated a so-called divergence indicator. This was an attempt to compensate for the fact that a country whose currency had a large weight in the ECU basket would, so to speak, when pursuing deviant policies, drag the whole system with it for a certain distance before encountering its exchange rate boundary. The idea was to identify the phenomenon from a currency's movement in terms of the ECU basket, with a presumption to modify the policies in question when a divergence threshold was reached. The main potential culprit was, of course, a deflationary Germany.

The indicator was an ingenious pioneering effort, but could not have been expected to play more than a very subsidiary role in altering the balance of national economic policies. The exchange market behaviour which it was intended to record was quite remote from policy actions and subject to numerous other influences. As it happens, the details of the indicator's construction were also defective, notably in failing to distinguish adequately between absolute and proportionate exchange rate movements and to allow for the effect of including non-members of the ERM (sterling) and semi-members (Italy, with its wider margins) in the ECU basket. (See Spaventa 1982; Artis 1985).

For all its technical complexities, the EMS agreement stands out as a rare episode of creative common sense between the follies of the Werner Report a decade earlier and those of the Delors Report a decade later, the latter giving rise in turn to the Treaty of Maastricht in 1992. In contrast to Werner and Delors, the creators of the EMS did not proclaim the goal of monetary union. While the immediate objective was 'to establish a greater measure of monetary stability in the Community', its wider significance was seen in terms not of one-sided extrapolation to monetary union but of a broad range of Community objectives in which money had no special priority.

It should be seen as a fundamental component of a more comprehensive strategy aimed at lasting growth with stability, a progressive return to full employment, the harmonisation of living standards and the lessening of regional disparities in the Community. The European Monetary System will facilitate the convergence of economic development and give fresh impetus to the process of European Union.

(*European Economy*, 3, July 1979, 46, quoted in Ungerer *et al.* 1983)

Moreover, these wider objectives were kept in view for much of the 1980s, notably in the Single European Act of 1985, and its programme 'to complete the internal market' by 1992.

The difficulty was to accept the EMS itself as a quasi-permanent rather than an interim arrangement. The 1978 agreement envisaged the system as proceeding within two years to a second and (be it noted) final phase, in which the EMCF would be transformed into a European Monetary Fund, with a more independent role regionally analogous to that of the IMF. This proved unrealistic and the system continued to operate under its initial supposedly interim provisions.

In addition, the system was not – could not be – well designed to meet Chancellor Schmidt's objective of monetary burden-sharing in the face of dollar weakness, i.e. to promote conditions in which the European counterpart of such weakness would be not a disproportionate appreciation of the D-mark but a more even appreciation of a wider range of currencies. Other currencies could take the place of D-marks in global portfolios only if exchange rate changes between them and the D-mark looked less and less likely in the future – if, in other words, the system was seen as clearly on the road to monetary union. This condition was plainly not fulfilled for the first eight years or so (1979–87) of the EMS's operation, which witnessed altogether eleven central rate realignments, albeit of decreasing frequency and in three cases involving only a single currency (Table 5.1).

Chancellor Schmidt's anxieties were allayed by other means. The dollar ceased to be weak. And major industrial countries, their resolve bolstered by the second oil-price shock of 1979–80, undertook a synchronised (though not coordinated) attack on inflation in the 1980s. Both changes were signalled, or symbolised, by President Carter's appointment in mid-1979 of Paul Volcker as Chairman of The Federal Reserve System. Volcker moved decisively to tighten US monetary policy and maintained this stance – with some moderation after the onset of the third-world debt crisis in August 1982 – for more than five years. The result was to put the dollar on a continuous upward trend from autumn 1979 until the first quarter of 1985.

At the same time average inflation rates in industrial countries declined from 8–10 per cent at the start of the 1980s to around 3 per cent in the second half of the decade (Table 5.2).

The convergence of inflation rates on the (low) German level was the main

Table 5.1 EMS central-rate realignments, 1979–90 (percentage change; minus sign denotes a devaluation)

Currency	24 Sept 1979	30 Nov 1979	23 Mar 1981	5 Oct 1981	22 Feb 1982	14 June 1982	21 Mar 1983	22 July 1985	7 April 1986	4 August 1986	12 Jan 1987	8 Jan 1990[a]
Deutschmark	+2.0			+5.5		+4.25	+5.5	+2.0	+3.0		+3.0	
French franc				-3.0		-5.75	-2.5	+2.0	-3.0			
Netherlands guilder				+5.5		+4.25	+3.5	+2.0	+3.0		+3.0	
Belgian and Luxembourg franc					-8.5		+1.5	+2.0	+1.0		+2.0	
Italian lira			-6.0	-3.0		-2.75	-2.5	-6.2				-3.0
Danish krone	-2.9	-4.8			-3.0		+2.5	+2.0	+1 0			
Irish punt							-3.5	+2.0		-8.0		
Spanish peseta[b]												
Pound sterling[c]												

Source: Eurostat, cited in Tsoukalis (1991).

Notes

a On this date the Italian lira moved from wide fluctuation bands of ± 6 per cent around its central rate to narrow fluctuation bands of ± 2.25 per cent.
b The peseta joined the ERM on 19 June 1989 with a wide band of ± 6 per cent around its central rates.
c The pound entered the ERM on 8 October 1990 with a fluctuation band of ± 6 per cent around its central rates.

reason for the much diminished frequency of EMS exchange rate realignments in the later 1980s. How much credit can the EMS itself, or rather the ERM, claim for the conquest of inflation? The answer is – only a modest amount. Basically, ending inflation was a global, not a regional phenomenon. It owed quite a lot to the recession-induced weakness of commodity prices (Beckerman and Jenkinson 1986) and especially to the turn-round in the oil market, where a variety of economies and substitution processes on both the demand and the supply side came to fruition in the early 1980s. A buyer's market for oil re-emerged, as OPEC sales tumbled from over thirty million barrels a day in 1980 to under twenty million in 1982. OPEC countries for a while managed by dint of output restrictions, mostly on the part of Saudi Arabia, to prevent a major price collapse. But these arrangements broke down and in early 1986 the price dropped from $28 to around $16 a barrel, remaining at this level for most of the following decade.

Within Europe, it may be said, the desire to maintain pegged exchange rates stiffened the anti-inflationary resolve of ERM participants, partly because Germany was at once the biggest economy in the system and the one with the best established commitment to price stability. Even so, the 'sacrifice ratios' (short-run relationships between inflation decline and unemployment increase) were not

Table 5.2 Inflation rates, 1980–9 (private consumption deflator; annual percentage change)

	1980	1981	1982	1983	1984	1985	1986	1987	1988	1989
Belgium	6.5	8.6	7.8	7.2	5.7	5.9	0.3	1.8	1.8	3.1
Denmark	10.7	12.0	10.2	6.8	6.4	4.3	3.5	4.4	4.9	5.0
Germany	5.8	6.0	4.7	3.2	2.5	2.1	-0.2	0.8	1.3	3.1
Spain	15.6	14.3	14.5	12.3	11.0	8.2	8.7	5.4	5.1	6.6
France	13.2	13.4	11.8	9.7	7.9	6.0	2.9	3.3	3.0	3.5
Ireland	18.6	19.6	14.9	9.2	7.6	4.7	4.0	2.6	2.5	4.1
Italy	20.2	18.2	16.9	15.1	11.9	9.0	5.7	5.0	4.8	6.0
Luxembourg	7.7	8.7	10.6	8.5	6.9	4.5	1.2	1.5	2.6	3.4
Netherlands	6.9	5.8	5.5	2.9	2.2	2.2	0.2	-0.4	0.7	1.1
Greece	21.2	22.7	20.7	18.1	17.9	18.3	22.0	15.6	14.0	13.8
Portugal	22.3	20.2	20.3	25.8	28.5	19.4	13.8	10.0	10.0	12.8
United Kingdom	16.4	11.2	8.7	5.0	5.1	5.2	4.4	3.9	5.0	5.8
	Weighted average									
EC-12	13.2	12.1	10.7	8.6	7.3	5.9	3.8	3.5	3.7	4.8
ERM-8[a]	11.6	11.7	10.3	8.4	6.7	5.2	2.4	2.7	2.8	3.9
ERM-9[b]		12.0	10.8	8.9	7.2	5.6	3.1	3.0	3.0	4.2

Source: Commission of the EC, cited in Tsoukalis (1991).
Notes
a   ERM-8: Belgium, Denmark, Germany, France, Ireland, Italy, Luxembourg and the Netherlands.
b   ERM-9: The above countries plus Spain.

necessarily more favourable in ERM than in other industrial countries – Ireland being a striking case in point, despite earlier optimism (Dornbusch 1989).

At the same time, Europe's reactions to Germany's example and behaviour were by no means uniformly approving. There were complaints from both academics (e.g. de Grauwe 1987) and policy makers about 'asymmetries' and deflationary bias in the operation of the EMS. It was felt after 1981 that more than lip service should be paid to the principle of collective decision making on exchange rate realignments and related measures (Padoa-Schioppa 1985). The resulting politicisation and bureaucratisation of decision making on exchange rates constituted a second significant brake on EMS realignments – and, unlike the convergence of inflation rates, a basically undesirable one. The key influence of France is noted below.

A further stage in the process was reached in 1987. The practice of intra-marginal exchange market interventions by ERM participants had not only put a further nail into the coffin of the divergence indicator, but had also rendered inoperative the provisions for very short-term ECU credits through the EMCF. The Basle-Nyborg Agreement concluded in September 1987 was a renewed attempt to remedy the associated asymmetries. It was agreed that EMCF credits would be available – up to a specified but fairly generous limit – to finance intra-marginal interventions. At the same time, however, participants stated their intention to make parity realignments as small and infrequent as possible, and less than fully compensatory for inflation differentials (i.e. so as to encourage convergent price- or cost-level behaviour). The latter feature carried the danger of allowing currency misalignments to become persistent.

The long-continuing debate about biases and asymmetries in the ERM itself gives the lie to suggestions that the EMS was a simple D-mark zone or that membership automatically allowed countries to benefit from the Bundesbank's anti-inflation credibility (Giavazzi and Pagano 1988). It is evident that the German authorities exercised greater autonomy in macroeconomic and especially in monetary policy than other members (Giavazzi and Giovannini 1989). But they had no desire to direct other countries' policies nor to preserve a given set of exchange rates through thick and thin.[12] They were certainly conscious of the possibility of inflationary impacts upon Germany emanating from other participants' economies. If the EMS began as an attempt by Helmut Schmidt to promote monetary burden-sharing across the EC, it had developed a decade later into an attempt by (mainly) France and Italy to compel Germany to subordinate its financial policies to the preservation of a fixed-rate system. The German authorities, especially the Bundesbank, were understandably reluctant.

FRANCE (II)

France was the key case of a country whose anti-inflationary orientation came to be founded on EMS membership. This emerged after the French authorities had come close to repeating the country's in-out performance with the 'snake' of the 1970s.

The initial decision of President Giscard d'Estaing and Prime Minister Barre to join in establishing the Exchange Rate Mechanism in 1979 was called into question following the election of a socialist administration under President Mitterrand in May 1981. Rather than maintain the restrictive financial policies inherited from his predecessor, Mitterrand sought at first to revert to an expansionary strategy in search of higher employment and economic growth, despite the fact that France's inflation rate in 1981–2 was running at over 12 per cent per annum, more than double that of Germany.

An ERM realignment in October 1981, with the French franc and lira devaluing by 3 per cent while the D-mark and Dutch guilder both upvalued by 5 per cent, was taken by the Government in its stride. In June 1982, however, the process was repeated with the franc dropping 5.75 per cent and the D-mark rising 4.25 per cent. The Government wavered. There was a three-month wage and price freeze, higher social security contributions and a budget deficit target of 3 per cent of GDP (Sachs and Wyplosz 1986). The dénouement came with the third franc devaluation in March 1983. The Government faced a choice between abandoning either its expansionary strategy or its commitment to the ERM and even, on a partial or temporary basis, to free trade and liberalised markets within the European Community. France's partnership with Germany would have been put at risk. This was seen as unacceptable. France's macroeconomic strategy accordingly underwent an about-turn. The commitment to the ERM was reaffirmed, financial austerity imposed and *le franc fort* became the watchword of French financial policy. While the unemployment rate rose from 8 per cent in 1983 to over 10 per cent in 1986, annual inflation came down to 3 per cent.

At the same time French willingness to accept further exchange rate realignments rapidly diminished. It was common knowledge that the Bundesbank wanted a further upvaluation of the D-mark in 1988–9 and that this was vetoed by the German government at France's insistence. France thus bears principal responsibility for the freezing of ERM exchange parities after 1987, a move which among other things hardened the Bundesbank's attitude to European monetary union and thereby influenced the terms of the Maastricht Treaty (1991–2) and the European Union Stability Pact (1996) in a deflationary direction. Germany's inflation rate rose from zero in 1986–7 to 3.1 per cent in 1989 on the eve of reunification; and this movement would very probably have been dampened by additional D-mark appreciation.

UNITED KINGDOM (II)

Like France, Britain had more than one bite at the EMS cherry. Having declined to enter the ERM in 1978–9, the authorities with much delay and hesitation

came round to joining it in October 1990. Two factors played a part in the decision. One was politics. The Conservative government and party were notoriously
divided in their attitude to European integration, Mrs Thatcher being on the
Euro-sceptic side and her successive Chancellors of the Exchequer (first Howe,
then Lawson, then Major) being either pro-European or middle-of-the-road.

The second factor was economic management and especially the control of
inflation. The Medium-Term Financial Strategy followed by the Thatcher
government in its early years (1979–82) centred on the targeting of money
supply growth and, in a subordinate capacity, of the public sector deficit. The
policy pursued was extremely tight. This was indicated by the increase in, and
level of, both interest rates and the sterling exchange rate. It led to a ferocious
squeeze on profits and liquidity in the corporate sector, and thence to a deep
recession and a 30 per cent fall in manufacturing employment. Unfortunately, or
amusingly, these developments went together with a substantial overshoot of the
financial aggregates, caused by distress borrowing from the banking sector and
automatic stabiliser effects on the budget. Although the financial numbers were
eventually brought into line – in the medium term, in fact; but that is not what
the Strategy was supposed to mean – their use as policy anchors was discredited.

Policy was relaxed and economic recovery gathered pace in the middle years
of the decade. Chancellor Nigel Lawson embarked early in 1987 on a policy of
'shadowing the Deutschmark' without any formal or public declaration of
exchange rate fixity. The policy was sustained for a year. It broke down because
the rate chosen – a little under DM3 to the pound – turned out to be too low in
the face of vigorous credit demand in the UK economy which pulled in funds
from abroad.[13] In other words, instead of acting as a brake on UK monetary
growth, the undeclared peg facilitated it. And, of course, the problem with an
undeclared peg is that the peg cannot be altered without the policy as a whole
collapsing.

Circumstances alter cases. In 1980–2, with a floating exchange rate, excessive-
looking growth of bank credit was a sign of extreme monetary tightness. In
1987–8, with an undeclared pegged rate, excessive-looking growth of bank
credit – 20 per cent per annum – was a sign of just that. Lawson was saying one
thing (paying lip service to the priority of price stability as a policy goal) and
doing another (permitting an unrestrained credit boom, analogous to those of
Maudling in 1964 and Heath-Barber in 1971–3). At the same time the anti-
inflation benefits of the ERM were looking more impressive, largely because of
the turn-round in France's and Italy's performance. The lesson drawn in political
circles was that an opportunity should be taken to put sterling on a declared
pegged rate within the ERM. The fact that the clandestine D-mark peg in 1987
had proved, contrary to expectations, to be too low for equilibrium must have
been seen as arguing in favour of a high ('overvalued') parity for sterling when
the moment came.

A further misguided argument in the same direction was the extreme version
of the Giavazzi-Pagano (1988) idea that the mere declaration of a D-mark peg

would give immediate anti-inflation credibility, reducing at a stroke the expected future rate of UK price increases and enabling interest rates – including the politically crucial mortgage rate – to be reduced correspondingly. Carried to its logical conclusion the argument implied that the United Kingdom could bring about any price level it wanted merely by choosing an appropriately high sterling peg to the D-mark. This has the same gimmicky quality as the faith of some of Mrs Thatcher's colleagues ten years earlier that the Medium-Term Financial Strategy would produce an instant turn-round in inflationary expectations. Samuel Brittan has referred to belief in gimmicks as an unfortunate (if unintended) aspect of Keynes's legacy to economic policy makers. It was certainly very much in evidence among UK monetarist politicians in the 1980s.

John Major as Chancellor of the Exchequer finally announced Britain's entry to the ERM – with the wider fluctuation band of ±6 per cent – in October 1990. The fact that the announcement referred to a D-mark rather than an ECU parity was consistent both with the anti-inflation objective that underlay the British decision and with the 'shadow' episode in 1987 which itself had been conducted in relation to the German currency alone. On the other hand, the unilateral nature of the announcement, without consultation of Britain's European partners, surely reflected Britain's reluctance to shift a growing range of economic policy decisions from the national to the Community level.

SPAIN

Britain was not the only latter-day entrant to the ERM. Spain had joined some fifteen months earlier, in June 1989, also with the wider (6 per cent) band of fluctuation. But Spain's membership of the European Community as a whole dated only from 1986, and its adherence to the exchange rate mechanism was part and parcel of its adaptation to Community institutions. This had three main aspects: financial stability, political integration and the unified market.

As regards financial stability, the Spanish authorities – notably the central bank, which was the main protagonist of EMS membership – were aiming to consolidate progress made since 1985 in reducing the rate of inflation and the volatility of the exchange rate, both nominal and real. A further goal was to bring down the level of real interest rates with the help of much greater external financial integration.

Spain's inflation rate in the first half of the 1980s averaged about 14 per cent per annum; by 1987–9 the figure had come down to 6 per cent. At the same time, the authorities succeeded in keeping the fluctuating rate of the peseta within 6 per cent of the EMS currencies during 1986–8, while at the same time (slightly earlier in fact, in 1985–7) substantially abolishing currency regulations and liberalising financial markets (Viñals 1990; Artus and Dupuy 1992). The long-term nominal interest rate, however, declined less than the rate of inflation – from 16 per cent to about 11 per cent.

As regards trade in goods and services, Spain had before joining the EC in 1986 already eliminated most quantitative restrictions on European trade, as well as more than half of its 14 per cent basic tariff. The remaining trade barriers had been largely removed by 1989.

The main difficulty which the country faced on joining the EMS was that its entry encouraged a wave of semi-speculative capital inflows, both portfolio investment and short-term lending. The boom which this helped to finance not only put the balance of payments into large current deficit – from modest surplus in the mid-1980s – but also, more important, obstructed further lowering of the rate of inflation. With a fixed peg *vis-à-vis* other EMS currencies, the peseta was bound to become increasingly overvalued; the position was sustainable to begin with partly because Spain's competitiveness had benefited significantly from currency depreciations in the earlier 1980s (Tsoukalis 1997: 154).

PORTUGAL

Portugal entered the European Community together with Spain in 1986, but the ERM only in April 1992. The difference was entirely a matter of the inflation rate. There was widespread consensus among Portuguese politicians and economists that the country should indeed join the ERM as soon as circumstances permitted: there was everything to gain in terms of external trade and foreign investment from participating as fully as possible in the process of European economic and monetary integration. In addition, the monetary discipline implied by an exchange rate peg would give potentially decisive help in the curbing of inflation. The difficulty was to bring the initial inflation rate to a point where the country could plausibly commit itself to a stationary peg in the first place. In the early 1980s Portuguese prices were rising by well over 20 per cent per annum; in 1986–90 the average rate was still around 11 per cent. It was only just in single figures when the entry to ERM was announced.

Exchange rate policy had gone through corresponding phases. For more than a decade up to 1989 the country used a crawling-peg system, with pre-announced monthly devaluation targets designed to cover all or most of the excess of Portugal's inflation over that of its main trading partners (da Silva Lopes 1993). In 1989 this was replaced by a less specific policy of managed float. As a result the nominal exchange rate of the escudo in terms of other EMS currencies and the ECU showed little net change over the next three years; in other words, the rate could have been readily accommodated during that period within a ±6 per cent ERM band. This signified, however, a real appreciation of about 25 per cent, with the prospect of more to come even if inflation declined further in the aftermath of entry.

In these circumstances proponents of early entry were evidently banking – or gambling – on both the directly favourable effects of exchange rate stability on domestic prices and the indirect disciplinary influence upon fiscal policy, industrial pricing and wage negotiations. Encouragement was drawn from the 1992 wage round, which produced agreed target figures of 8 per cent pay increases with 2 per cent productivity gains, compared with wage rises of 15+ per cent in 1991. The inflation rate did indeed decline to 6 per cent in 1993–4.

EPILOGUE: THE BUNDESBANK'S REVENGE

From 1987 to 1992 there were no parity realignments within the ERM, apart from a slight reduction for the lira in January 1990 on the occasion of its moving from the 6 per cent to the 2.5 per cent band of fluctuation. This period witnessed the European Council meeting in Hanover (1988), which set up the Committee for the Study of Economic and Monetary Union (the Delors Committee), whose report in 1989 led in turn, via an Intergovernmental Conference in 1990, to the Treaty of Maastricht signed in January 1992. Political motives were of course paramount in these developments. But it seems also that on the economic side governments had been misled by the substantial reduction and convergence of European inflation rates during the 1980s into overlooking symptoms of vulnerability in the exchange rate structure.

Convergence of inflation rates, though substantial, was not complete. At low rates of inflation, systematic inter-country differences of one or two per cent per annum will, if not halted or reversed, make realignments necessary eventually. In addition, there was a legacy of accumulated differences in cost or competitiveness *levels*, which would be preserved rather than eliminated by uniform rates of inflation. This was indicated by, for example, the conspicuous variation in standardised unemployment levels between, on one side, West Germany (6 per cent) and on the other, France and Italy (10–11 per cent). United Kingdom unemployment, too, exceeded 10 per cent in 1992–3. The fact that the Bundesbank had been frustrated in its wish to secure further upvaluation of the D-mark was also significant. In short, the danger signals were clear enough for those who wished to observe them, and it is not only with hindsight, *pace* the comments of Tsoukalis (1997: 148) and of Artis and Lewis (1993), that the exchange rate pattern appeared rigid rather than stable.[14]

Against this background the principal factor making for realignment was the firm monetary policy maintained by the Bundesbank in the period 1990–2. This *pis aller* for the revaluation which the Bundesbank had sought earlier was doubly warranted by economic circumstances in Germany. The country's reunification, formally accomplished in October 1990, prolonged and intensified the economic upswing. Real GDP rose by more than 5 per cent in 1990 compared with 1980, and by a further 3.7 per cent in 1991; the corresponding average figures for the rest of western Europe were under 3 per cent and about 0.8 per cent respectively, despite some spillover of Germany's boom to its neighbours. German growth fell away in 1992, leaving however a pronounced inflationary legacy, with prices rising by 4.5 per cent per annum and trade unions seeking large wage increases. Money and credit aggregates were continuing to expand rapidly – e.g. bank credit to the private sector by nearly 10 per cent per annum. Furthermore, the public sector accounts had deteriorated as a result of the Federal Government's refusal to raise taxes sufficiently to cover the expenditure increases arising from reunification (essentially subsidies of one kind or another to the former East Germany).

Thus the German policy mix was one of fiscal stimulus combined with monetary restraint. Even so, the restraint remained quite moderate. Nominal short-term interest rates climbed steadily from 8 per cent at the start of 1990 to nearly 10 per cent in mid-1992; this meant real rates fluctuating around 5.5 per cent. At the same time, however, long-term rates both nominal and real were falling from summer 1990 onwards; the real rate was in the neighbourhood of 4.5 per cent by summer 1992.

A further feature of Germany's economic position after reunification was that its current balance of payments had moved into deficit to the tune of $20 billion a year, reflecting the huge excess of absorption over production in the new eastern Länder. This was a factor diminishing the desirability of D-mark revaluation. Recovery of output in eastern Germany was already handicapped by the high level of unit labour costs compared with those in other ex-communist territories such as the Czech Republic. The current payments deficit also made it easy for Germany to accommodate a large inflow of funds from the United States, where the currency was weakened by a sharp easing of monetary conditions in 1991–2 – an instructive contrast with the episode of dollar weakness at the time of the EMS's creation in 1978, when the German authorities were trying to fend off the movement of funds into D-marks.

The prolonged nature of the currency confusions in Europe in 1992–3 was partly due to the sheer number of currencies involved. Apart from the member countries of the ERM, three Nordic non-members had declared their currencies pegged in terms of the ECU: Norway in 1990, Finland and Sweden in 1991. The Finnish markka had then undergone an exchange market crisis in November 1991, only five months after pegging to the ECU. A massive outflow of funds, triggered in part by anxiety over Finland's commercial prospects in the face of the impending disintegration of the Soviet Union, had been halted by a temporary (one-day) float and a devaluation of 12.3 per cent of the markka's central ECU rate.[15] This episode turned out to be a pointer to the events beginning in September 1992, rather as in 1980 the crisis over Poland's external indebtedness presaged the wider international debt crisis after August 1982.

As it happened, the markka was the first currency to be forced off its ECU peg in early September 1992, following the breakdown of a negotiated wage agreement. But the Swedish and Norwegian currencies, as well as the lira and sterling, were also perceived as vulnerable, after the failure of European Community finance ministers and of the ECOFIN Council to secure an early lowering of German interest rates (the Bundesbank having indeed raised its discount rate from 8.0 to 8.75 per cent in mid-July). The narrow rejection of the

Maastricht Treaty in the first Danish referendum in June had also contributed to the sense of fragility.

In any event, between September 1992 and May 1993 eleven fixed or pegged European currencies came under repeated downward pressure in the exchange markets of unprecedented severity. Eight of them (the lira, sterling, the punt, the Swedish and Norwegian krone, the markka, the peseta and the escudo) were either devalued, in some cases more than once, or floated. The only ones to hold the line were the French and Belgian francs and the Danish krone. The D-mark and the Dutch guilder, of course, were subject to corresponding upward pressure. Finally, at the end of July 1993, renewed selling of the French and other currencies led the European authorities to announce a 'temporary' widening of the ERM's margins of fluctuation (except between the D-mark and the guilder) to ±15 per cent.[16]

Thereafter a calmer period set in. The new 15 per cent bands were not seriously tested – the bandwidth actually exploited seldom reached even 8 per cent over the following two years. In March 1995 the peseta was devalued – for the fourth time since its ERM entry – by 7 per cent; and the escudo – for the third time since its entry – by 3.5 per cent. In January 1995 Austria had formally joined the 'new' ERM. Finland and Italy (re)joined it in autumn 1996, largely with a view to seeking eligibility for adherence to the single European currency in 1999.

As one would expect, the real effective exchange rate changes which resulted from these events in the medium term were quite limited in size and in no way commensurate with the market upheavals. The latter proved unavoidable because the authorities in the ERM countries had rejected the idea of orderly general realignments. So they were faced with a succession of speculative attacks affecting one currency after another in domino fashion. Once the turmoil started, events had to take their course. The authorities could not have quietened the markets by declaring a new set of parities. The episode demonstrates, first of all, the futility of tying one's hands. Premature attempts to freeze exchange rates end by destroying the credibility of the pegged-rate system. At the same time, there was no damage to price stabilisation efforts. Annual inflation rates in the European Union averaged 3 per cent in 1994–5 – at least 0.5 per cent less than in 1992–3.

Beyond this, opposite lessons may be drawn. Probably the more common is to strengthen the belief that an adjustable-peg system is incompatible with substantial freedom of international capital movements. This is argued on two counts. First, efforts to maintain exchange rate pegs are liable to be defeated by speculation. Second, with pegged exchanges markets tend to equalise nominal rather than real interest rates in different member countries, which is destabilising because it implies that real rates are held below their equilibrium level in (relatively) high-inflation countries and above it in low-inflation countries.

If this line of reasoning is accepted, there is no halfway house between floating and full monetary union. But the reasoning is not conclusive. The opposite view is that adjustable pegs form a viable system, provided realignments are managed so that speculators are unable to make large profits by anticipating them. This means keeping parity changes small, preferably no greater than the width of the normal band of fluctuation around parity. A realignment can then be announced with no simultaneous movement in market rates. To be both small and adequate, however, parity changes must be timely. Delay tends to magnify the underlying disequilibrium as well as any associated speculation. On this view, the problem with the EMS (as with Bretton Woods before it) was the tendency for parities to become frozen and changes in them viewed as a measure of last resort.

As for the supposed equalisation of nominal rather than real interest rates, this has simply not been the historical experience. Nominal interest rate differentials between other European countries and the D-mark in the 1980s appear to have fully reflected expected national differences in inflation rates and, by the same token, expected long-term movements in exchange rates (de Grauwe 1990).

Difficulties arise because the movement of exchange rates is not continuous or monotonic. One is never in a perfect steady state. So there will be times when, for example, the Italian lira is expected to depreciate over the next three years but not over the next three or six months, and the interest rate obtainable on six-month lira deposits consequently looks very attractive to D-mark portfolio managers. The result is a rush of money into the lira, further strengthening the currency and encouraging a speculative bubble against the trend of fundamentals (Giavazzi and Spaventa 1990). Conversely, at other times a flood of money in the opposite direction may put premature downward pressure on the lira and pull Italian interest rates above trend.

If such pressures interfere with domestic stabilisation efforts, greater reliance has to be placed for this purpose upon fiscal policy. Fiscal policy is less flexible in operation than monetary policy, and in addition its use for stabilisation purposes has been unfashionable in recent years, so governments are inclined to plead impotence. There is, however, no escape from the constraint that, in a system of pegged exchange rates with capital mobility, balance-of-payments needs must if necessary have first call on interest rate policy in the short run.[17]

Each type of currency regime has shortcomings. Permanent fixity of exchange rates means unification of monetary policy, regardless of differences in financial mechanisms or economic structures. Floating means exposure to possibly extreme fluctuations in exchange rates and hence in the profitability of different industrial sectors. Even if the core countries of the EMS proceed to monetary union along Maastricht lines, the question of exchange rate relations between 'Euro' countries and outsiders will remain on the agenda, and with it the search for a viable compromise between floating and permanent fixity.

NOTES

1 I am grateful for excellent research assistance to Mark Carney and Ildikó Taksz.

2 The three IMF Occasional Papers by Ungerer *et al.* (no. 19 in 1987, no. 48 in 1986 and no. 73 in 1990) are particularly valuable for their description and analysis of the EMS and its progress. See also Gros and Thygesen (1988).

3 This adverse impact, it may be noted, is quite compatible with the textbook theorem that a floating exchange rate insulates a country from external monetary conditions. The theorem is applicable *in steady state*. (Country *x* can have steady-state price inflation of 2 per cent per annum while the rest of the world inflates at 5 per cent per annum and *x*'s currency appreciates by 3 per cent per annum.) It is not applicable in the face of unforeseen shocks or transitions from one policy regime to another, when some variant of the Dornbusch 'overshooting' model is relevant (Dornbusch 1976).

4 The IMF Articles of Agreement laid down a maximum margin of 1 per cent on either side of a currency's par value, the latter defined in gold or, more normally, in US dollars. The scope for fluctuation in the relative rate of two non-dollar currencies was then a maximum of 4 per cent (currency A rising from its lowest to its highest point in terms of the dollar, while currency B moved in the opposite direction). In practice many countries did not avail themselves of the full 1 per cent on either side permitted by the Articles of Agreement. Amusingly, the Smithsonian Agreement of December 1971, besides devaluing the dollar, also widened its agreed margins of fluctuation in terms of other currencies to 2.25 per cent on either side. But by then the formal abrogation in August 1971 of the dollar's gold convertibility had already ensured that the global system of pegged exchange rates was doomed.

5 See Ludlow 1982: 636. Besides fiscal and monetary issues, subjects of dispute included US objections to German trade with eastern Europe and questions of nuclear defence.

6 In Cooper *et al.* (1989) some one hundred and fifty pages of analysis of the Bonn Summit scarcely mention the EMS. Conversely, Tsoukalis (1991) makes no mention of the Bonn summit in his discussion of the origins of the European Monetary System. See also various contributions in Guerrieri and Padoan (eds) (1989). The two are explicitly connected in Forder and Oppenheimer (1995).

7 Quoted in Ludlow 1982: 200. See also Story (1988) and *The Economist*, 12 January 1979, 'Survey of France', 12.

8 A striking early instance of failure to resolve this dilemma was the debate over the proposed European Defence Community in 1954. In the early 1990s, President Mitterrand struggled to prevent Germany from effectively determining European Community policy towards the former Yugoslavia.

9 Ludlow 1982: 174. The figure was accompanied by a detailed list of infrastructure projects for which assistance would be used.

10 Peter Ludlow's comment (Ludlow 1982: 269) is well taken:
    'Several if not all of Mr Callaghan's colleagues, not least Mr Schmidt, believed from what the British PM told them that it was only a matter of time before the UK entered. If this actually happened, the Irish government knew that it would have no alternative but to enter itself. Better then to enter when there was cash and kudos on offer, than to creep in on the coat-tails of the British government at a moment of their choosing'.

11 See Dell (1991) and Burk and Cairncross (1992) for full-length accounts of this episode.

12 It may be noted also that no ERM country held the bulk of its exchange reserves in D-marks (contrast the historical examples of the franc zone or the sterling area). The expanded role of the D-mark as a reserve currency was global rather than an exclusively regional phenomenon. Kenen (1996) guesstimated that D-marks comprised about 25 per cent of the currency reserves of EU countries other than Germany in the mid-1990s.

13 The strength of demand itself stemmed from a policy of credit market deregulation, defended at the time by the Chancellor and his advisers with the bizarre and unhistorical argument that, so long as the government was not a borrower (the public accounts were moving into surplus), there could be no problem of excessive credit expansion for the economy as a whole.

14 The matter has been well summarised by the Bank for International Settlements (*Annual Report*, 1993: 199):

'The 1992–3 European currency turmoil was fundamentally the result of the fact that, despite the impressive convergence of inflation performances, several countries' real exchange rates had become misaligned, and at a time when European economies were displaying signs of more or less severe weakness and/or financial fragility'.

Needless to say, until the crisis broke, it was not possible for officialdom, least of all central-banking officialdom, to admit that the existing state of affairs might conceivably prove unsustainable. It is therefore naive of Artis and Lewis to cite as evidence statements made in 1991–2 first by the Deputy Director General of the Bank of Italy and then by the Bank of England to the effect that the system was sound and the authorities well able to forestall destabilising speculation by demonstrating commitment. One may as well ask a military commander on the eve of battle about the morale of his troops.

15 'The Bank of Finland later revealed that in 1991 as a whole gross official sales of foreign currencies (including forward transactions) had amounted to the equivalent of 17 per cent of the country's GDP, or nearly 80 per cent of its (reduced) annual exports of goods and services' (Bank for International Settlements 1993: 196).

16 For a detailed account see Bank for International Settlements 1993, 1994.

17 Neither this constraint nor the abovementioned need for parity changes to be small and timely can be lessened by recourse to devices such as a 'Tobin tax' on foreign-exchange-market transactions or heavy marginal reserve requirements on banks adopting open foreign exchange positions (see Mahbub ul Haq *et al.* (1996) for a useful, balanced collection of papers on these proposals). The bursts of speculation which triggered the collapse of global pegged exchange rates in the early 1970s occurred despite a far wider range of controls then still in place on international capital movements. If exchange rate misalignment is allowed to become blatant and offer speculators a short-term one-way option, no feasible system of taxation or bank reserve requirements will provide an effective barrier. Of course, containment of speculation is not the only possible purpose of a Tobin tax; another one is enhancement of government revenues.

BIBLIOGRAPHY

Almancha Barudo, A. (ed.) (1993) *Spain and EC Membership Evaluated*, London: Pinter.

Artis, M. J. (1985) 'Comment on Padoa-Schioppa', in W. H. Buiter and R. C. Marston (eds) *International Economic Policy Coordination*, Cambridge: Cambridge University Press.

——(1987) 'The European Monetary System: an evaluation', *Journal of Policy Modelling*, 9, 1: 175–98.

——(1992) 'Monetary policy', in S. Bulmer, S. George and A. Scott (eds) *The United Kingdom and EC Membership Evaluated*, London: Pinter.

Artis, M. J. and Lewis, M. K. (1993) 'Après le déluge: monetary and exchange rate policy in Britain and Europe', *Oxford Review of Economic Policy*, 9, 3.

Artus, P. and Dupuy, C. (1992) 'The entry of the southern countries into the European Monetary System', in E. Baltensberger and H.-W. Sinn (eds) *Exchange Rate Regimes and Currency Union*, London: St Martin's Press.

Bank for International Settlements, Basle, *Annual Report*, various years.

Beckerman, W. and Jenkinson, T. (1986) 'What stopped the inflation? Unemployment or commodity prices?', *Economic Journal*, 96.

Begg, D. (1988) 'Comment on Giavazzi, Francesco and Marco Pagano, 1988, "The Advantage of Tying One's Hands" ', *European Economic Review*, 32: 1075–7.

Bilger, F. (1993) 'The European Monetary System and French monetary policy', in F. Dreyfus and J. Morizet (eds) *France and EC Membership Evaluated*, London: Pinter.

Burk, K. and Caincross, A. K. (1992) *Good-bye, Great Britain!*, London and New Haven: Yale University Press.

Cobham, D. (1989) 'Strategies for monetary integration revisited', *Journal of Common Market Studies*, 17.

Cooper, R. N., Eichengreen, B., Holtham, G., Putnam, R. D. and Randall Henning, C. (1989) *Can Nations Agree?*, Washington DC: Brookings Institution.

da Silva Lopes, J. (ed) (1993) *Portugal and EC Membership Evaluated*, London: Pinter.

de Cecco, M. (1989) 'The European Monetary Systems and national interests', in P. Guerrieri and P. C. Padoan (eds) (1989) *The Political Economy of European Integration*, Hemel Hempstead: Harvester Wheatsheaf.

de Grauwe, P. (1987) 'International trade and economic growth in the EMS', *European Economic Review*, 31.

——(1990) 'Liberalisation of capital movements and the EMS', in *The Macroeconomics of 1992*, CEPS Policy Studies Paper no. 42: Brussels.

de Grauwe, P. and Papademos, L. (eds) (1990) *The European Monetary System in the 1990s*, London: Longman for CEPS and the Bank of Greece.

Dell, E. (1991) *A Hard Pounding*, Oxford: Oxford University Press.

Dornbusch, R. (1976) 'Expectations and exchange rate dynamics', *Journal of Political Economy*.

——(1989) 'Ireland's failed stabilization', *Economic Policy*, 8: 173–201.

——(1990) 'Two-track EMU, now!', in *Britain and the EMU*, London: Centre for Economic Performance.

Euromoney (1992) 'Lisbon builds new bridges', June.

Forder, J. and Oppenheimer, P. M. (1995) in J. E. S. Hayward (ed.) *Elitism, Populism and European Politics*, Oxford: Oxford University Press.

Giavazzi, F., Micossi, S. and Miller, M. (1988) *The European Monetary System*, Cambridge: Cambridge University Press.

Giavazzi, F. and Giovannini, A. (1989) *Limiting Exchange Rate Flexibility: The European Monetary System*, Cambridge, MA: MIT Press.

Giavazzi, F. and Pagano, M. (1988) 'The advantage of tying one's hands: EMS disciplines and central bank credibility', *European Economic Review*, 32.

Giavazzi, F. and Spaventa, L. (1990) *The 'New' EMS*, CEPR Discussion Paper no. 369; and in P. de Grauwe and L. Papademos (eds) (1990).

Gros, D. and Thygesen, N. (1988) *The EMS: Achievements, Current Issues and Directions for the Future*, CEPS Policy Studies Paper no. 35: Brussels.

Guerrieri P. and Padoan, P.-C. (eds) (1989) *The Political Economy of European Integration*, Hemel Hempstead: Harvester Wheatsheaf.

Kenen, P. B. (1996) 'Sorting out some EMU issues', *Reprints in International Finance*, 29, Princeton, NJ: International Finance Section.

Ludlow, P. (1982) *The Making of the European Monetary System*, London: Butterworth.

O'Donnell, R. (1991) 'Monetary policy', in P. Keatinge (ed.) *Ireland and EC Membership Evaluated*, London: Pinter.

Oppenheimer, P. M. (1989) 'External impacts of US financial policies', in O. F. Hamouda *et al.* (eds) *The Future of the International Monetary System*, London: Edward Elgar.

——(1991) 'Historical development of the EMS and the UK decision to join the Exchange Rate Mechanism', in J. Driffill and M. Baker (eds) *A Currency for Europe*, London: Lothian Foundation.

Padoa-Schioppa, T. (1985) 'Policy cooperation and the EMS experience', in W. H. Buiter and R. E. Marston (eds) *International Economic Policy Coordination*, Cambridge: Cambridge University Press.

Pohl, K. O. (1990) 'The prospects for the European Monetary Union', in *Britain and the EMU*, London: Centre for Economic Performance.

Sachs, J. and Wyplosz, C. (1986) 'The economic consequences of President Mitterrand', *Economic Policy*, 2: 261–322.

Schmidt, H. (1985) 'The EMS: proposals for further progress', *The World Today*, 41.

Spaventa, L. (1980) 'Italy joins the EMS – a political history', Johns Hopkins University Bologna Centre, *Occasional Paper*, 32.

Story, J. (1988) 'The launching of the EMS: an analysis of change in foreign economic policy', *Policy Studies*

Thiel, E. (1989) 'Macroeconomic policy preferences and coordination: a view from Germany', in P. Guerrieri and P-C. Padoan (eds) (1989) *The Political Economy of European Integration*, Hemel Hempstead: Harvester Wheatsheaf.

Tsoukalis, L. (1991) *The New European Economy*, Oxford: Oxford University Press.

——(1997)*The New European Economy Revisited*, Oxford: Oxford University Press.

ul Haq, M., Kaul, I. and Grunberg, I. (eds) (1996) *The Tobin Tax: Coping with Financial Volatility*, New York: Oxford University Press.

Ungerer, H., Evans, O. and Nyberg, P. (1983) 'The European Monetary System: the experience, 1979–82', *International Monetary Fund Occasional Paper*, 19.

Ungerer, H., Evans, O., Mayer, T. and Young, P. (1986) 'The European Monetary System: recent developments', *International Monetary Fund Occasional Paper*, 48.

Ungerer, H. *et al.* (1990) 'The European Monetary System: developments and perspectives', *International Monetary Fund Occasional Paper*, 73.

Viñals, J. (1990) 'The EMS, Spain and macroeconomic policy', *CEPR Discussion Paper*, 389, London: CEPR.

Part II

POLICY IN FOUR MEMBER STATES

6

FRANCE

Jacques Reland

INTRODUCTION

When, on 26 October 1995, President Chirac announced a two-year austerity plan intended to help France reduce its budget deficit, many observers were reminded of Mitterrand's 1983 commitment to EMS discipline and the restrictive economic policies that accompanied it. In the same way as Mitterrand had finally to abandon the reflationary policies adopted in 1981, Chirac was forced to renege on the wild economic promises of his election campaign. His denunciations, prior to the 1995 Presidential election, of *la pensée unique* (orthodox monetarist economic thinking) and of the constraints it imposed on economic policy, along with his affirmation that with imagination and willpower it was possible to conduct *une autre politique* – a different, more growth-oriented policy than the competitive disinflation of the previous twelve years – found a receptive ear among the voters and secured his election. But after he came to power there developed an awareness that governmental autonomy in economic policy making was seriously constrained.

The fact that the October announcement came the day after an important meeting with Chancellor Kohl on the future of European integration, and that the main objective of the announced sacrifices was the reduction of the budget deficit to bring it in line with the Maastricht convergence criteria, led many to believe that these measures were imposed by the need or the desire to achieve EMU. This view is, however, as misleading as that which attempts to explain the competitive disinflation pursued by French governments after 1983 simply as a function of Mitterrand's European enthusiasm. EMS discipline was good for France and for Mitterrand. What the government lost in terms of policy autonomy was largely compensated for by the economic benefits the country derived from EMS membership and the gains made by the Socialists in terms of governmental credibility. Upon realising in 1982 the weight of the international constraint on national economic policy, the President chose, in 1983, to remain in the EMS and to participate fully in the ERM not only in the name of his undoubted European commitment, but also, and above all else, in the name of the national economic interest and therefore of his own political survival. The EMS framework was therefore perceived not simply as a constraint reducing the economic policy-making autonomy of the government, but as both a spring-board and a shield enabling the government to carry out drastic reforms considered necessary by the majority of France's decision makers. Linking the disinflation policy to Europe had the dual advantage of providing both a clear and credible framework – that of the D-mark-dominated EMS – and a political justification for the painful but necessary measures to be enacted.

The same caveat applies to the view which uses the French authorities' desire to achieve EMU to explain France's obsession with maintaining at all costs the franc's EMS parity with the D-mark. The drive towards EMU certainly played a part in the determination with which the Bérégovoy and Balladur governments pursued the *franc fort* policy. However, their monetary dogmatism can be more satisfactorily explained as a result of reforms decided on before 1989. The reasons why France has had to maintain such high real interest rates, so detri-mental to activity and employment levels, stem from a combination of factors linked both to European integration and to the need to modernise the French financial markets. The mid-1980s reform of the French financial system, which the Fabius and Chirac governments so enthusiastically implemented, and the adoption of the Directive of 24 June 1988 completely liberalising capital move-ments within the European Union (which Mitterrand accepted uncritically) were to have as much, if not more, of an impact on French governments' autonomy in economic policy making than the oft-mentioned Maastricht criteria. Maastricht or not, as a result of decisions made in the heady atmosphere of Euro-enthusiasm and improved competitiveness, French governments have found themselves obliged to pursue an orthodox economic policy. Maastricht has also impacted on autonomy in one other crucial respect: the freedom of French governments has been further curtailed by the decision to grant the Banque de France its independence.

EMS AS A SHIELD

A necessary choice

It is often argued that François Mitterrand finally allowed Prime Minister Mauroy's government to embark on the well-documented March 1983 economic U-turn in the name of Europe. However, even though Mitterrand's European credentials are undoubted, this view ignores how marginal a consid-eration Europe was in France at the time. When, after a prolonged period of hesitation, Mitterrand finally decided in 1983 to keep the franc in the EMS and to accept its macroeconomic discipline, he did so for domestic reasons, political as well as economic. Ultimately it was domestic politics that led to the view that the government had no other option, just as the first Mauroy government had no other choice in 1981 than to overturn the Barre government's austerity policy.

In the wake of Mitterrand's 1981 electoral victory, Prime Minister Mauroy's first government had to change this policy, as the Socialists had been brought to power to fight unemployment. It made political sense and appeared economically possible, given the then current forecasts of an international recovery scheduled for 1982, and also the healthy French fiscal situation arising from the 1980 balanced budget. A momentary deterioration of France's public finances and trade balance seemed bearable. In the belief that they could engineer employment-creating growth, the Mauroy administration embarked on a go-it-alone Keynesian reflationary policy and reactivated the tools which had served France so well in the postwar reconstruction effort, namely planning and nationalisations of large industrial groups and of financial institutions. The well documented failure of their first year's economic management (Machin and Wright 1985) made the government realise that political will was no longer sufficient and that the state was no longer able effectively to implement the Fordist model of growth which had been at the root of the *trente glorieuses*. Their hopes of boosting activity and mission to 'reconquer the domestic market' floundered in the face of internal and external constraints.

The government had underestimated the structural weaknesses of the French economy, its inadequate and uncompetitive industrial supply, the low level of corporate profitability and investment and the financial backwardness of a capitalist France short of capital. Moreover, its macroeconomic strategy, which overlooked the inbuilt inflationary pressure arising from index-linked wage agreements, was no longer suited to the new international economic environment. France had done well until the mid-1970s, thanks to a stop-go approach involving a tolerance of inflation and frequent recourse to devaluations to restore price competitiveness. This was, however, no longer possible at a time when France's main trading partners had adopted a completely different economic strategy. Following the G7 Tokyo meeting of 1979, defeating inflation had become the new international priority, leading the major powers to adopt restrictive budgetary, wage and monetary policies allowing them to cut inflation and to restore corporate profitability and national competitiveness. French economic policy was therefore out of step with the tight economic management of its major European partners, especially Germany and the UK.

The Mauroy government's decision to increase the wages of the lower-paid, with a 10 per cent increase of the legal minimum wage (*Salaire Minimum Interprofessionnel de Croissance*) and to improve social justice through the upgrading of social benefits helped to boost the purchasing power of households by 2.6 per cent in 1981 and 2.5 per cent in 1982. The 3 per cent rise in household consumption in 1981 and 1982 benefited French manufacturers less than their European counterparts, especially the Germans, who saw their exports to France rise spectacularly. France's rising labour costs and higher inflation (running at around 14 per cent in the 1980–2 period) combined with its neighbours' deflationary policies to cause a loss of export competitiveness, not restored by the 4 October 1981 devaluation, while increased French demand boosted imports. Demand from OPEC countries and a rising food and drinks surplus had helped to decrease the trade deficit from F62 billion the year before to F56 billion in 1981. In 1982, however, the deepening world recession and the impact of the rise of the dollar on the price of oil added to continually high French demand and decreasing competitiveness to cause a spectacular deterioration of the trade deficit, which jumped to F92 billion. Public finances plunged into the red with an F80.8 billion budget deficit in 1981, rising to F98.9 billion the following year. Awareness of this deterioration of France's trade balance and public finances forced Finance Minister Delors to call for a 'pause' in 1982. The franc was devalued again, but, unlike 1981 when devaluation was a means to correct the overvaluing of the franc and was not accompanied by restrictive measures, that of 1982 led to the adoption of austerity measures.

Although fairly harsh, the 1982 *plan de rigueur* did not prove successful. France's accounts were plunging deeper into the red, as was the credibility of the government. France faced a choice of either adapting to the new international economic environment or embarking on a protectionist course. Having decided that the latter option was a dead-end which could only have wreaked economic havoc and undermined the credibility of the Socialists as a governing party, Mitterrand chose to keep the French currency in the ERM. The 'French authorities then decided that, given the growing internationalisation of the economy and the ensuing loss of economic policy autonomy, it was preferable to accept EMS discipline and constraint rather than vainly oppose structural integration trends' (De Boissieu and Duprat 1990: 71).

The drama surrounding the decision, as well as the apparently prolonged hesitation by Mitterrand, gave the choice a strong resonance (Favier and Martin-Roland 1990: 465–93; Elgie 1993: 124–30). France had to be in line with its European trading partners, had to try to emulate virtuous Germany and conduct a monetary policy enabling it to defeat inflation and reduce budget deficits. Linking the necessary sacrifices to EMS membership was economically significant and politically symbolic. It put the issue of European integration back on the agenda and monetary policy at the forefront of French economic policy making.

For Mitterrand and his supporters, the 1983 choice was a response to external pressures which France could no longer ignore if it wanted to remain an economically competitive and politically influential power. Committed membership of the EMS was a lifejacket which was understandably seized, albeit reluctantly, by politicians who were aware of its potential as a straitjacket. Due to its lack of credibility in currency matters, and given the suspicion under which the socialist government was held by the markets, it would have been far more difficult and painful for France to implement the necessary disinflation process without externally imposed discipline, as Fabius later acknowledged: 'We would have been obliged to be much more rigorous [*faire des kilomètres de rigueur en plus*] just to appear to be rigorous' (*Le Nouvel Observateur*, 2–8 May 1991). Staying within the EMS framework and deciding to peg the franc to the strongest currency within the ERM was going to allow France to 'import the credibility' of the German monetary policy tradition in the manner described by Giavazzi and Pagano (1988). ERM discipline implied a loss of economic autonomy, but only insofar as it forced France to adapt to its partners' restrictive economic strategy.

Disinflation and how to achieve it

Disinflation became the cornerstone of French economic policy, the aim being to eliminate the inflation differential with Germany so as to remove pressures against the franc. The strong measures taken in 1983 were to lay the foundations for a successful fight against inflation and for the restoration of France's competitiveness, which the pursuance of a tight monetary policy would allow. Inflation fell quickly from 14 per cent in the spring of 1982 to 9.3 per cent in 1983, 6.7 per cent in 1984, 4.7 per cent in 1985, and thanks to the fall in oil prices, down to 2.1 per cent in 1986. While between 1980 and 1985 the French 9.6 per cent average annual rate of inflation was 5.7 percentage points above that of Germany, the all-important inflation differential shrank to 1.7 percentage points between 1985 and 1990, at the end of which period the 3.4 per cent French inflation rate was just above the 2.8 per cent German performance.

Jean-Claude Trichet, who became Governor of the Banque de France in September 1993, later defined the components of the macroeconomic policy followed by successive French governments of the 1980s as 'the four pillars of competitive disinflation' (Trichet 1992: 28). These consisted of wage moderation, structural reforms of the productive apparatus, a balanced budget and a monetary policy aiming at defeating inflation.

> Low inflation and currency [parity] are instruments in the service of an economic strategy of growth and job-creation . . . because in a completely open economy . . . our economy must manufacture its goods and produce its services at a lower cost, and therefore at a better price than our partners' economies.
>
> (Trichet 1992: 28)

Wage moderation became a prerequisite for restoring French competitiveness and corporate profitability. It would allow France to improve its trade position through a combination of weaker consumer demand for imports and improved sales abroad, and provide French companies with the financial means to start investing again. This would create domestic demand for capital goods, a rise in which had contributed initially to the deterioration of the manufactured goods trade balance.

This approach paid off. From 1983 to 1989, French wages increased by only 6 per cent in real terms, the lowest in the EC. This wage restraint has been maintained since, as shown by 1995 OECD statistics (OECD 1995) which indicate that the 3.9 per cent average annual increase in wages over the last five years was the lowest in the OECD after the US and the Netherlands. The share of wages in the added value of companies, which had reached its highest ever level (69.8 per cent) in 1982, had fallen to just over 66 per cent in 1984 before tumbling down to 62 per cent in 1986 and 59.8 per cent by 1989. Corporate profitability, measured in terms of gross profit margin over added value, which had fallen to 22.5 per cent in 1981 and 1982, crept back up to around 25 per cent in 1984–5 before rising to 31.9 per cent in 1989, the highest level ever recorded. The impact on corporate investment of the improvement of the French companies' financial situation, however, took a longer time to register. Initially, investment fell markedly, by an annual average of 2.6 per cent between 1980 and 1985, before recovering in the second half of the 1980s when it grew at an average of 7.5 per cent.

The fourth pillar, monetary policy, did not, however, initially play the central role in defeating inflation. In postwar France, monetary policy had rarely been used in this way (Delpit and Schwartz 1993: 25). In keeping with the French Keynesian approach to monetary policy, it had been used by Prime Minister Chirac in the 1974–6 period in an expansionary fashion. It was not until Barre took over as Prime Minister in 1976 that, in an effort to curb monetary expansion, France posted for the first time a monetary objective, a 12.5 per cent M2 aggregate growth for 1977. Because of the highly administered nature of the French financial system, interest rates could only play a minor role in meeting that objective. Instead, France relied on *l'encadrement du crédit*, credit controls, 'which applied to each bank and combined ceilings on credit growth and penalties, consisting of legal reserve requirements, whenever the limit on credit growth was violated' (De Boissieu and Duprat 1990: 62). The need to use monetary policy as the main instrument to stifle inflationary pressures and the unsatisfactory nature of credit controls as its main instrument were going to push the French authorities to completely reorganise the French financial system. The government had announced its intention to dismantle *encadrement du crédit* as early as 1984, but would not be able to do so until the French money market had been sufficiently transformed to enable the Banque de France to conduct a 'market-based monetary policy' relying almost exclusively on the use of short-term interest rates.

EUROPE AND FINANCIAL DEREGULATION

If the goal of more efficiently applying a monetarist policy was not used as a justification by newly appointed Finance Minister Bérégovoy when he set about shaking up French financial institutions in late 1984, neither was Europe. Yet the European integration process and the will to preserve the franc's ERM parity against the D-mark were to underpin and hasten the pace of French financial reforms. The need to reduce the budget deficit as well as the 25 June 1980 European Directive (updated on 24 July 1985) limiting the ability of the state to fund state-owned companies (Zerah 1993: 174) were soon going to act as a spur to decrease the role of the state in the financing of the economy. The need to finance nationalised companies outside the budget had already led to the first Socialist financial innovation, the creation, through the 'Delors Act' of January 1983, of several new financial instruments in the form of investment certificates and contingent value rights which allowed these companies to increase their capital without changing the structure of ownership, as they were bereft of voting rights. The Single European Act, insofar as it aimed to create a common market in financial services and to remove exchange controls, made it imperative to improve the competitiveness of the French financial sector. Moreover, the prospect of the Single Market required French companies to have the means to finance their internal and external development so as to be in a position to face up to increased competition.

However, the European constraint only added urgency to the major motive behind the zeal with which the French financial authorities deregulated the financial sector: cheaper and easier access to capital (Virard 1993: 110–14). In 1981 and 1982, the great majority of French financial institutions had been nationalised with a view to improving the financing of investments so as to create employment. The failure of the nationalisation of credit as an instrument for boosting investment had convinced the Minister and Jean-Charles Naouri, his key adviser, of the need to transform the whole French financial system. Under the existing regime, raising capital was not only expensive but also difficult because of the compartmentalisation and specialisation of the French banking system. The problem was compounded by the existence of the aforementioned quantitative credit controls which had been used intermittently in the 1958–70 period, and constantly from 1970 to 1985, before being abolished on 1 January 1987, and by exchange controls, except for a short interlude between 1966 and 1968, which limited access to foreign capital.

The Banking Act of 1984 brought the French financial services sector in line with the requirements outlined in the 12 December 1977 European Directive, which would subsequently allow French companies to trade freely in any other European country following the adoption of the 15 December 1989 directive (Perrut 1993: 22–6). It abolished the distinction between *banques de dépôt*, which collected most of the deposits but had only been allowed to grant short-term loans to companies, and *banques d'affaires*, able to hold stakes in companies or to give them long-term loans. Both categories now fell under the European status of *établissements de crédit* (credit institutions), institutions which carry out at least one of three activities: collecting deposits from the public, granting credits and issuing means of payments such as credit cards, travellers' cheques and bankers' drafts. The harmonisation of the financial system created a level playing field, enabling every institution to have increased access to capital and to offer the same services under the same regulatory conditions; this helped achieve the government's objective of increasing competition and making credit cheaper.

The same motive applied to the reform of the financial market: 'The logic of improved efficiency and increased competition presided over the reform of both financial institutions and financial instruments . . . so as to lower the costs and improve the service' (Delpit and Schwartz 1993: 42). In keeping with what De Boissieu calls the French tradition of 'public financial innovations', the state authorities were instrumental in introducing new financial instruments which, even if they 'satisfied a demand, explicit or latent, by private operators, resulted from a centralised process' (De Boissieu and Duprat 1990: 56). However, if the authorities wanted to improve the access of companies to liquidity, 'their main concern was to make the financing of public borrowing easier by attracting foreign capital' (Fitoussi 1995: 203). This is also the view of De Boissieu and Duprat, who identify three reasons behind the acceleration of the financial innovation process besides the factors common to all OECD countries: 'the external, fiscal and financing constraints' (1990: 57). The first refers to the need to maintain the competitiveness of the French banking system and the role of Paris as a financial centre, the second to the government's need to finance public sector deficits through non-monetary means, and the third to the need to finance the development of small and medium-sized enterprises and of nationalised firms. This analysis was shared by OECD experts, who in their 1987 survey argued that the first motive of the government was to 'limit money financing of the public deficit and surges in inflation'; the second 'to improve the efficiency of the banking system and reduce the financing costs of intermediation'; the third to 'make Paris a major financial market and so benefit from the income and job-creating opportunities arising from financial activities'; and the last to ease 'the controls over the financing of the economy' (OECD 1987: 50).

Unification was the keyword for the reform of the capital market, the aim being to create a huge unified money market accessible to all economic actors and able to offer the financial products best suited to their needs. It involved:

> the opening up of a new range of debt instruments, including the creation of a commercial paper market in December 1985. The new markets gave companies direct access to funding by issuing their own short or long-term securities, cutting down the banks' direct lending activity in a process of disintermediation.
>
> *(Financial Times* 2 December 1987)

Bank intermediation in corporate financing dropped from 64 per cent in 1982 to 20 per cent in 1986. This share however rose in the following years and eventually stabilised at around 45 per cent in 1991. However, this disintermediation process has not been sustained by private companies which have considerably reduced their issuing of securities and other commercial papers and have instead called on short-term securities and on banks to organise and manage their financing.

The securitisation process has been kept up by the initiator and main beneficiary of the financial deregulation process, the state, which became the biggest borrower in the Paris markets as a result of the structural transformation of French government debt since 1985. The auction technique, which had applied to current account Treasury bills since 1973, was extended to three newly created categories of standardised securities: OATs (*obligations assimilables du trésor*) which are long-term fungible treasury bonds with maturities of up to thirty years; medium-term BTANs (*Bons du trésor à taux fixe et à intérêt annuel*) which are fixed-rate Treasury notes with maturities of between two to five years; and BTFs (*Bons du trésor à taux fixe et à intérêt annuel*) which are fixed rate short-term treasury bills with a maximum maturity of one year (Ministère de l'Economie 1995: 6). These became very attractive to foreign investors and were to experience such a spectacular growth that state issues alone accounted for 48.2 per cent of the French bond market in 1992 against 25.9 per cent in 1982 (*Les Echos*, 2 March 1993, 9). However, as we will see later, this reliance on direct funding and to a large extent on foreign capital proved to be a major constraint on the government's autonomy in monetary policy making.

ERM, deregulation and monetary policy

EMS discipline and financial deregulation had a strong impact on the instruments of French monetary policy making and also on the autonomy of the government in its conduct. The level of expertise required to conduct monetary policy in this new, restricted and open environment gave the French central bank more influence in monetary policy making:

> As recently as 1983, France had tight capital controls, interest rates were administered by the treasury, financial instruments were few, and banks were subjected to *encadrement du crédit*. Today, capital controls are gone, the only administered rates concern bank deposits, a host of new financial instruments has emerged and there is no *encadrement*. The essential instrument of monetary policy is the short-term interest rate.
>
> (Melitz 1990: 1)

Until the mid-1980s, the existing system allowed the Banque de France to separate control of the money supply from interest rate policy. It also enabled the authorities to manipulate interest rates in accordance with their objectives. France had three main interest rates. On the bond market, they were kept artificially low to stimulate investment and growth. The bank credit rate was determined by the Banque de France intervention rate and the level of the 'compulsory reserves' they were obliged to maintain. On the money market, rates were high so as to keep the franc up (De Boissieu and Duprat 1990: 53). The reforms undertaken would eventually allow the Banque de France to adopt a market-based monetary policy. The Bank reformed its mode of intervention in the money market in 1986. The manipulation of short-term interest rates, namely the call (bottom) and repo (ceiling) rates became the main instrument of monetary policy for influencing the exchange rate of the French currency and the evolution of the quantity of money. Its 'application required a very profound knowledge of the financial markets . . . [which] served to strengthen the role of the Banque de France' (Eizenga 1990: 6) and contributed to reducing the government's margin of manoeuvre in monetary policy making, especially as 'participation in the Exchange Rate Mechanism of the EMS required more flexible and timely intervention by the monetary authorities, all the more as capital controls were progressively removed after spring 1986' (*ECU newsletter*, September 1993, 18).

The task of the Banque de France was to watch over currency and credit. In its pursuit of monetary policy, the Bank contributed to the preparation and participated in the implementation of government policy, but was 'subordinate to the general policy formulated by the government and [had] no specific duties in the monetary sphere' (Eizenga 1990: 5). Actual practice, however, involved closer cooperation between the Governor, appointed by the French Council of Ministers, the Finance Minister, with whom he held weekly meetings, and the Treasury officials who dictated the policy line within the framework of the government's political aims. Their combined monetary expertise was crucial to the government's monetary policy making and meant that decisions, on interest rates especially, were actually made by the Governor, but 'made public by the Minister of Finance' (Eizenga 1990: 6).

Monetary policy, industrial policy and the Single Market

The adoption of a restrictive monetary policy not only helped to compress demand and prop up the currency in the EMS, but also to prepare French industry for the SEA. Not only did it suppress imported inflation, but it was also a spur for companies to improve their productivity, as they could no longer count on devaluations to restore their competitiveness (Forbes and Howlett 1994: 216).

Old habits die hard, however, and this lesson would take some time for French firms to learn. When the Chirac government devalued the franc in April 1986 – an unavoidable measure following market speculation based on evidence of a widening of the production costs differential with Germany – the trade deficit with Germany rose as French firms chose to increase their profit margin rather than cut their prices. However, their attitude changed following France's November 1988 decision to match the German increase in interest rates, thus demonstrating their determination to pursue the *franc fort* policy.

The high interest rates required to preserve the parity of the currency also helped to streamline or modernise domestic industry (Crozet 1994: 158), a non-negligible side-effect given the SEM. From 1984 to 1989, real interest rates hovered around the 5 per cent mark, a departure from the period between the mid-1970s and 1981, when they were mostly negative. As few productive invest-ments can match the rate of returns on financial investments, activities which are not very profitable curtail their investment programmes. A natural selection process occurs which allows for the survival of only the fittest companies and leads them to divest themselves of their least profitable activities in order to concentrate on the most potentially rewarding segments of the market. France's growing trade surplus and the improvement of company profitability bear this out. One danger is that if the least profitable activities are sacrificed or delo-calised, France could end up with an under-dimensioned industrial base compared to the needs of the country. The most visible downside of this produc-tivity drive, however, was obviously a rise in unemployment which culminated at 10.5 per cent of the working population in early 1987, before dropping to a low of 8.9 per cent in July 1990. However, as a result of their streamlining, French companies were now ready to tackle not just the Single Market, but also the world, as seen by the rash of international acquisitions and mergers completed after 1988, especially by state-owned companies, for example, Péchiney's acquisi-tion of American Can and Rhone-Poulenc's purchase of Rorer.

MORE EUROPE, ALWAYS MORE EUROPE!

Towards EMU

By 1988, the EMS gamble had paid off. France's economy had become competi-tive, its fundamentals were sound, its financial markets were sophisticated and its companies felt able to capitalise on the Single Market. By then, the European ideal had made great strides. More Europe became the mantra, the new 'ardent obligation', or as Mitterrand reiterated in his *Lettre aux Français*, his 1988 electoral manifesto, 'La France est notre patrie, L'Europe est notre avenir' (*Libération*, 7 April 1988, 14).

High but falling unemployment and the high level of real interest rates were seen as a small price to pay for the benefits France's socialist administration reaped from swapping its socialist principles for the tenets of the Common Market, as it was still known at the time. Taking a leaf out of the German book on inflation control and currency stability, France had, in the opinion of Rowley (1992: 45) abandoned the two postwar tenets of economic policy making – social regulation through inflation and the preservation of employment. The economic role of government was now to provide the right macroeconomic environment, to ensure that the fundamentals were sound enough to guarantee what the much-criticised Raymond Barre had identified as the new national imperative, 'the competitiveness of the economy'.

Framing this policy in a European context provided the Socialists with a new rallying cry. In their 1984 European manifesto, the Socialists had claimed that no 'government in Europe has done more to save the EEC and to redress it. France is acknowledged today as the decisive actor within the European Community' (Saint-Ouen 1986: 208). Not only did Europe provide a worthwhile political justification for harsh economic policies, but it also helped to quieten political opposition, especially from the Union pour la Démocratie Française. Simone Veil, for instance, claimed in May 1994 that 'Europe is our guarantee. Thanks to her, we stayed in the EMS and have not drifted into generalised "étatisation" ' (Saint-Ouen 1986: 208).

Mitterrand had used Europe as a means of helping his re-election campaign. It had brought the President the tacit backing of many UDF members, but also of much of the French administrative and business elites who shared his desire for further European economic integration and the consequent need for coordinating economic policy making in line with German discipline. Beyond pro-European political quarters, in industrial, financial and technocratic circles, Europe's potential as a springboard had been quickly perceived, especially following the launch of the SEM, which the French so readily embraced.

> Europe is perceived as a way of preserving France's rank, no longer through domination and *ad extra* projection, but through an *ad intra* modernisation and adaptation to the world order. . . . Community rules are seen as a way to 'cleanse and rationalise obsolete domestic laws and to offer France better conditions for facing international competition'.
>
> (Lequesne 1994: 54)

Mitterrand's Euro-enthusiasm led him to accept at the June 1988 Hanover summit the removal of exchange controls on capital movements from 1 July 1990, without demanding the achievement of capital tax harmonisation as a prerequisite. The President went against the advice of some leading Socialists, Bérégovoy in particular, who pointed out that capital liberalisation would force France to cut its tax on capital gains, tighten its budgetary policy and strengthen its currency policy, because at the same summit, his partners agreed to his proposal to set EMU in motion.

EMU was accepted by the majority of European countries as a natural complement to the SEM, and also as a way to give Europe more weight in international currency markets against the dominant dollar, whose vagaries were felt to be responsible for many European economic problems. For France, EMU also implied other benefits. Politically, given the prospect of German unification, it was considered as a way to tie Germany to Europe. EMU also represented a way to limit the power of the D-mark and of the Bundesbank, so painfully felt by France through its dedication to EMS and the *franc fort*. Although the Maastricht convergence criteria are legitimately perceived as a constraint reducing national governments' autonomy in macroeconomic policy making, the rationale behind them, i.e. a single currency and a shift in monetary power from the Bundesbank to a European central bank, was seen by many European governments as the best way 'to recover a lost sovereignty' (Fitoussi and Muet 1993: 10).

Waiting for EMU

The worst of both worlds

Without EMU, France has the worst of both worlds. Even though EMU implies a transfer to community level of monetary instruments and tough fiscal constraints, financial deregulation and globalisation meant that these constraints were there before the Maastricht criteria were adopted. 'These constraints stem less from EMU than from the financial deregulation of the eighties. . . . The macro-economic disciplines of EMU will not be fundamentally different from those now followed by the major industrial powers' (Commissariat Général du Plan 1993: 224). Economic and monetary union would, on the other hand, give participating European countries more monetary weight and therefore more influence on interest rates. Meanwhile, the prospect of EMU and the convergence criteria set by the Maastricht treaty were bound to lead to complete domination by the D-mark for the rest of the decade and therefore to more instability within the EMS, as shown by the September 1992 and July 1993 currency crises:

> The asymmetry of the EMS and the leadership of the Deutschmark have severely limited the ability of the French authorities to run an autonomous monetary policy. While during the eighties this helped France pursue its target of reducing the inflation rate by borrowing the Bundesbank credibility, after German unification, as French inflation fell below Germany's and the economy slipped into recession, the conflict between the external constraint posed through the ERM by tight German monetary policy and the need to prop up domestic recovery by lowering interest rates has gradually weakened the position of the French authorities, prompting a series of attacks against the franc since October 1992.
>
> (*ECU Newsletter*, September 1993, 19)

The cost of the unification of Germany and the decision to convert eastern marks at an apparently favourable rate led to fears of inflation. This, combined with an increase in domestic demand and a growing budget deficit, led the Bundesbank, in pursuit of price stability, to raise its short-term interest rates. Although this policy made sense for Germany, its impact on its EMS partners could only be negative. The French authorities did not seem to realise the economic implications of such a historical event. They turned down German proposals of a readjustment of parities within the EMS which would have been good for both countries. Instead, they chose to match German interest rate increases in an attempt to prevent the franc coming under attack. As a result, while real French interest rates had been on a par with Germany in the 1981–8 period when German inflation was lower, in the 1989–94 period, when France had lower inflation than Germany, their real interest rates averaged 6 per cent, against 4 per cent in Germany. In the light of this, one must ask why the French rejected the German proposal of an ERM realignment.

French fears that a realignment would undermine the EMU did play their part but were misplaced, especially as in all other respects France was meeting the convergence criteria. The unavoidable readjustment of September 1992 and the August 1993 broadening of the ERM Band to 15 per cent have not stalled the EMU process. Therefore, though it was used as an 'alibi' (Fitoussi 1995: 106) the European constraint was not the overriding factor behind France's tightening of its monetary policy: 'They took the risk of an economic slowdown in order to reaffirm their commitment to the continuity of their anti-inflation and currency stability policy and therefore to reinforce medium-term growth' (Commissariat Général du Plan 1993: 26). In other words, given the importance for the French economy of long-term interest rates (see below), the French monetary authorities were more concerned about their *franc fort* credibility than about a short-term improvement in economic activity. This view is shared by Fitoussi (1995: 86–8) who argues that the *franc fort* dogmatism stems from the French authorities' 'obsession with credibility', from their desire to be considered as a fully committed strong currency country. Markets are meant to have a long memory and five years of sacrifices on the altar of currency stability is too short. Further proof that French monetary policy is less constrained by Europe than by concerns about long-term interest rates was supplied when France did not take advantage of the August 1993 widening of the ERM band to 15 per cent, which would have allowed for cuts in short-term rates. Instead they have since striven to bring the franc back into the old 2.25 per cent band.

The cost of foreign capital

The remarkable liquidity of the French government bond market, 'one of the most liquid of its kind in the world' (*Financial Times*, 20 December 1991) has attracted foreign investors, as have the fluidity and technical efficiency of other markets, such as the Bourse, the MONEP and the MATIF. They have been all the more welcome as the French economy finds it difficult to raise capital, especially long-term capital, due to the shortage of adequate savings, itself due to the lack of pension funds. A sophisticated and liquid market, the absence of exchange controls and the shortage of domestic capital to fulfil the financial needs of the major borrowers, principally the state, have therefore made the French capital markets reliant on foreign capital. Each day around $25 billion is traded on the Paris market, an amount which can double in times of turmoil such as September 1992 and January and July 1993, and non-residents are very active. In 1993, foreign pension funds, insurance companies, mutual funds and financial institutions held 800 billion francs worth of government bonds (a 40 per cent share) and a third of the equity listed on the Paris Bourse, as well as a quarter of the short-term investment funds (SICAV, OPCVMs, currency unit trusts). These foreign financial investments amounted to 2,000 billion francs, equivalent to 30 per cent of French GDP, and their owners are obviously very concerned about the stability of the franc as they do not wish their assets to depreciate. This was one of the major reasons for the *franc fort* dogmatism of the early 1990s which led the French monetary authorities to keep real interest rates higher than in Germany, even though French inflation was lower. It was a kind of risk premium on investments in a currency not endowed with the magical quality of the D-mark. Bérégovoy and Balladur discovered this unpleasant truth when they tried to bring nominal interest rates below German ones in the autumn of 1991 and in July 1993. The theory that a country cannot reconcile the three aims of monetary independence, stable parity with its trading partners and free movement of capital is further strengthened when a country is heavily dependent on foreign capital.

A vicious circle

Ironically, the state's need for foreign capital has been exacerbated by France's *franc fort* policy. The need to keep interest rates high in order to maintain the parity of the currency and therefore foreign investors' confidence has led to an economic slowdown and a rise in unemployment, thus undermining France's fiscal position. Falling levels of activity and employment have contributed to a shortfall in tax and social contributions revenue, whilst the electoral calendar (March 1993 parliamentary elections and May 1995 presidential ballot) was not conducive to cuts in public spending. Consequently, in an unsuccessful effort to limit the deterioration of the budget balance, the Bérégovoy and Balladur governments increased their borrowing, principally through OATs (long-term treasury bonds), BTANs (medium-term treasury bonds) and to a lesser extent, BTFs (short-term treasury bonds). In 1992 the Treasury issued 168 billion francs worth of OATs, 152 billion francs in BTANs and 80 billion francs of BTFs. France's government debt therefore increased from F1,500 billion in 1988 to F2,100 billion at the end of 1992. By the end of 1994, thanks mostly to the issuing of 500 billion francs of OATs and BTNs, the total government debt had jumped to F2,900 billion, of which F2,479 billion were in a negotiable form, 63 per cent in long-dated debt and 37 per cent short and medium-term treasury notes (Ministère de l'Economie 1995). The gross cost of servicing that debt rose from F174 billion in 1992 to F206 billion in 1994 and F226.4 billion in 1996. This amounts to nearly 15 per cent of budget expenditure, against 10.5 per cent in 1990, making debt repayment the second largest item in the budget after education.

Consequently, French efforts to bring down the budget deficit in order to satisfy the markets and lately the Maastricht convergence criteria, have forced successive governments to limit the growth of public spending by keeping public sector wages low and to raise taxes, thus further inhibiting consumer demand and business confidence and therefore economic activity, employment and tax revenue. The economic slowdown and the relentless rise of the jobless total which have followed Juppé's August 1995 VAT rise and public sector wage freeze are a perfect illustration of the point, as was the 1993 recession caused by Balladur's initial attempt at belt-tightening.

The rapid deterioration of public finances has been closely watched by the markets and has had a doubly negative impact. Not only did it make it difficult to implement a much-needed relaxation of France's short-term rates policy, but it also amplified the 1994 withdrawal of foreign capital caused by anxieties over the international bond market and the increase in US interest rates. Non-resident holdings of Treasury bonds fell from close to F800 billion in January 1994 to F600 billion at the end of the year (Ministère de l'Economie 1995), before picking up again in 1995. As currency stability and credibility have become an almost structural need for the French financial markets, it was hoped that granting independence to the Banque de France would help to achieve that aim while at the same time paving the way for the European Central Bank and therefore convincing the Germans of the seriousness of French intentions.

An independent Banque de France

'An independent Banque de France? I am not sure that it is a good thing, but it was the prerequisite set by the Germans for voting the Maastricht treaty': Bérégovoy's remark has often been quoted (*Nouvel Observateur*, 5 August 1993, 27). Events were to show that his reservations, which centred around the potential for further reduction of the government's autonomy in economic policy making, were fully justified.

Articles 108 and 109E of the Maastricht Treaty require the achievement of independence for the central banks of the countries participating in EMU by the date of the inception of the European Central Bank, i.e. 1 January 1997 or 1999. Mitterrand stressed in a speech he made on 27 January 1994, the day of the installation of the Conseil de la Politique Monétaire, that, in spite of his reservations about the risks inherent in central bank independence, it was justified by 'the need for France to move quickly towards a single currency' and to achieve a 'higher objective . . . EMU as the only way to turn Europe into a major power in all areas, economic and monetary especially' (*Bulletin de la Banque de France*, no. 2, February 1994, 78). However, for the French monetary authorities, even though 'the Maastricht treaty played an important part in the decision to grant the Banque de France its independence . . . there were other reasons to grant it immediately' (Trichet in *Les Echos*, 28 January 1994). Indeed, whilst an 'independent BdF is the cornerstone of the Maastricht Treaty, it could have waited. Independence was also and mainly a requirement for sound monetary management' (Ferman in *Bulletin de la Banque de France*, no. 3, March 1994, 80).

Immediate independence was perceived as a way to enhance the sought-after credibility of French monetary policy, a justification which recurs time and time again in all the writings or speeches made by Banque de France representatives.

The fact that French monetary policy is now in the hands of a credible institution and no longer subject to the whims of the politicians is meant to give markets the extra confidence which will help to lower the risk premium and interest rates (Trichet 1994: 10). Of course, long before the Bank gained its independence, its governor's role in monetary policy making had begun to grow, especially after Bérégovoy took over as Finance Minister in 1984. The new status of the Bank gave it clearer responsibilities, as well as independence. Since its inception on 1 January 1994, the newly independent bank's Monetary Policy Council (CPM) has a statutory obligation (Law no. 93.980, 4 August 1993) to:

- 'define and implement monetary policy with the objective of maintaining price stability' (Article 1); and
- 'achieve the exchange rate regime and the parity of the franc decided by the government' (Article 2) through the fixing of central bank rates and the determination of monetary policy objectives (Article 3).

The CPM comprises nine members, whose autonomy is guaranteed by the fact that the Governor and two under-governors are appointed for a six-year renewable term, whilst the other six members are appointed for a non-renewable nine-year term. They meet at least once a month and take majority decisions, on a one-person-one-vote basis, in meetings which the Prime Minister and the Finance Minister, or their representatives, can attend and in which they can propose topics for deliberation. The September 1993 appointment of Jean-Claude Trichet as Governor of the Banque de France and head of the CPM showed that there would be a strong continuity in France's monetary policy. The ultra-orthodox Trichet had been, with the previous Banque governor De la Rosière, one of the key architects of the *franc fort* policy. Their views are also shared by a majority of the CPM members.

If, as CPM member Michel Albert stated in a speech in Toulouse, the Balladur government had granted the Bank its independence 'because it felt that it was in the national interest' (Banque de France Toulouse no. 85, 15 March 1995, 2), it was going to quickly realise that the Bank did not see its role as simply to conduct monetary policy and that its actions could go against the short-term political interest of the government. The Bank soon used its power to set interest rates as a way of influencing the government's economic policy. At the end of 1994, the CPM made its voice heard to the Balladur government and to all future candidates in the forthcoming presidential election through a Trichet press conference (*Oxford Analytica Daily Brief*, 13 January 1995, III) in which he rebuked the government over the worrying extent of the public deficits. Also, by stating that, as French fundamentals were sound, the franc was in his opinion undervalued against the mark, he confirmed that the CPM would keep on using the short-term interest rates weapon to maintain the franc within the old 2.25 per cent ERM band. The determined tone and the clear monetary objectives set by the CPM were a clear signal that the bank would not willingly depart from its stance.

Further proof that the Banque de France was seriously trying to emulate the Bundesbank and play an increased role in economic policy making came in the wake of the 1995 presidential election. Chirac's campaign promises had worried the markets, leading the CPM to raise its repo rate to 8 per cent in March. The Chirac administration would have liked to cut the cost of borrowing in order to boost activity, but the CPM wanted the government to show its commitment to a more orthodox fiscal policy. It waited until the June mini-budget presentation, stressing the government's will to reduce the budget deficit to 5 per cent of GDP in 1995, 4 per cent in 1996 and 3 per cent by 1997, before embarking on a careful step-by-step trimming of its short-term rates. In four steps from 22 June, the CPM brought down its repo rate from 8 per cent to 6.5 per cent in August. However, the CPM shared the markets' scepticism of Chirac's commitment to fiscal rectitude and were particularly worried by the 2 per cent increase in the top (in effect, standard) VAT rate in August. They considered that increasing taxation was not only harmful to economic activity, but also, along with the growth in public spending, conducive to inflationary pressure. The CPM chose to stop the downward spiral of interest rates and, following the bad reception by markets of Juppé's September presentation of the 1996 budget, increased the call and repo rates to stem speculation against the currency.

Chirac finally surrendered in a television interview on 28 October 1995, committing himself to deficit reduction and, in effect, to the abandonment of his manifesto. The CPM however waited until Juppé announced his proposals for social security reforms on 14 November before condescending to welcome the government's social deficit reduction programme with a modest quarter point rate-cut. Even though the need to meet the Maastricht criteria was the declared aim of this public deficits reduction exercise, Chirac and Juppé's commitment to fiscal rectitude was, in the short-term, motivated more by the watchfulness of the financial markets than by the desire to promote European construction. A few weeks later, Chirac was reported to have said that his objective in the interview was to provoke a cut in interest rates: 'I do everything I can for that purpose. It is not in order to respect I don't know what kind of Maastricht dogma, but in order to reduce social tensions' (*Libération*, 21 November 1995). Unable to carry out the 'other policy' advocated during the campaign, Chirac had to admit that the government's autonomy was limited by structural factors which forced him first to cut the budget deficit before embarking on a more proactive employment policy. Thus his initially reluctant endorsement of the Maastricht criteria had less to do with Europe than with the acceptance that France is an ordinary player on the global marketplace, whose rules it has to observe.

CONCLUSION

The *franc fort* policy originating in the policy change of 1983 allowed the French economy to become more liberal, open and competitive than it had ever been:

however, since the early 1990s, its weaknesses in terms of economic slowdown, rising unemployment and bulging borrowing have cast doubts on its validity. Mirroring that evolution, the European monetary integration process, which was initially perceived as a necessary and ultimately beneficial constraint, has now become a convenient scapegoat on which to place the blame for high unemployment and cuts in public spending. It is undeniable that France's desire to maintain the parity of the franc in a D-mark-dominated EMS has limited its ability to lead a more independent economic and monetary policy, but this loss of sovereignty stems less from the European constraint than from financial globalisation.

Concerns about France's commitment to EMU emerged following the election of Jacques Chirac. They were partly based upon the fact that his electoral promises were going to be hard to deliver within the framework of the Maastricht convergence criteria calendar, but also on Chirac's perceived lack of Euro-enthusiasm. Since then, the President has jettisoned his promise to carry out *une autre politique* and reaffirmed France's commitment to EMU and its calendar. In the final approach to 1999, French policy revolves around meeting the convergence criteria, not just because they match those of the financial markets, but because it is convinced that EMU is in its interests. As French elites share Fitoussi's view that 'EMU is not only a way for European countries to recover a lost sovereignty, but also a way to gain a new one' (Fitoussi 1995: 281), they have worked hard to convince the current administration of its benefits for France. Ironically, in the same way as economic realities had led the Mitterrand Socialist administration to accept market forces, they have turned the Euro-sceptic Gaullists into strong advocates of European Monetary Union and the single currency, as is shown by Chirac's efforts to convince British leaders of its merits during his official visit of May 1996.

With EMU, national governments will be deprived of macroeconomic instruments to boost medium-term growth, such as devaluations, low or negative real interest rates and increases in the budget deficit, but reliance on foreign capital and financial globalisation have already reduced the French authorities' autonomy. A single currency and a European central bank would give Europe more weight in international currency matters, and in reducing the Bundesbank's domination would give France more say in European monetary policy. Combined with French proposals to balance the bank's powers by making it more subservient to the wishes of the participating countries' finance ministers, monetary policy would be at the service of an economic policy closer to the economic and social concerns of governments. The single currency would therefore be, as stated by Chirac in an interview published by *Libération* on 25 March 1996, the main weapon to promote and defend the 'European social model' in the face of global market forces. Europe has often been used as a justification for the last fifteen years' financial deregulation and capital liberalisation, but a stronger united Europe could help to 'put the genie back in the bottle' and help governments regain some of the tools of economic policy making which they have lost to the markets.

BIBLIOGRAPHY

Commissariat Général du Plan (1993) *L'Economie Française en Perspective*, Paris: La Découverte/La Documentation Française.

Crozet, Y. (1994) *Inflation ou Déflation*, Paris: Nathan.

De Boissieu, C. and Duprat, M-H. (1990) 'French monetary policy in the light of European monetary and financial integration', in H. Sherman (ed.) *Monetary Implications of the 1992 Process*, London: Pinter.

Delpit, B. and Schwartz, M. (1993) *Le Système Financier Français*, Paris: Montchrestien.

ECU Newsletter (1993) 'The central bank's operating procedures and the transmission of monetary policy in France', September, Turin: San Paolo Bank Holding SpA.

Eizenga, W (1990) 'The Banque de France and monetary policy', in *SUERF Papers on Monetary Policy and Financial Systems*, no. 8, The Hague: SUERF.

Elgie, R. (1993) *The role of the Prime Minister in France, 1981–91*, London: Macmillan.

Favier, P. and Martin-Roland, M. (1990) *La Décennie Mitterrand, vol. 1: Les Ruptures*, Paris: Seuil.

Fitoussi, J-P. (1995) *Le Débat Interdit*, Paris: Arléa.

Fitoussi, J-P. and Muet, P-A. (1993) 'Les enjeux de l'Europe', *Observations et Diagnostics Economiques*, no. 43, Paris.

Forbes, J. and Howlett, N. (1994) *Contemporary France*, London: Longman.

Giacobbi, M. and Gronier, A-M. (1994) *Monnaie Monnaies*, Paris: Le Monde Marabout.

Giavazzi, F. and Pagano, M. (1988) 'The advantage of tying one's hands', *European Economic Review*, 32: 1055–82.

Lequesne, C. (1993) *Paris Bruxelles*, Paris: Presses de la Fondation Nationale des Sciences Politiques.

Machin, H. and Wright, V. (1985) *Economic Policy and Policy Making under the Mitterrand Presidency, 1981–4*, London: Pinter.

Melitz, J. (1991) 'Monetary policy in France', *CEPR Discussion paper*, no. 509, London, CEPR.

Ministère de l'Economie (1995) *French Government Securities: 1994 Annual Report*, Paris: Ministère de l'Economie.

OECD, *Economic Surveys France*, January 1987, March 1994, September 1995, Paris: OECD.

Perrut, D. (1993) *L'Europe Financière et Monétaire*, Paris: Nathan.

Rowley, A. (1992) 'Les Français dans la crise', *Histoire Economique de la France au XXᵉ siècle*, Paris: Cahiers Français, no. 255.

Saint-Ouen, F. (1986) 'Les partis politiques Français et l'Europe', *Revue Française de Science Politique*, vol. 36, no. 2.

Trichet, J-C. (1992) *Les Notes Bleues de Bercy*, 16–31 October 1992, Paris: Ministère de l'Economie.

——(1994) 'La Banque de France: son nouveau statut', *Economie et Culture*, 10 April 1994.

Virard, M-P., (1993) *Comment Mitterrand a Découvert l'Economie*, Paris: Albin Michel.

Zerah, D. (1993) *Le Système Financier Français*, Paris: La Documentation Française.

7

GERMANY

Elke Thiel and Ingeborg Schroeder

INTRODUCTION

European unification has always been a pre-eminent goal of German policy. The country has assumed a pivotal role in promoting the deepening of monetary integration in the European Union (EU). Germany, in close cooperation with France, initiated the European Monetary System (EMS) in 1979, and Economic and Monetary Union (EMU) in 1988. Both projects became feasible due to a convergence of policies among EU members. Germany has both contributed to and benefited from these developments. Given this basically positive premise, German monetary policy will be analysed on the basis of the following three questions. First, what is the relationship between autonomy and sovereignty in domestic monetary policy and to what extent can these be preserved in the face of growing regional economic interdependence? Second, how did EMS membership interfere with autonomy in setting domestic monetary policy and how did German policy respond to this problem? Third, given that all member states have to surrender sovereignty in EMU, how is this issue being dealt with by Germany?

THE NATURE OF AUTONOMY IN THE MONETARY REALM

Monetary policy is a most delicate issue. Its conduct has a decisive impact on a country's economic welfare and social peace. Due to past experiences and traditions, the monetary constitutions of the member states of the European Union (EU) differ. In Germany, the Deutsche Bundesbank is responsible for setting monetary policy. Its independent status enables the Bundesbank to maintain its commitment to securing price stability without political interference.

This independence and the priority given to assuring price stability, both of which are written into the constitution of the Bundesbank, insulate monetary policy from undue influence by interest groups. This stance has been accepted as a value *per se* and internalised by the German people to the extent that an equal level of independence for the European Central Bank is a necessary condition for German acceptance of EMU.

However, the autonomy to set an independent monetary course is, as described in the introduction, circumscribed by the interdependence of the global financial market. Monetary policy has a vulnerable flank. Its stability-orientated course can be easily undermined by external forces. The impact of these forces on the domestic economy depends on the exchange rate regime. There are in principle two regimes: managed floating and fixed rates. The fixed system constrains the autonomy of policy formulation more because of the necessity of supporting the fixed rates in the event of speculative attack. Germany became aware of the costs of this regime as early as the 1960s when the effects of the D-mark functioning as a haven for capital flight out of the dollar placed definite constraints on policy discretion. The Bundesbank was obliged, under the rules of the Bretton Woods System, to buy dollars in large amounts, which made it much more difficult to control West German inflation.

The change in the international monetary regime from a system of fixed rates to floating exchange rates heightened the degree of independence each country had in setting its macroeconomic policy. However, not even large countries like the United States can neglect the exchange rate in favour of a monetary policy set exclusively in the interests of domestic policy. A large country with a substantial domestic market and therefore a certain resistance to the influence of exchange rates on production levels is still affected by the movements of the global capital markets, especially since these have become so immensely powerful.

Within the European internal market the freedom to set an autonomous policy is even more restricted than in the global system. The international system did sometimes allow a country temporarily to secure its independent national objectives by means of floating exchange rates. This instrument is of little use, however, to countries in the internal market. The larger member states carry out more than half their foreign trade with their partners in the internal market. In the case of the smaller member states this figure can represent up to 70 per cent of their foreign trade. In these circumstances exchange rate fluctuations have important domestic implications.

The European Monetary System was introduced in 1979 in order to provide the Common Market with a 'zone of stable currency relations'. At the heart of this system was the Exchange Rate Mechanism (ERM) which pegged the currencies of those who joined in a fixed exchange rate regime. The EMS was successful in that it promoted an increasing convergence in policy. Moreover, the loss of autonomy due to the fixed exchange rates was made acceptable to member states by the fact that their economic priorities became more compatible over time. This was particularly true of German monetary policy. The foremost priority of German monetary policy, price stability, was gradually taken on by other nations in the EMS as a goal worth striving for. Due to both the fact that Germany was able to convince the other members of the validity of its priority on price stability and the fact that the D-mark functioned as the key currency or anchor within the ERM, Germany was able to preserve a somewhat greater independence in setting its monetary policy.

Economic and Monetary Union goes further than did the EMS. In addition to a loss of autonomy in setting policy, EMU requires member states formally to transfer sovereignty to EU institutions. Thus the autonomy circumscribed by external constraints is formally surrendered. All responsibility for setting monetary policy must be transferred to the European Central Bank. The remaining autonomy that Germany had within the EMS will have to be legally and formally surrendered to the European Union in terms of a transfer of sovereignty. Even in the realm of fiscal policy, the individual nation's sovereignty is curtailed by the rules of Article 104c of the Treaty. On the other hand, this autonomy is then returned collectively by way of participation in the decision-making process in the Council of the European Central Bank (Schonfelder and Thiel 1996: 146–8). Furthermore, the EU/EMU provides more room for manoeuvre in the international system by virtue of the size of the internal economic and financial market.

GERMAN MONETARY POLICY IN THE EMS

The Bundesbank's dilemma

The EMS was launched by a common Franco-German initiative of President Giscard d'Estaing and Chancellor Helmut Schmidt. It was a political decision that altered the conditions for German monetary policy. The Bundesbank was obliged to accept this new system, since its independence does not include the choice of the exchange rate regime.

Instead of tying the D-mark tightly to the French franc, the Italian lira and other EC currencies in the EMS, the Bundesbank probably would have preferred the British method of unilateral floating. The D-mark already belonged to a small group of pegged exchange rates at that time – the remains of the European 'snake'. In that exchange rate regime, since the D-mark by virtue of its weight in the currency system was in a position to set the trends for the other, much smaller currencies in the system, German monetary policy autonomy was not infringed.

The EMS was rather different in this respect. Both France and Italy had pursued macroeconomic policies in the past which were quite different from German policies. Inflation was much higher in these countries and their currencies were frequently under pressure from financial markets. Under these circumstances, pegging them to one another was quite risky. The Bundesbank was contractually obliged to support the weaker currencies of the EMS by selling D-marks, which made it more difficult to follow a tight anti-inflationary monetary course at home.

Linking their currencies to the stronger D-mark was also risky for France and Italy. In order to keep in line with the D-mark, they had to deflate their domestic economies, not an easy task for societies accustomed to glossing over distributive conflicts by tolerating increased inflation. If they did not adjust their policies to more stringent anti-inflation criteria, however, their currency would be under frequent pressure to devalue. In retrospect, France in particular contributed much to the success of the EMS by altering its macroeconomic policy so that the economic performance of the two largest currencies in the system could converge.

When the EMS was introduced, inflation rates differed widely among the member states, by up to more than 10 per cent between the lowest and highest levels. Many German economic experts, therefore, suspected that divergencies would soon cause the system to fail. If the system survived, it was feared that price levels would converge at the upper end of the spectrum. Anxious not to lose control over inflation, the Bundesbank reached an informal understanding with the German government for opting out. In a situation where a severe conflict arose between the obligation to intervene in EMS currency markets and its commitment to price stability, the Bundesbank was anxious to retain control over the level of its involvement. It wanted to have the right to cease intervention in currency markets should that be absolutely necessary.

This was a security measure. The Bundesbank wanted to avoid situations in which it would be obliged to provide unlimited support to weak currencies in the EMS. Such a situation could have occurred, given the fact that decisions on the realignment of the currencies were taken by the political authorities. The Bundesbank could thus have been placed in a position in which it was forced to defend existing parities between currencies, even if these were deemed by capital markets to be unsustainable and vulnerable to attack.

The Bundesbank never did opt out, however. In fact it went to great lengths to ensure the smooth functioning of the EMS. In particular, it tried to ameliorate the EMS crises of 1992–3 with substantial intervention in the currency market. In the course of only one month – from the end of August to the end of September 1992 – the Bundesbank had to absorb an influx of capital amounting to DM92 billion as a result of exchange market interventions (Deutsche Bundesbank 1992). The Bundesbank did, however, express the opinion that the political decision makers in the EU should open up the possibility of instituting a realignment before the overvalued currency was forced into a crisis situation by capital markets. It attempted to use its influence to achieve an improvement in this aspect of the functioning of the EMS.

Converging policies

The European Monetary System functioned much better than many observers had expected. Inflation gradually declined in the participating countries. For

German monetary policy, this was a positive development as it reduced the risk of importing inflation.

At the beginning of the 1980s there was a gradual shift in the dominant paradigm and a growing consensus that price stability was a worthwhile goal. Those nations whose currencies had been subject to frequent depreciation in 1970s began to realise the value of pegging their currencies to a more stable 'anchor'. The D-mark provided such an anchor currency. This is one reason France and Italy were interested in joining the EMS. On the other hand, achieving price stability for themselves required them to follow policies more convergent with the German monetary course. Due to its anchor function, the Bundesbank could preserve more room for manoeuvre in pursuing an autonomous monetary course than could other members. This gave rise to the oft-used phrase that monetary decision making in the EMS takes place in Frankfurt.

This phrase indicates that German autonomy in setting monetary policy was often felt to be extensive and to be pursued at the expense of the autonomy of other members of the EMS. This is debatable. Despite the stability-oriented course of Bundesbank policies, the system also had its impact on German policy. While the internal management of EMS exchange rates was largely carried out by means of intra-marginal interventions on the part of the weaker currency members, exchange rate management between the EMS as a whole and the dollar was the Bundesbank's responsibility. Frankfurt had to cooperate closely with the other EMS central banks in order to keep the system together, internally and externally.

The complaints reveal the dilemma of German policy in the EMS. The Bundesbank is not a European central bank. Bound by the statutes of its constitution, the Bundesbank bears responsibility for domestic economic performance. It can give support to the EMS as far as this is compatible with its constitutional commitments, and this it has done.[1] In general, the pre-eminent aim of the Bundesbank in the EMS has been to strengthen the core of strong currencies in the system. The reasons for this are obvious: to the extent that the anchor function currently exercised by the D-mark is more equally shared with others, policy autonomy might shrink, but price stability becomes easier to achieve.

GERMAN POLICY IN THE FRAMING OF EMU

The political decision

For Germany the decision to pursue EMU was a political one, taken to promote integration. The project was an initiative of the Foreign Minister Hans-Dietrich Genscher, presented at the European summit in Hanover in June 1988. The so-called Delors Committee was set up on his advice and given the Chancellor's full support. The finance ministry, the economic ministry and the Bundesbank were rather more sceptical and pointed out that, prior to an institutionalisation of monetary union, economic convergence in the EMS ought to be strengthened. However, rather than attempting to disrupt the project, the ministries and the Bundesbank concentrated on constructing the legal and institutional framework in such a way as to assure that it conformed to the German priority of price stability. Given the German Chancellor's determination to further economic and political integration, policy makers focused on the way in which EMU was implemented, as opposed to debating joining EMU.

In Germany a high value is placed on the goal of integration. EMU can be seen as a natural continuation of the Treaty of Rome's integrational teleology and the functional path toward integration which was chosen at its inception. There is understandably a stronger consensus within the original signatories of the Treaty on the value of this goal than among some of the more recent entrants. As in the case of the founding of the EMS, two considerations played a central role in the German EMU initiative: strengthening Franco-German cooperation and providing the process of integration with a new momentum. The project was supposed to revitalise the dynamic force of the internal market.

As a system of fixed exchange rates, the European Monetary System offered only very limited scope for evolution. The EMS was to have entered a second stage after two years, in which a European Monetary Fund would have been created. One of this fund's main purposes would have been the coordination of exchange rates between the EMS and third currencies. The member states would have placed a portion of their currency reserves at the disposal of this central fund. Neither the German government nor the Bundesbank could have been entirely happy with such a structure because no regulations for ensuring price stability were envisioned in its planning.

Plans for adapting the EMS to the requirements of the internal market had also reached stalemate. In 1987 the mutual credit mechanism was strengthened in order to improve the defence of EMS currencies in light of the approaching liberalisation of capital flows. The completion of the internal market had required all restrictions on the movement of capital to be dismantled and further speculative attacks on the weaker currencies were expected. The Bundesbank worried that the commitment it had already assumed in support of the weaker currencies in the system would interfere with its constitutional commitment to securing price stability. Although supportive of the EMS, Frankfurt was unwilling to extend its obligations for exchange market interventions beyond what had already been agreed upon.[2]

Moreover, France and Italy had spent heavily in supporting their weaker currencies on the foreign exchange markets in order to stay within their margins. Unless the currency had reached the bottom of its margin, when the Bundesbank stepped in to help support it, each member was responsible for maintaining the value of its own currency. This led to an asymmetry in the amount of foreign exchange market intervention the various central banks were obliged to undertake, because the weaker currencies required much more intervention than the stronger ones. Consequently there were calls for a strengthening and reform of the structure of the EMS.

France and other members wanted more say in the common monetary policy within the EMS. An independent central bank appeared to be the only solution to the impasse. Such an institution was a means of safeguarding German stability priorities while allowing other EMS partners more say in decisions which affected them equally. However, this solution was only possible by virtue of the fact that Germany was, in contrast to the United Kingdom, prepared in principle to accept a loss of sovereignty as a consequence of deeper integration.

On the other hand, the loss of sovereignty was only acceptable to the German electorate if accompanied by assurances that the European Central Bank (ECB) would uphold the same priority as the Bundesbank and the EMU would be equipped with measures to guarantee its stability. On this point the German Federal Government and the Bundesbank were in complete agreement. Bundesbank officials were involved in formulating the German position for the EMU negotiations from the start. The Bundesbank was also involved at the Community level. Having worked closely together during the years of the European Monetary System, a kind of congeniality had evolved among the national central banks. Their presidents worked together in the Delors Committee, not in their official capacities but *ad personam*. They unanimously approved the three-step approach to EMU. The Committee of Central Bank Governors later drafted the constitutions for the ECB and the European System of Central Banks (ESCB). The drafts of these constitutions were taken up in the final version of the Treaty with very few changes. Thus the Bundesbank had a strong impact on the final concept.

Surrendering sovereignty

EMU is to be implemented in three stages. Stage one began on 1 July 1990 and stage two came into force on 1 January 1994. Neither of these first two stages requires members to surrender sovereignty to a supranational organisation. With the beginning of the final stage, however, monetary decision making will be transferred *in toto* to a common body, the European System of Central Banks.

The national central banks are an integral part of the ESCB. They will be represented by their governors on the Council of the European Central Bank, which also includes the president, the vice-president and the other four members of the ECB executive board. All EMU members will thus have a say in the formulation of European monetary policy.

The framework of the ECB will be quite different from the national institutions with which most member states are familiar. As they become integral parts of the independent ESCB, national central banks will have to become independent of their governments. Votes will not be weighted in accordance with the weight of their countries; instead all ECB Council members will have only one vote. They will be independent personalities, to whom the political authorities of the European Union and the member states are not allowed to give advice.

Given the spectrum of types of national institution, surrendering sovereignty to the Central Bank has different implications for the individual member states. It is largely held that Germany, as the anchor currency country, will have to give up more in terms of actual sovereignty than others. The Bundesbank will be one among equals in the ESCB and could be outvoted in the Council. On the other hand, the ECB as it stands corresponds in its legal and institutional structure to the German system.

Member states who have complained of being obliged to hand monetary decision making over to Frankfurt could collectively regain sovereignty in the ESCB. But this regained sovereignty will not benefit national governments, since they have to grant their central banks independence. Thus it is not surprising that opposition to EMU centres on the independence of central banks in those countries accustomed to a different model. Overall, therefore, and given the close correlation between existing German and future European institutional structures and practices, it may be said that the losses of sovereignty are balanced rather evenly in the final EMU.

While the European Monetary System had a strong impact on the member states' monetary policies, fiscal policies were only indirectly affected. As a result, the current fiscal policy performances of the various nations diverge much more than their monetary performance. This will have to change in view of EMU. Member states have submitted so-called convergence programmes which oblige them to achieve more budget consolidation. They will have to qualify for the final stage of EMU in terms of both price stability and fiscal balance. Most member states – including Germany – may find it difficult to meet the fiscal criteria. Given the fact that public deficits and debts must be reduced, EMU already infringes upon member states' fiscal policy and will continue to do so. Sovereignty will remain intact only to the extent that member states are able to conduct their fiscal policy within the constraints set by the Treaty's guidelines for fiscal discipline.

Nonetheless, among all the Community's plans for strengthening the European Monetary System, EMU was the most logical. All other proposals for implementing an improved EMS were vague and ambiguous in their commitment to price stability. They focused on the common management of the external exchange rate and on the pooling of currency reserves. The German government and the Bundesbank were unable to approve such plans, leaving the Union with little choice but to forge ahead with full monetary union.

The *modus operandi* of EMU

Having committed themselves to EMU, the important question for the German government and Bundesbank was how and according to which paradigm EMU would be implemented and function. From a German point of view, it was vital that the political independence of the ECB and the national central banks, as well as the primacy of price stability, be expressed in the constitutional foundation of EMU.

It was equally important that during the transitional period responsibility for monetary policy should not be shared by several institutions. Thus, although this task is to be entirely transferred to the European System of Central Banks at the final stage of EMU, it must remain solely in the hands of the national monetary authorities until that time. In other words, sovereignty cannot be submitted gradually or piecemeal. In order to ensure the price stability orientation of monetary policy, a single organ of authority must have charge.

The Major plan for a so-called 'hard ECU' did not receive German approval because it would have divided monetary responsibility between the national monetary decision makers and a common one.[3] There would be no central authority to guard against creeping inflation in one or more of the member states which would result in a *sub rosa* hollowing out of the currency's value. A further problem with the hard ECU was that any one of the currencies making up the basket currency could succumb to inflationary habits and thus affect the price of the ECU, at least to the extent of that nation's weight in the basket. The ECU would become a parallel currency which Europeans could freely choose. However, there would be no incentive to choose a basket currency which would necessarily be weaker than the strongest currency in the basket.

While a complete transfer of sovereignty in monetary policy takes place in the final stage of EMU, the framework for fiscal policy is more complex. Fiscal policy will basically remain in the hands of the member states. Yet regulations have been introduced that are designed to reduce the risks which fiscal policy can pose for monetary stability, with member states being required to avoid excessive public deficits and debts.

The question as to how fiscal discipline should be maintained after EMU was extensively debated during the EMU negotiations, even more so than the issue of the European Central Bank. All member states were very anxious to preserve their budget autonomy, although there was a general understanding that some rules were necessary. On this issue, the community of economic experts is split into two schools of thought. Some hold the view that monetary union must be accompanied by a centralised economic and fiscal policy, which would also necessitate a substantial increase in the Union's budget. The majority of nations are not in favour of this idea as it would contradict the subsidarity principle and lead to excessive centralisation. Another school of thought tends to believe that a common monetary policy will itself exert sufficient pressure to keep member states' policies on a converging path. In this view, a stability-oriented monetary policy will automatically restrain public deficits and debts. In the German domestic debate, the Advisory Council to the Ministry of Economics, for instance, was among the advocates of the latter view (Bundesminister für Wirtschaft 1989).

In the absence of regulations for securing fiscal discipline, however, the entire burden of defending price stability is borne by monetary policy. The German government and the Bundesbank therefore strongly supported incorporating rules governing fiscal policy. The member states should not be allowed to run up excessive deficits. The negative consequences of such deficits within EMU would affect all members. These consequences include the fact that governments draw upon the domestic savings of all the member states in order to finance their deficits. High public deficits would also have the effect of pushing interest rates up. Moreover, between the governments' borrowing on capital markets and the higher interest rates, private investment would be crowded out, with the attendant effects for economic growth.

There remains a question as to how to enforce these criteria after a country has joined EMU. The 3 per cent of GDP is meant to be the ceiling for a government's deficit, which implies that in times of normal economic growth deficits should be much smaller. At present, almost all the potential candidates are having substantial difficulties in bringing their deficits down to the region of 3 per cent, much less succeeding in keeping them generally below that level. It is important to avoid the situation where a potential member achieves the required fiscal position until being accepted into EMU, after which it relapses into old habits.

Therefore the German Minister of Finance, Theo Waigel, proposed that the countries joining the final stage of EMU should commit themselves to a so-called stability pact comprised of stricter rules for fiscal policy than those contained in the Treaty of Maastricht. The stability pact aims to encourage and if necessary enforce true reform of national budgets to avoid a situation in which problems in the area of fiscal policy put pressure on monetary policy within EMU.

The Treaty of Maastricht includes a timetable for implementation of EMU. The final stage will start at the latest in 1999, with a membership comprised of those nations who fulfil the criteria. Germany supported such a concrete timetable so that EMU would not become mired in stages one or two. A common institution, the European Monetary Institute (EMI), was created to handle the technical preparations of the final stage. Its mandate does not extend beyond the second stage of EMU, and it will be replaced in the final stage by the European Central Bank. The possibility cannot be ruled out that if EMU were to be halted before its final stage, the EMI would take on monetary tasks for which it lacks all legitimacy. Germany has favoured a short second stage for this reason.

Criticism and acceptance of EMU

Ever since EMU was launched, the academic economic community has for the most part questioned the key premise on which German support for the project is based, namely the feasibility of an anti-inflationary approach to EMU. Many consider EMU to be a very risky undertaking for Germany.[4]

The reaction of the German population has been mixed. On the one hand, the feeling fostered since the beginning of the Federal Republic, that the closer Germany is integrated into western Europe the better, is prevalent. On the other there is a sense of insecurity concerning EMU. Giving up the D-mark, one of the most powerful symbols of Germany's peace and prosperity since the Second World War, is not an easy task for the German electorate. The stringent anti-inflationary attitude, a reaction to the extremely destructive hyperinflation of the 1920s, has been internalised as a value *per se* and generations who have no recollection of that period in history are nonetheless adamantly opposed to allowing their currency to be undermined by inflationary policies. Only when the Germans are convinced the ECU will be as 'hard' as the D-mark will they be prepared to relinquish the latter. The warning that the ECU will be less stable than the D-mark has issued from German academic economists and the media. The so-called 'D-mark Party' was formed especially to oppose the Maastricht Treaty. Despite this party's attempt to achieve political gains by exploiting fears about the consequences of EMU, it received only a tiny percentage of the vote in the 1994 European election.

The German business and banking community has adopted a more favourable attitude towards EMU and has started with the technical preparations for a single currency. The trade unions, too, see distinct benefits in a common currency. But all of these groups are adamant that the priority of price stability be upheld – a precondition shared by all EMU proponents. The Bundesbank has approved the Maastricht framework – to which it made a substantial contribution – as an appropriate approach for creating a strong European currency. But members of the Bundesbank's board of governors have repeatedly insisted that the provisions of the treaty must be strictly applied.

The Bundestag ratified the Treaty of Maastricht by an overwhelming majority in December 1992,[5] with unanimous approval also given by the Bundesrat. In its ruling on the Treaty, the German constitutional court concluded that EMU has been conceived as a *Stabilitätsgemeinschaft*, i.e. a community of stability. As is underscored in this ruling, the stability approach of EMU is the foundation on which the German law ratifying the Treaty of Maastricht is based. Unlike the situation in the United Kingdom, the final stage of EMU will not need to be handled as a new case for approval by the German legislature. According to the ratification law, however, the Bundestag and the Bundesrat will address the issue with respect to the entrance criteria that the member states must fulfil. Before the issue is decided at the level of the European Union, they will vote on the matter. The German government will respect the decision of the parliament and this will be reflected in the government's vote in the Council.

The German government has tried to promote confidence in the stability of the future currency. Political authorities have repeatedly stated that the convergence criteria will be strictly upheld and the fulfilment of these criteria will take precedence over the timetable. As a means of enhancing fiscal discipline in the final stage of EMU, the stability pact is also likely to reduce the population's distrust of EMU. German negotiators were also interested in a new name for the single currency. The term ECU retained associations with the 'basket' currency, which, as it had gradually lost value against the D-mark, was not symbolic of a strong currency. The fact that the Central Bank will be located in Frankfurt should further reassure Germans that an atmosphere favourable to monetary stability will surround it.

CONCLUSIONS

For a long time, the independent status of the Deutsche Bundesbank and its constitutional commitment to price stability distinguished German monetary policy from that of most other EU members. However, in the past decade these distinguishing characteristics of German policy have slowly been integrated into the policies of other member states. The Banque de France has already become independent of the government and other central banks are about to follow. The commitment to striving for low inflation rates has generally become more common, especially amongst the founding members of the European Monetary System.

Due to the standing of the Bundesbank, Germany was able to assume a leading role in the EMS. Because the D-mark became the anchor currency, German monetary policy was able to pursue an autonomous course while other members had to adjust their policies to keep in line. It should be remembered, however, that the EMS became feasible and sustainable solely due to a reversal in the policies pursued by Germany's partners. It was a change in economic thinking and attitudes that helped the Bundesbank to combine its commitment to price stability with its support for the EMS.

With respect to Economic and Monetary Union, the pre-eminent German concern regards its implementation. German and British views, while often similar, generally differ on this subject. Among the reasons for this are diverging perceptions of monetary policy. From a German point of view, the responsibility for a stability-oriented monetary policy can not be shared by several authorities. There can be no half-measures, as the Major plan for a hard ECU seems to suggest. In order to ensure stability in EMU, monetary sovereignty has to be transferred *in toto*. German policy has therefore concentrated on shaping the institutional framework of EMU. While the British are anxious not to surrender sovereignty in Economic and Monetary Union, the Germans are anxious not to sacrifice stability.

This emphasis on stability as the highest priority is based on an enduring consensus between the government and the Bundesbank in Germany, which allowed them to present a united front during the negotiations for EMU. These integrationist ambitions and support for further integration of the European Union consistently given by the government do not negate the primacy of the stable monetary policy or the independence of the German central bank.

Economic and Monetary Union is held by the political elite, the central bankers and important interests groups alike to be feasible only if based on a stable and enduring foundation that guarantees long-term price stability. The fact that unemployment is high in Germany and that this presents a problem for policy makers could have caused conflict between the political authorities and the central bank in Germany, but in fact it has not. There is a widely held tenet, to which the political elites also subscribe, that monetary policy is not an appropriate instrument for ameliorating unemployment. The tradeoff between inflation and unemployment is discounted as an option in Germany and is thus unlikely to become a factor undermining Germany's support for EMU. On the contrary, distrust or critique of EMU among German elites and the populace are more apt to be concerned that the EMU will not be tough enough on inflation, not that it will increase unemployment.

Many commentators have indicated that Germany, of all prospective members of a possible single currency, stands to lose most in terms of autonomy under such arrangements. What this chapter has illustrated, however, is that whilst this may indeed be the case, German policy in the run-up to the creation of such a currency has centred on ensuring that monetary sovereignty is sacrificed in such a way as to ensure that the European-level arrangements finally arrived at impinge as little as possible on autonomy. Far from limiting the ability of the German state to translate its preferences into policy, EMU should be organised, as far as Bonn is concerned, in such a way as to guarantee not only the continuance of those policies, but, further, their implementation on a Europe-wide scale.

NOTES

1 For German policy see also Thiel 1989a; 1988.
2 See also Thiel 1989b.
3 See also Hasse and Koch 1991.
4 For the German academic debate on EMU see also Hrbek 1992; 1993.
5 Of the 568 votes cast, 543 were 'yes' against seventeen 'no' and eight abstentions.

BIBLIOGRAPHY

Bundesminister für Wirtschaft (1989) *Europäische Währungsordnung, Gutachten des Wissenschaftlichen Beirats beim Bundesministerium für Wirtschaft*, Bonn, Studienreihe 61.

Deutsche Bundesbank (1992) *Monthly Report*, 44, 10.

Hasse, R. H. and Koch, T. (1991) 'The hard ECU – a substitute for the D-Mark or a Trojan Horse?', *Intereconomics*, 26, 4: 159–66.

Hrbek, R. (1992) 'Kontroversen und Manifeste zum Vertrag von Maastricht', *Integration*, 15, 4: 225–45.

Hrbek, R. (ed.) (1993) *Die Entwicklung der EG zur Politischen Union und zur Wirtschafts- und Währungsunion unter der Sonde der Wissenschaft*, Baden-Baden.

Schönfelder, W. and Thiel, E.(1996) 'Ein Markt – eine Währung', *Nomos Verlagsgesellschaft*, 146–8.

Thiel, E. (1988) 'West Germany's role in the international economy', *Journal of International Affairs*, 42, 1: 53–73.

——(1989a) 'Macroeconomic policy preferences and coordination: a view from Germany', in P. Guerrieri and P. C. Padoan (eds) *The Political Economy of European Integration*, Hemel Hempstead: Harvester Wheatsheaf.

——(1989b) 'From the Internal Market to an economic and monetary union', *Außenpolitik*, German foreign affairs review, 40, 1: 66–75.

8

ITALY

EMS discipline, fiscal imbalance

Giacomo Vaciago

INTRODUCTION

The paper is divided into two parts. The first reviews the benefits of EMS membership by considering the main changes that Italy had to accept in order to sustain a gradually higher degree of exchange rate stability. The second assesses the implications of the various EU constraints on Italian policy making. Among European countries Italy is probably the one which has most consistently used EU membership to justify the adoption of particular, allegedly 'correct' policy stances. The EMS (since 1979) has been seen as an instrument to achieve low inflation; while Maastricht (since 1992) has been accepted as a check on fiscal imbalances.

Membership of the European Monetary System has had many important consequences for Italy's macroeconomic policies. Some have been entirely positive. Others have had more questionable features. The need to achieve exchange rate stability and therefore reduce domestic inflation led to a gradual tightening of monetary policy. But the strategy of tight money with a strong currency that produced disinflation also led to higher interest rates and therefore to rising government outlays and a rising debt-to-GDP ratio, since the discipline exerted by the EMS did not extend to fiscal policy. On the contrary, the 'credibility' of the lira in the ERM promoted a relatively low-cost means of funding of the PSBR, at least until the summer of 1992 when EMS discipline and fiscal imbalance finally came into conflict.

At that time the Italian government was still focusing on the original goals of the EMS – the elimination of inflation differentials aimed at guaranteeing exchange rate stability – but financial markets had started to take into account the new Maastricht criteria of non-excessive fiscal deficits. The previous successes of monetary policy were therefore ignored. Membership of the ERM had to be suspended, not because of any unsustainable loss of competitiveness, but due to the fiscal imbalance which had accumulated in

119

the previous ten years. In this sense, EMS discipline turned out to have been self-defeating.

THE BENEFITS OF EMS MEMBERSHIP

After the ERM's introduction in March 1979, Italy's monetary policy had to be progressively tightened to prevent excessive pressures on the exchange rate. After barely a year, and notwithstanding the wider (6 per cent) band granted to the lira, the exchange rate weakened and the Bank of Italy experienced problems in controlling domestic liquidity, essentially because of the size of the public deficit. The 'divorce' between the Treasury and the Bank of Italy which was announced in July 1981 meant that the Bank was freed from the previous agreement to purchase all unsold treasury bills. Under that agreement the Treasury would auction bills up to a ceiling that fixed maximum yields. Any excess supply – due to yields lower than required by market demand – would then lead to Bank of Italy purchases. In other words, the Treasury would decide short-term rates and the central bank would then step in and – at least initially – create liquidity if those rates were below market equilibrium. Discontinuation of the agreement after the 1981 'divorce' therefore strengthened the Bank of Italy's control over short-term interest rates. A limitation remained, however, because the Treasury maintained a direct line of access to Bank of Italy short-term (current-account) credit, and therefore could still monetise some of its borrowing requirement. It was left to the Bank of Italy to try and sterilise any Treasury liquidity creation – something which was progressively achieved over the following ten years. The degree of monetary financing of the annual deficit was gradually reduced, and at the cost of higher real interest rates the Treasury gradually came to be funded exclusively through the sale of bills and bonds to the non-bank private sector.

The reduction in domestic inflation from the 20 per cent per annum of the late 1970s to the 5 per cent which on average prevailed in the following ten years was evidently linked to a similar deceleration in monetary growth, especially in the first part of the period when the decline in inflation was more marked (Figure 8.1).

Another indicator of the tightening of monetary policy from 1979 onwards can be seen in the fall of the M2/GDP ratio – from 85 per cent in 1978 to 60 per cent in 1987. But the reduction in the monetary financing of the Treasury deficit – from over 100 per cent down to zero (Figure 8.2) – was not without stressful consequences. First came the significant increase in real interest rates (Figure 8.2). This led to a marked increase of the annual government deficit in the period 1980–5 when money was tighter and disinflation greater. Thus a rising debt-to-GDP ratio (Figure 8.3) was the combined result of both the significant 'primary' (i.e. net of interest) deficit and high real interest rates. Conventional ways of treating debt arithmetic suggest that in order to stabilise the debt-to-GDP ratio at 100 per cent with a 5 per cent real interest rate and a 5

120

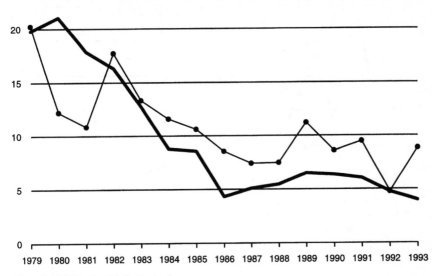

Figure 8.1 M2 (——)and inflation(——)

per cent primary-deficit-to-GDP ratio, a rate of growth of 10 per cent of real GDP is needed! The improvement which occurred in the annual deficit – down from 14 to 10 per cent of GDP – seems modest, but it is the outcome of a much greater improvement amounting to 8 per cent of GDP in the primary budget, half of which was however offset by higher interest payments.

The persistent non-accommodating stance of monetary policy was able to defend the stability of the lira in the ERM. The latter was at least partly an explicit 'intermediate' goal of the monetary authorities, in order to stabilise the economy and reduce inflation. The convergence of Italy's inflation towards the EU average has been impressive, especially in the first part of the 1980s: it was directly due to monetary tightening and to the impact of exchange rate stability on the price competitiveness of tradeables (mostly manufactured goods). Both these positive effects were somewhat less effective in the second half of the 1980s in moderating cost and price pressures in public and private services, i.e. in the non-tradeable sectors.

In addition to the cost in terms of a higher government debt, disinflation achieved through tighter monetary policy also had a cost in terms of higher unemployment (Figure 8.4). But one could argue that in other European countries this cost was in fact greater: the trade off in terms of lower inflation (down from 20 per cent to 5 per cent) but higher unemployment (up from 8 per cent to 12 per cent) was no worse than in most other countries.

In summary, therefore, the EMS discipline did produce positive effects in terms of disinflation, and the credibility of that discipline did also lower the costs

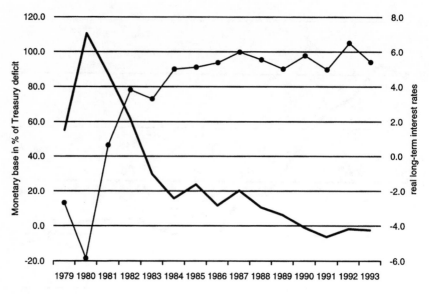

Figure 8.2 Monetisation of the treasury deficit (━)and real interest rates(-•-)

of disinflation in terms of lost output and employment. But the underlying fiscal imbalance was not cured. On the contrary, the widening public deficit was associated with its foreign counterpart (the 'twin deficits') and in the second part of the 1980s the net external position of Italy started to deteriorate drastically.

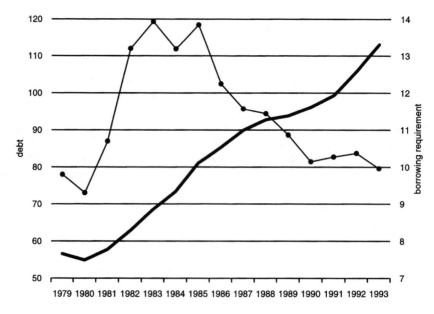

Figure 8.3 Public debt (━)and borrowing requirement (-•-)

The turning point is to be found in the Danish referendum of June 1992, which belatedly, if illogically, convinced the markets that an early ERM realignment was after all feasible and in fact likely. Prospective candidates for devaluation were therefore shortlisted and the lira was certainly in the first group, given its cumulated real appreciation and above all given the widespread belief that it could not sustain any further increase in interest rates. Both the government and the corporate sectors in Italy were already burdened by very high interest rates. In the face of an expected large-scale devaluation of the lira, avoidance of a run on official reserves would have required an equivalent, exceptionally high, increase in interest rates. Yet by damaging the state of the economy and exacerbating the already grave debt imbalances of state and private firms, such an increase in interest rates could scarcely help to sustain the lira. On the contrary, the warranted rate of depreciation – to offset an otherwise deteriorating economy – would have increased.

Exit from the ERM has taken the lira drastically away from its previous trend. In terms of the CPI-deflated real exchange rate, the lira against the D-mark returned in 1993 exactly to where it was in 1980, at the beginning of this story. A different picture emerges from considering real exchange rates deflated by producer prices. The difference is, of course, due to increased productivity in manufacturing (tradeables), which explains an inflation rate systematically lower for producer than for consumer prices. Manufacturing has been given back some of its terms-of-trade loss *vis-à-vis* services.

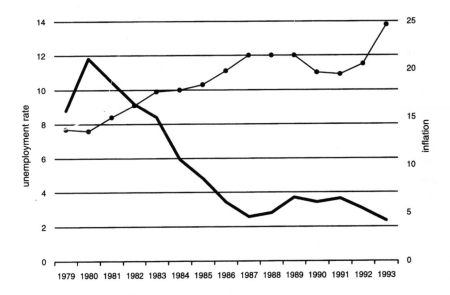

Figure 8.4 Unemployment rate (⟶) and inflation (⟶)

EU CONSTRAINTS ON POLICY MAKING

It can be argued that EU membership has always imposed constraints which were in Italy's own interest, and which were in this sense self-imposed. At one level, Italy's position was therefore no different from that of every west European state excepting Norway and Switzerland, since each has freely come to the conclusion that the constraints on autonomy implied by membership have outweighed the disadvantages of exclusion. Where Italy does differ is that some adjustments, particularly in the fiscal area, but also in others, such as state aids or financial-market regulation, have had to be especially large. Equally, however, they have been changes which many policy makers would have fought for in the name of improvements to the operation of markets or to macroeconomic management, whatever external constraints were operating. Because some such changes would have been difficult to accept and thus, in Italy's complex policy-making environment, politically difficult to agree upon unless conducted in the name of the wider benefits of EU membership, it was positively advantageous to present membership as implying extensive obligations and policy adjustments. It was also advantageous to have externally imposed timetables. These timetables have not always been respected, and Italy has often found itself in difficulty with the European Commission and the European Court of Justice as well as with the judgements of financial markets, but they have on at least some occasions been a sterner master than the pressure of domestic political opinion.

For these reasons it is sometimes difficult to distinguish between EU constraints on Italian policy-making autonomy, and those which would eventually have existed for other reasons. What is clear, throughout the 1980s and 1990s, is that Italy has accepted the EU timetable and the EU policy framework for responding to those constraints, and that it is Italian political life and the policy agenda which has adjusted to that timetable, rather than vice versa. Even when Italy has experienced difficulty in meeting the agenda requirements, it has rarely been suggested that the requirements or the timetable were at fault.

Thus the decision to participate in the EMS in the final months of 1978 had extensive political implications. It led to the departure from the majority supporting the government of the then Communist Party (since 1990 reborn as the PDS) which was not prepared to follow orthodox policies for returning to a low-inflation scenario. With inflation – after two oil shocks and a perverse price-wage spiral – reaching 20 per cent, the need to moderate price increases in order to protect savers and resume growth received political priority. The fight against inflation had its cornerstone in the EMS pact for nominal exchange rate stability. To prevent further depreciation of the currency, the inflation differential *vis-à-vis* other countries needed to be eliminated. A tight monetary policy was required and the necessary conditions for its implementation had to be in place. In the first phase, policy was gradually adapted in order to prevent monetary financing of the public deficit, and changes in the institutional process were adopted to reinforce Bank of Italy autonomy.

By 1984, with inflation already down from 20 to 10 per cent, a second phase had been reached. The need to tackle Italy's rigidly entrenched system of wage indexation, and more generally to moderate the inflationary expectations still prominent in labour relations and wage negotiations, was becoming unavoidable. The Craxi government was the first to attempt to confront this issue in a non-consensual manner. Its unilateral suspension of the automatic wage-indexation mechanism (the so-called *scala mobile*) in 1984, in the face of a bitter campaign of direct action by the trades union confederations and the Communist opposition, led directly to a referendum (on a Communist proposition to force employers to repay the price compensation lost by the government's action). Hitherto Italy's wage-indexation mechanism had been among the strongest in western Europe, especially for the lower paid. Along with other measures, it reduced differentials and was not only inflationary, but also a strong deterrent to labour mobility and productivity incentives. The system had been supplemented in the mid-1970s, in a major agreement with employers, by an expensive system of temporary redundancy payments (the so-called *cassa integrazione*), which added to labour market costs and rigidities.

It would be wrong to suggest that the 1985 referendum solved all the problems posed by the wage-indexation system. The battle to abolish the system was only won with the Incomes Policy Accords of July 1992 and July 1993, which drew a line under the *scala mobile*, imposing a good deal more flexibility into the wage-setting mechanism. Nevertheless, the mid-1980s represented an important turning point. The unity of the trade union movement itself was broken, and thereafter changing labour market conditions, lower levels of unionisation, and much stiffer government and employer resolve, combined to alter the balance of forces in the government-union-employer relationship in ways that signalled to labour market actors that the accommodating stance of the authorities had definitively ended. Thus if the fight against inflation was not over by the mid-1980s, it was greatly assisted by the gradual adaptation to the prevailing conditions of other EU countries, by tight monetary policy and an increasingly independent central bank, and by the gradual elimination of wage indexation accompanied by other labour market measures.

In the later 1980s however, a new, more important problem had started to emerge. The reduction in inflation, helped by the very high interest rates, was producing a rapid accumulation of government debt. Italy's most pressing problem was no longer domestic inflation (which was stabilising at around 5 per cent), but the fast increase in public debt, as measured by a rising debt-to-GDP ratio. It was precisely then that the Treaty of Maastricht shifted the perspective. The new goal was that of reducing so-called 'excessive' public deficits and therefore lowering the debt-to-GDP ratio. Measures to tackle the deficit, and in fact more directly to reduce the net-of-interest borrowing requirement (Figure 8.5), became necessary after the summer 1992 crisis. Stabilising the public debt so as to restore a badly shaken external equilibrium (Figure 8.6) became a top priority for the 1992 government as well as for subsequent administrations. In forcing policies and institutions to adapt to the need for monetary stability, fifteen years of EMS membership had made a major contribution to the control of inflation. The same process, starting in the early 1990s, now had to be implemented with regard to fiscal balance. In the present decade, the main challenge – not only for Italy – has thus been that of complying with Maastricht rules which, for better or worse, place so much stress on fiscal equilibrium.

The five convergence criteria of the Maastricht Treaty (Article 109j) require exchange rate stability, inflation and long-term interest rates within fixed parameters of the best performers, and low deficit- and debt-to-GDP ratios (respectively less than 3 per cent and 60 per cent). It might be argued that the safest route to achieving all these goals simultaneously would be by way of a specific order and timetable. The first step would be to bring the fiscal imbalance under control so as to stabilise the debt ratio (a primary surplus equivalent to any excess of the yield on government debt over GDP growth). While the fiscal balance is being achieved, monetary policy would be tightened so as to reduce domestic inflation. The success achieved on these two fronts would then allow the complete liberalisation of capital movements and the abolition of all exchange controls. In Italy a more risky path was initially followed: for too long tight money was adopted as a substitute for fiscal balance. The elimination of capital controls was meant to convince markets of the need for fiscal consolidation, but it proved insufficient to achieve this.

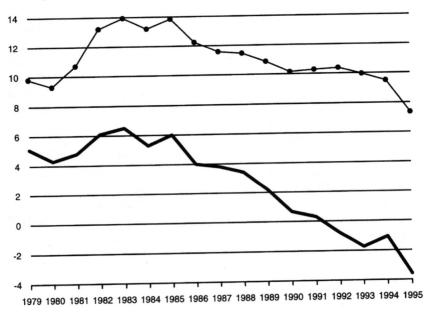

Figure 8.5 State sector borrowing requirement (--•--total; ▬ net of interest)

Only after the 1992 crisis has the right order of priorities been followed. Freed from the straitjacket of misguided exchange rate rigidity, Italy has been able to achieve a significant correction in its fiscal deficit. As in the past, the EU has thus imposed a constraint which has been openly embraced by those who have feared a drift away from Europe. The re-entry of the lira to the ERM has been decoupled from monetary policy and has been achieved following the success of the Prodi government's 1997 budget, which itself has built upon those of successive administrations since 1992, each of which has made a significant contribution to regaining fiscal balance.

As in the case of wage inflation, and in an even more dramatic manner, the recovery of fiscal balance has been achieved thanks to a major reconstruction of both the political order and the policy mix. There has been much, largely unfruitful, attention paid in recent years to the real causes of the dramatic collapse of the old party system after 1992. Certainly, the causes go well beyond the problem of budgetary imbalance, and encompass the long-term immobility of party politics, the extensive levels of political corruption and the consequences of major resource transfers between north and south. Ultimately, however, the impossibility of sustaining long-established distributional outcomes – especially those benefiting the public sector and southern voters – stemmed from the budgetary crisis ushered in by the Maastricht criteria. The governments that succeeded one another after 1992 – especially those of Giuliano Amato, Carlo Azeglio Ciampi and Lamberto Dini – were different from their predecessors not just in terms of the party composition of the governing majority, but

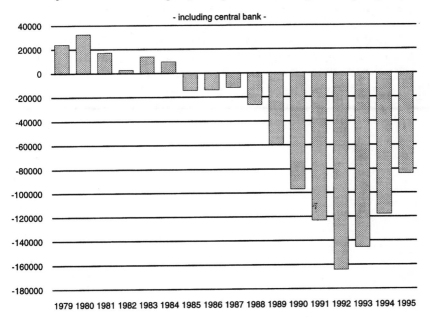

Figure 8.6 External position (end-of-period outstanding claims in billions of lire)

also in terms of the balance of power between, on the one hand, the technocrats of the Treasury and the Bank of Italy, their advisors and consultants, and on the other, the spending lobbies within Parliament, which had traditionally reshaped budgets in the parliamentary budget cycle in ways which blunted their purpose.

CONCLUSION

The EMS was 'invented' to ensure stable (nominal and real) exchange rates and thus favour integration in Europe. Italy was initially granted a wider 6 per cent band so as to manage more effectively the changes in parities expected on account of its original large inflation differential. But in order to resist devaluation the interest rate differential was maintained well above the corresponding inflation differential. This monetary 'success', however, led to the failure to discipline the state budget and its deficit. It was the latter that eventually made unsustainable the lira's membership of the ERM. The policy adjustments made since 1992 have therefore been even more dramatic, and more telescoped, than those made between 1979 and the start of the present decade. Whether they have been sufficient to achieve their ultimate goal of Italian qualification for first-phase EMU membership is, at the time of writing, still unclear. Whether the speed and distribution of their impact will have deleterious or indeed perverse consequences is also unclear, though by 1997 this question was beginning to be debated in Italy in a more open and critical manner than hitherto. Whether the budgetary choices made after 1992 were the right ones may also be disputed – in general they have relied heavily on the revenue rather than the expenditure side of the fiscal equation, with changes to some of the key areas – pensions in particular – coming only painfully slowly. What is not in doubt however, is the extent to which Italy's objective of remaining a key part of the European Union's core membership had imposed constraints on fundamental issues of labour market and budgetary management, with consequences that reverberated throughout the political system.

9

THE UNITED KINGDOM

M. J. Artis

INTRODUCTION

No EC regulations or directives have so far had any significant impact on monetary policy in the United Kingdom, whilst the UK's participation in the operation of the Exchange Rate Mechanism (ERM) of the European Monetary System (EMS) was of relatively short duration. So, for example, where the development of monetary policy in some other EU countries may have been substantially affected by the requirement under Single European Market legislation to remove exchange controls, the United Kingdom had already removed such controls at the outset of the 1980s. It is doubtful whether the EC banking directives had any discernible effect on banking regulation in the UK, which had already been radically revised in a series of steps from the reforms of 1971 to those of 1981.[1] And where other countries participated with enthusiasm in the ERM from the outset, the UK stood on the sidelines, only formally taking part in the period from October 1990 to September 1992. Aside from this latter episode we are left with nuances rather than strong and clear effects.

Two points stand out for elaboration. First, the 'optimal peg' literature indicates that the direction of trade provides an important criterion of choice when it comes to choosing an exchange rate target. With the evolution of trade links between the UK and the rest of the EC it would be natural to expect on this basis that an exchange rate pole of attraction rival to the US dollar would reveal itself. Second, the success (or erstwhile success) of the Exchange Rate Mechanism (ERM) of the European Monetary System was read as providing some instructive lessons to the UK, both influencing the nature of monetary policy pursued outside the framework of the ERM and attracting its eventual, if short-lived, formal participation in it.

In the following section I will comment briefly on the fundamentals behind the emergence of an alternative pole of attraction; I will then discuss the arguments for exchange rate targeting and the implications for monetary policy.

Finally, I will discuss the evolution of views in the light of experience about participation in the ERM.

THE D-MARK AS RIVAL TO THE DOLLAR

By the trade criterion, the UK has traditionally been placed in a position of ambiguity. If it were to choose to peg sterling to a single currency, the US dollar and the D-mark would be close rivals. At least after taking into account the fact that a number of other currencies are already aligned to one or other of the two leading currencies, the trade criterion has often failed to provide a clear discriminator. The growing orientation of UK trade towards Europe, together with the success of the EMS in tying other European currencies to the D-mark, has changed matters. Three decades ago the UK belonged to the US-dollar-based Bretton Woods System; two decades ago the UK had flirted briefly with the D-mark via its participation in the 'snake'. During the latter half of the 1980s the dominant question was whether and when the UK would announce its formal participation in the ERM. A useful summary of the shift in fundamentals underlying this transition is provided by the change in the weighting of the official Effective Exchange Rate (EER) index. The EER is a weighted average of bilateral exchange rates, the weights coming from a formal model of trade flows (cruder versions simply use bilateral trade weights). Table 9.1 is drawn from the Bank of England's *Quarterly Bulletin* and simply lists the old and new weights when the index weighting was revised in 1988. The weights are based on recent but past experience, so the shift in weights is a lagging indicator. As can be seen from the table, the weight of the ERM currencies in the UK EER rose by some 10 percentage points between 1981 and 1988 whilst the weight of the D-mark alone nearly doubled. The weight of the dollar declined at the same time, from a value nearly twice as high as that of the D-mark in 1981 to one of about the same value in 1988. A similar strengthening of attachment to the D-mark and to ERM currencies is observable for the other countries also listed.

A further factor is of interest in this connection. It is derived from applying a methodology first suggested by Haldane and Hall in an article in the *Economic Journal* (Haldane and Hall 1991) and subsequently elaborated by Hall with other colleagues (Hall *et al.* 1992). The argument of Haldane and Hall was that if one contemplates a three-currency world comprising the US dollar, the D-mark and sterling, and wonders whether sterling has moved from the dollar pole to the D-mark pole, the answer can be obtained by performing two simple regressions, one in which the $/£ exchange rate is related to the DM/£ exchange rate, the other in which the DM/£ exchange rate is related to the DM/$ exchange rate. If in fact the pound sterling were attached to the dollar, then the first regression should show nothing whilst the second would indicate a strong correlation (movements in the DM/$ exchange rate would imply nothing for the $/£ rate, whilst shifts in the dollar's exchange rate with the D-mark would show up in

Table 9.1 Effective index weights (per cent)

	Old index				New index			
	$	DM	ERM	£	$	DM	ERM	£
UK	24.6	14.1	41.6	-	20.4	20.1	51.1	-
Belgium	16.2	23.2	62.0	2.1	9.2	27.6	65.8	10.1
Denmark	24.0	11.2	35.3	7.1	9.1	24.7	44.7	11.8
France	22.7	20.1	46.0	4.1	12.1	27.4	57.2	10.1
FRG	21.6	-	41.7	-4.8	13.4	-	46.7	10.9
Italy	20.7	27.8	48.5	5.1	11.6	27.6	57.6	9.3
Netherlands	19.3	20.2	54.6	3.2	10.2	31.0	62.4	10.9

Source: Quarterly Bulletin of the Bank of England, March 1981, November 1988.
Note
The figures show the weight in the index, for any country, for the currencies listed. ERM is the sum of the weights of the ERM countries (excluding Spain). The basis of the new and old indices is explained in the source of references. In the new index, introduced in November 1988, Australia was dropped from the list of countries involved.

similar shifts in the pound's exchange rate with the D-mark).[2] The data displayed in Figure 9.1 in fact indicate that, according to the test proposed, sterling slipped into the D-mark orbit[3] well before the period of formal participation in the ERM. This, of course, in part reflects conscious policy decisions taken by the UK monetary authorities (as described below), themselves based on an appreciation of the fundamentals. The robustness of the Hall criterion has not yet been widely investigated and it is as well to consult the underlying data series. Do these suggest a relative constancy in the £/DM exchange rate compared to the £/$ rate? The lower part of Figure 9.1 plots the time series of the two exchange rates. The greater relative constancy of the DM/£ rate is most obvious after 1986.

'THE' EXCHANGE RATE AS AN INTERMEDIATE TARGET VARIABLE

The significance of the exchange rate issue lies in the implications that exchange rate targeting has for monetary policy.

The immediate point of analytical significance is that it is not possible both to orient monetary policy at maintaining a particular exchange rate peg and independently to target a chosen value for the money supply (or its rate of growth) or a particular value for the rate of interest. Whilst it is always possible to target an exchange rate peg and to issue forecasts of what this may imply for the money supply or interest rates, these will be in the nature of forecast implications, not of independent targets. In an important sense, pegging an exchange rate reduces, to the point of eliminating, the scope for independence in monetary policy. This

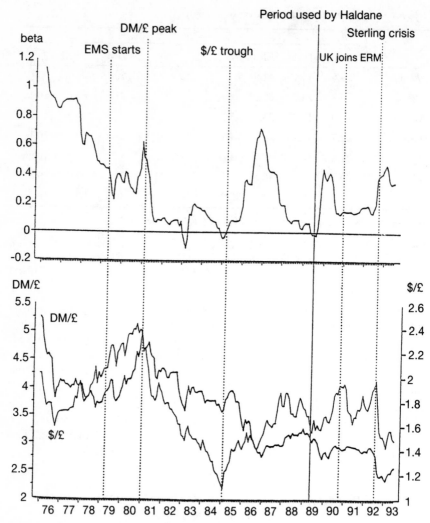

Figure 9.1 Time varying parameter (beta) and the movements of DM/£ and $/£

does not mean that it is not a good thing to do in some circumstances, and in any case there are ways of constructing useful compromises: the exchange rate peg may be described as a central rate peg plus a band of permitted fluctuations; exchange controls may introduce an extra degree of freedom into the decision-making environment; foreign exchange interventions may obviate the need for immediate instrument adjustment; the exchange rate peg may be a hard or a soft one (either a definite peg or simply a promise to 'consult' the exchange rate when contemplating a policy adjustment). The peg itself, finally, may be framed as a nominal peg or a real one (where the nominal exchange rate objective is revised in respect of relative inflation rates).

Successful exchange rate systems have historically combined a degree of inflation discipline effected through nominal exchange rate pegging against an 'anchor' low-inflation currency, with enough flexibility to dampen deviations in the real exchange rate (competitiveness). In the 1980s the success of the EMS was celebrated in these terms. The System allowed for realignments and, during the early period of high and widely dispersed inflation, realignments prevented real exchange rates from becoming locked into systematic drift. At the same time, the System evolved into a means of allowing countries to exert counterinflationary discipline, by placing primacy on the D-mark as the anchor currency and emphasising the commitment to maintain the bilateral D-mark exchange rate. This development offended the elaborately 'symmetrical' arrangements set out in the EMS statutes; for the point of the new arrangements was to privilege Germany as the anchor country. McKinnon (1993) sets this situation out in the perspective of the historical development of earlier exchange rate systems.[4]

Whilst the logic of targeting the exchange rate against the currency of a lowinflation country was always available, this logic was reinforced in important ways by the influence of the Barro-Gordon (1983a, 1983b) model of 'reputational policy'. This model stressed the importance of reputation and commitment in counter-inflationary policy; it led directly to the view that constitutional arrangements – such as the degree of independence of the central bank – were of paramount importance in counter-inflationary policy strategy. More immediately, it suggested that if a country were to attempt the control of inflation through exchange rate pegging, that country would do well to do so within the framework of an established system (as opposed to 'going it alone'). Participation in such a framework would maximise the credibility of the commitment both by harnessing the reputation of the past success of the system itself and also by raising the costs of reneging by the authorities: any reneging would be very public and would involve reneging against external commitments (i.e. commitments to other countries) as well as against those given to domestic agents. It seemed possible to short-circuit the need for domestic central bank autonomy; some observers described participation in the EMS as a means of 'importing the Bundesbank's credibility'.

It deserves particular emphasis, given the central theme of this book, that the availability of such a choice (of pegging to the D-mark through the ERM) represented in itself a strengthening of a country's ability to achieve its objectives. The pegging option was after all not compulsory. Countries were able to use it to bring inflation down, improving their position, and in principle at least, to reduce the cost (in terms of lost output and employment) of doing so. Evidence that the pegging option reduced the sacrifice of output and employment implied by counter-inflationary policy is in fact quite scarce. So it may be that the real value of the pegging option was simply that countries were enabled in this 'indirect' way to begin to tackle their inflationary problems, when a direct attempt to do so would have been foiled politically.

THE UK'S FORMAL POSITION

Upon assuming power in 1979, Mrs Thatcher's first Conservative administration had the opportunity to reverse the previous Labour government's decision not to participate in the ERM. But it did not do so. Where the Labour government had believed that the ERM would offer too rigid a commitment for the UK, which would stand to lose competitiveness, the Thatcher government wished to tackle inflation by 'monetarist means'. The Labour government had still been attached to the view that the state should pay attention to the exchange rate as a prime determinant of competitiveness and thus of employment. The Thatcher government's priorities were different. In particular, priority was to be given to the control of inflation. Much more firmly than under Labour, the commitment to full employment was jettisoned.[5] Given the priority attached to the control of inflation and the Thatcher government's additional belief in the monetarist method of effecting that control, rejection of membership of the ERM followed. Quite correctly, the Thatcher government appreciated the intrinsic inconsistency between a policy of money supply control and commitment to an exchange rate peg. The government's plan was to effect a reduction of the rate of growth of the money supply over a period of years. When the formal plan was set out in the first statement of the Medium Term Financial Strategy (MTFS), the reference to the exchange rate was that it 'is assumed to be determined by market forces' (*Financial Statement and Budget Report*, March 1980). A volte-face was to follow rather quickly.

This is not the place to document the failures of the MTFS (see Artis 1990 for a broader account); suffice to quote from the 1982 restatement of the MTFS:

> External or domestic developments that change the relationship between the domestic money supply and the exchange rate may . . . disturb the link between money and prices. Such changes cannot readily be taken into account in setting monetary targets. But they are a reason why the Government considers it appropriate to look at the exchange rate in monitoring domestic monetary conditions and in taking decisions about policy.

From entering the authorities' 'check list' of relevant indicators in this way, the exchange rate came to play a more prominent role in policy, leading finally to the episode of ERM participation. The motivating factors were on the one hand the failure of the money supply targeting strategy, and on the other the seeming success of the EMS. The availability of the pegging option thus relaxed a constraint (the difficulty of achieving monetary control) on the government's ability to realise its underlying objective.

There is a view (well articulated in McKinnon 1982) that in modern financial conditions, the attempt to control the growth of money supply in a single country is doomed to failure: instead, monetary control should be transferred to a higher level – to the level of the G3 or G7 or perhaps to the level of a sub-global regional grouping (like that formed by the countries of the ERM). However, most observers do not trace the failure of single-country monetary targeting to international currency substitution in the way that McKinnon does, and whilst modern financial conditions provide a number of reasons why monetary control in a single country might fail they do not in general point the finger at insularity, in McKinnon's sense, as the key to its failure.[6]

Whilst macroeconomic policy arguments are the most prominent in the record, however, one should presumably see the growing influence of the trade link behind the pressure from industrialists for a commitment to ERM membership: but the trade-based argument was never very prominent, partly because – as argued earlier – it could never be conclusive given the still-strong attachment of British trading interests to the dollar bloc.

Under cover of the global (G5) policy coordination exercise, the elevation of the exchange rate in British monetary policy making led to a false start under Mr Lawson's Chancellorship. For a period of approximately a year from February 1987 the UK independently targeted the D-mark exchange rate at a ceiling of 3DM to the pound. The point of this experiment was presumably to demonstrate that a full commitment to the ERM (to which Mrs Thatcher at this time remained opposed) would be entirely feasible and desirable.[7] However, any success in this respect is highly controversial.[8] The venture was cancelled amidst recriminations, and thereafter until October 1990 the exchange rate was relegated again to the position of a conditioning factor on monetary policy responses.

STERLING IN THE ERM

The decision finally to enter the ERM was determined at a time of political weakness on Mrs Thatcher's part and when the principal macroeconomic problem appeared to be one of grappling with a resurgence in inflation. By this time the monetarist prescription for dealing with inflation had been discredited; instead of appealing to an internal standard for the control of the price level, the solution now seemed to lie with the external standard of pegging the exchange rate of sterling against a hard currency (significantly, the British decision to enter the ERM was initially described officially in terms of pegging the D-mark, not the ECU). It was understood in this context that the central rate of exchange selected for the peg might be pitched 'on the high side', but the bands of fluctuation (±6 per cent) were wide (the ERM 'norm' being ±2.25 per cent) and, as it happened, this proved to be a time when inflation in Germany, following the unification 'shock', was unusually high. The Treasury noted formally that adherence to the exchange rate commitment might imply, sometimes, that interest rates might need to be higher (or lower) than those appropriate on strictly domestic grounds: 'There may be occasions when tensions arise between domestic conditions and ERM obligations' (HM Treasury 1991). This seemed entirely supportable during the first year of the ERM commitment. The anniversary of sterling's participation in the ERM was marked by an outburst of self-congratulatory articles in the press. Even the National Institute's sober assessment in its November *Economic Review* noted that 'the credibility of the exchange rate band itself seems to be well established'(HM Treasury 1991: 3) and, looking further ahead advised that 'The UK economy will reach a sufficient degree of convergence with the economies of the rest of Europe for full membership of an economic and monetary union to be a realistic aim by about 1997' (HM Treasury 1991: 4).

From this point on, membership of the ERM became increasingly less comfortable. The tie to the D-mark implied that the scope for interest rate reductions was limited. Whilst UK interest rates did begin to fall (and did so right through 1992 until the crisis), they did so against a background of rising unemployment, so that 'domestically desired' interest rates were in effect falling faster than actual rates. The eventual crisis, in September 1992, saw the withdrawal of sterling from the ERM. Looking back on this episode, it is easy to take undue advantage of hindsight. If it now seems 'obvious' that sterling was overvalued from the outset and that the UK policy cycle was mismatched to the German one, it should be recalled that those opinions were less than widely shared before the crisis.[9] An important part of the background, in fact, was the continued disappointment of persistent expectations of recovery – see Figure 9.2, which records the sad history of over-optimistic Treasury forecasts in the period. But for these faulty predictions, the government might not have persisted in the attempt to stay in the ERM; there might not have been a crisis. Credibility would not have been lost; continued membership of the ERM (at a lower rate) would have been possible.

As it is, of course, this episode ended in tears (or, from another point of view, in 'singing in the bath'). The lessons gratefully learned from the success of the EMS were summarily rejected.

The Bank of England now conducts counter-inflationary policy without the aid of an intermediate target variable like the money supply or the exchange rate. It does so, also, with the advantage of a degree of independence. Now, it targets 'expected inflation'. This method has hardly yet received a severe test. Ironically, now that the tight discipline of narrow ERM bands has given way to the tolerance of the wide ±15 per cent bands, introduced after the second ERM crisis of July 1993, there have been an increasing number of suggestions that the remaining ERM countries should target a value for inflation itself. The so-called 'monetarist approach' to the control of inflation via the seemingly 'premature' imposition of nominal exchange rate bands has been the main casualty of the crisis.

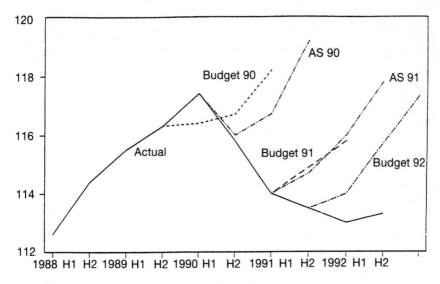

Figure 9.2 Treasury forecasts and actual GDP (1985 = 100)

CONCLUSION

Where does this leave us? On the one hand there is no doubt that the evolution of the EC as a trading bloc and the erstwhile success of the EMS have created for the UK an alternative exchange rate 'pole of attraction' to that provided by the US dollar. This has been important for the way in which it was possible to conduct monetary policy in Britain, not least – but not only – during the period of full formal commitment to the ERM. By contrast, formal regulations and directives affecting monetary and financial conduct in the EU have had little or no direct effect on the UK. Finally, there is the fact that the 1993 ERM crisis – which occurred after the UK had already left it – has served to weaken further the value of the ERM as a lesson for Britain.

NOTES

1   This statement may be too bald. As reported in Artis and Lewis (1991), 'Banking legislation was needed to comply with the First EEC Banking Directive of 1977'. However that Directive came in the wake of the Secondary Banking Crisis of 1974 and in the circumstances, 'fell on receptive ears' – that is, there would almost certainly have been some legislation in any case. In the event, the resultant 1979 Banking Act inaugurated a new phase of liberalisation in a framework of legislation which provided for effective supervision of a flexible type. Later on, the international concertation of capital adequacy measures – culminating in the Basle Agreement on this issue – was led by an initiative from the UK and the US.
2   More formally, the two regressions are:

$$\$/\pounds = a_{1t} + b_{1t} DM/\$ + e_{1t}$$

and

$$DM/\pounds = a_{2t} + b_{2t} DM/\$ + e_{2t}$$

In the case hypothesised in the text, where the £ is attached to the $, $b_1 \to 0$; and $b_2 \to 1$. In the alternative case, where the £ is attached to the DM, $b_1 \to -1$ and $b_2 \to 0$.

3   The figure shows recursive estimates of b_2 (see note 2 above), estimated on monthly data over a period expiring in September 1993. Haldane and Hall (1991) use daily data in a sample which terminates in March 1989.

4   In fact McKinnon makes it appear that nearly always formally symmetrical arrangements disguise a *de facto* asymmetric reality. It is possible that those countries which signed up for the EMS already discounted the formal symmetry of the system. However, I think not. This would give no room for what I believe was a real conversion of view among policy makers in the 1980s, first in the direction of prioritising the control of inflation, and second, in the direction of seeing central bank independence (or equivalent devices) as the key to achieving that priority. Thus there was some movement and a widening of the policy space which gave countries more power to realise their objectives: the asymmetry emerged from this.

5   This 'conversion' from policies based on a commitment to full employment to policies based on the control of inflation had, of course, already started under Labour. But the difference of view on exchange rate policy is symptomatic of the differences remaining between the two parties. Artis and Cobham (1991) provide additional evidence on this question.

6   For example, in the absence of exchange controls, monetary control exercised via credit rationing becomes unfeasible, as firms and individuals can resort to overseas sources of credit. The absence of exchange controls also inhibits central banks' ability to fend off speculative attacks on the currency because overseas speculators can borrow freely from banks in the country whose currency is under attack. Neither of these instances involves currency substitution in McKinnon's sense (where one money is 'as good as another' in the transactor's eyes).

7   This is Mrs Thatcher's interpretation (see Thatcher 1993: 699–705); remarkably, she claims not to have been aware of Mr Lawson's policy until November 1987 – some nine months after its inception.

8   Mr Lawson's policy of shadowing the D-mark has been held responsible for the subsequent resurgence of inflation. Certainly, the foreign exchange markets greeted the policy as a reason to hold sterling, thus forcing the exchange rate towards its ceiling and inhibiting the authorities from making the increases in interest rates that they should (in retrospect) have been making at the time. It was not until this conflict became unbearable that the cap was lifted. The fact that the ceiling for the D-mark in this episode had proven to be 'too low' led City commentators subsequently to warn that the entry of sterling into the ERM at the rates prevailing in 1989 would produce a 'wall of money'; it is plausible that the experience of the shadowing period and the City's warnings then led the authorities to err on the side of joining at 'too high' a rate in October 1990.

9   The market did not find the continued presence of sterling in the ERM incredible until very shortly before the crisis. See for example Rose and Svensson 1994.

BIBLIOGRAPHY

Artis, M. J. (1990) 'The United Kingdom and the EMS', in P. De Grauwe and L. Papademos (eds) *The European Monetary System in the 1990s*, London: Longman.

Artis, M. J. and Cobham D. (eds) (1991) *Labour's Economic Policies*, Manchester: Manchester University Press.

Artis, M. J. and Lewis, M. K. (1991) *Money in Britain*, Hemel Hempstead: Philip Allan.

Barro, R. and Gordon, D. (1983a) 'A positive theory of monetary policy in a natural rate model', *Journal of Political Economy*, 91, 4: 589–609.

——(1983b) 'Rules, discretion and reputation in a model of monetary policy', *Journal of Monetary Economics*, 12: 101–21.

HM Treasury (1980) *Financial Statement and Budget Report*, March 1980.

——(1991) *Financial Statement and Budget Report*.

Haldane, A. G. and Hall, S. G. (1991) 'Sterling's relationship with the Dollar and the Deutschmark, 1976–89', *Economic Journal*, 10, 406: 436–43.

Hall, S. G., Robertson, D. and Wickens, M. (1992) 'Measuring convergence of the EC economies', *The Manchester School*, IX, supplement: 99–111.

McKinnon, R. I. (1982) 'The exchange rate and macroeconomic policy: changing postwar perspectives', *Journal of Economic Literature*, XIX: 531–57.

——(1993) 'The rules of the game: international money in historical perspective', *Journal of Economic Literature*, XXXI, March: 1–44.

Rose, A. K. and Svensson, L. E. O. (1994) 'European exchange rate credibility before the fall', *European Economic Review*.

Thatcher, M. (1993) *The Downing Street Years*, London: Harper Collins.

Part III

SPECIFIC ISSUES

10

SHOULD UNEMPLOYMENT CONVERGENCE PRECEDE MONETARY UNION?[1]

Andrea Boltho

INTRODUCTION

European Monetary Union is, in principle, open to all the European Union's members, and to listen to the politicians, it would appear that most countries are eager to join it. Economists feel, however, that membership of a monetary union requires more than mere political willingness. After all, union will imply the pooling of a very important instrument of economic policy making. Hence a presumption that the eventual participants should share some common economic features and 'feel comfortable' with each other. To this effect, the Maastricht Treaty set up a number of prerequisites designed to limit access to countries fulfilling some particular financial and economic criteria.[2] These criteria have, however, been heavily criticised by economists. For one thing, they encompass an uneasy mixture of policy instruments (such as the interest rate), intermediate targets (such as the budget deficit and possibly the exchange rate) and ultimate objectives (such as inflation). For another, it has been argued that the fiscal rules 'are badly motivated, poorly designed and apt to lead to unnecessary hardship if pursued mechanically' (Buiter *et al.* 1993: 87).[3] As for the nominal convergence criteria on inflation or interest rates: 'it is wholly unrealistic to impose [them] as conditions for entry when in all likelihood these conditions can only be fulfilled after the monetary union has been realized' (De Grauwe 1994: 161–2).

By contrast, the authors of the relevant passages of the Maastricht Treaty seem to have paid little attention to what the older literature on the theory of optimum currency areas has suggested as reasonable criteria for the formation of a monetary union. Indeed, the Commission seems to admit as much: 'The optimum currency area approach provides useful insights but cannot be considered a comprehensive framework. . . . Empirical applications of this approach are scarce and hardly conclusive' (Commission of the European Communities 1990: 46).

This brief chapter looks at whether such a dismissal is warranted. The first section considers some of the ideas which have been put forward in the literature and tries to see how far they apply to the member countries of the EU. Its tentative conclusion is that some justification can, after all, be found for the Maastricht Treaty's much maligned criteria. Drawing on this discussion, the second section argues, however, that one additional and important criterion ought to have been considered.

THE OPTIMUM CURRENCY AREA LITERATURE

The optimum currency area literature of the 1960s and 1970s has put forward a number of possible criteria that countries should ideally fulfil in order to ensure a successful monetary union (for a survey, see Ishiyama 1975). At the risk of over-simplification, these will be divided into three main groups:

1   The degree of openness and integration of various economies
2   The similarity of their economic structures
3   The similarity of their policy preferences.

Openness

Put simply, the argument about openness is that the more open and internationally integrated an economy is, the greater, *ceteris paribus*, are the benefits it will reap, and the smaller are the costs it will incur, from union with its partners. Thus the gains from eliminating exchange rate uncertainty are bound to be larger the larger is the share of international transactions in output; while the unemployment costs of, for instance, eliminating an external deficit should diminish as the importance of foreign trade rises (Krugman 1990). More importantly, increasing openness is likely to reduce the effectiveness of the exchange rate instrument in offsetting shocks to the economy, while raising the speed of the inflationary pass through from, say, depreciation (McKinnon 1963). At the limit, in a very open economy, nominal exchange rate changes could be wholly ineffective in influencing real variables. In such circumstances, relinquishing the use of domestic monetary policy would involve virtually no economic costs to the country and joining a monetary union would appear to be clearly desirable.

While apparently sensible, this rule provides little operational guidance. Luxembourg at one extreme, the United States at the other, would seem to be countries that should respectively abandon and maintain an independent exchange rate, as they have indeed done through much of this century.[4] But uncertainty immediately surfaces when considering Europe's other, somewhat larger but still relatively open, economies in which the share of intra-EU trade in GDP goes from some 10 per cent in the major countries to 30–35 per cent in the Netherlands or Ireland. Behaviour in these countries over the last fifty years has shown a preference for relative exchange rate stability (with Britain as a possible exception). Yet this stability was also interrupted by realignments, not all of which were imposed by the market, and some of which (when in a downward direction) seem to have been successful in improving competitiveness, raising employment and stimulating growth over a significant number of years. Possible examples are France after 1957–8 (Mistral 1975), the United Kingdom after 1967 (Artus 1975), Belgium after 1982 (De Grauwe 1992), and, at least so far, Britain, Italy, Spain or Sweden after 1992 (Dornbusch 1996).

In other words, the exchange rate instrument may still be a potentially useful tool, even in conditions of very great openness such as those of a country like Belgium, provided it is not used too frequently and is accompanied by incomes policies and/or contractionary macroeconomic policies, as it was in all the episodes just listed. Notwithstanding the claims of mainstream theory, which assumes that money is always neutral and that purchasing power parity always holds, experience suggests that exceptions to these 'rules' are frequent and can last for periods that go well beyond the 'short-run'.[5] Indeed, on the strength of this evidence, it could be argued that most European countries, despite their openness, still represent optimum currency areas.

Similarities in economic structures

Retaining an instrument that can have significant real effects makes sense provided, of course, that such an instrument will be needed. A second strand of the literature discusses the conditions under which such needs are likely to be minimised. Broadly, this would be the case if the major characteristics of the various economies forming a union (e.g. production structures, or labour and financial market institutions) are similar, or operate in similar ways. If this is so, then there should be less danger that changes in the Union's monetary policies, or in demand and supply conditions in the world economy, would impinge asymmetrically on, or would elicit asymmetric responses from, individual countries. This in turn would diminish the need for a country-specific tool such as the exchange rate.

The degree of product diversification matters, for instance, in assessing the probability of asymmetric demand shocks hitting a particular country (Kenen 1969). Well diversified economies, it is argued, are better able to relinquish the exchange rate instrument, since microeconomic shifts in demand would be likely to offset each other, thus leaving domestic inflation or unemployment broadly unchanged. The opposite would be the case in highly specialised economies. In these, however, a high degree of inter-country labour mobility could still accommodate the effects of diverging demand trends (Mundell 1961). The structure of labour markets and the responsiveness of financial markets matter in assessing the likelihood of asymmetric responses. Highly centralised labour markets, for instance, may be more able to cope with macroeconomic disturbances than less centralised ones; similarly, some countries may react more rapidly than others to changes in area-wide, monetary policy instruments. Asymmetric adjustments of this kind to what could be symmetric impulses, might thus also require the use of an independent monetary policy.

Uncertainty prevails as to whether the EU countries qualify or not for EMU membership on these various counts. Clearly, the production structures of Finland or Greece seem less diversified than those of France or Germany. Similarly, the labour markets of Austria or Denmark are more centralised/corporatist than those of Italy, let alone Britain (Calmfors and Driffill 1988; Soskice 1990). And the transmission from short-term interest rate changes to the real economy is likely to be much more rapid in the United Kingdom than on most of the continent.[6] Such lists, however, beyond stating that Europe's economies differ, provide little guidance to policy decisions.

Proponents of EMU have usually taken a broadly optimistic line and argued that Europe's economies are either rather similar already, or will become increasingly so thanks to EMU itself. Thus the Commission, while accepting that intra-European labour mobility is limited, states, for instance, that 'EC countries typically have highly diversified industrial structures' (Commission of the EC 1990: 46) and argues that increasing intra-industry specialisation, consequent upon monetary union, will further raise inter-country similarities in this area (1990: 142–3). It also holds that differential labour market responses are likely to be eroded as EMU-induced credibility effects will persuade wage-earners to behave in similar ways across Europe. Differences in financial market structures are not addressed.

Much of this may be too optimistic. Even if economies enjoy a substantial amount of product diversification today, United States experience suggests that the operation of a monetary union may diminish this, rather than increase it (Krugman 1993): 'The move towards a common currency will lead to the increased specialisation of member countries, hence to greater asymmetric shocks, which constitutes an argument against a common currency' (Blanchard 1992: 152).

As for the credibility effects of the adoption of radically new policies on labour (as opposed to financial) markets, the available evidence suggests that this has been negligible so far in a variety of instances in which the policy makers had hoped to obtain significant effects (Buiter and Miller 1981; Blanchard 1984; Egebo and Englander 1992).

Somewhat firmer conclusions can be reached in one area thanks to the availability of quantitative work. Thus an analysis comparing the strength of supply and demand shocks to regions of the United States and European countries suggests that both areas 'appear to divide themselves into a "core" of regions characterised by relatively symmetric behaviour and a "periphery" in which disturbances are more loosely correlated with those experienced by the centre' (Bayoumi and Eichengreen 1993: 211–12).

The 'core' countries isolated by this study are France, Germany, Benelux and Denmark which, interestingly, also show slightly more rapid adjustments to shocks than do the 'peripheral' countries of Britain, Italy, Spain, Greece, Ireland and Portugal. For the new entrants, a much simpler analysis of cyclical behaviour *vis-à-vis* that of the EU as a whole, suggests that Austria and Sweden could also be part of the 'core', while Finland would clearly seem to belong to the 'periphery' (CEPR 1992).

Similarities in policy preferences

A third criterion which has received relatively little attention in the recent debate on EMU is that of similarity in policy preferences. Yet this surely seems just as important, if not more so, than the other criteria so far discussed. After all, it would seem essential for a successful monetary union that countries which are about to pool an important instrument of demand management share some basic policy attitudes:

> Perhaps of *primary importance* for a successful currency area . . . is that there be a reasonable degree of compatibility between the member countries' attitudes towards growth of inflation and unemployment. . . . A nation with a low tolerance for unemployment . . . would make a poor partner for a country with a low tolerance of inflation.

(Willett and Tower 1970: 411; emphasis added)

This would seem to be particularly important in the European context. Most EU members already share a number of common economic and political goals – e.g. free internal trade and factor movements, continuing integration in the economic and social spheres, and a will to gradually build a more united Europe. EMU would extend this consensus by creating a common monetary policy which would, presumably, be used to pursue common aims. In some ways, the Maastricht Treaty works in this direction by strengthening the move to convergence in several macroeconomic areas. Reducing fiscal imbalances and inflation is a way of imposing a particular set of common policy attitudes. Interpreted in this way, the Maastricht criteria could find some justification (even if the particular values chosen, notably on the fiscal front, still seem arbitrary). If all countries do subscribe to policies of eradicating inflation even prior to relinquishing their monetary policy autonomy, and are prepared to meet economic (and political) costs in order to reduce their public sector deficit and debt levels, then such a similarity in goals could well be as, if not more, important than any dissimilarity in other areas.

It is true, of course, that the criteria chosen strongly reflect Germany's preferences for sound finance and price stability, and that a different set of preferences, embodying, for instance, growth or employment targets, might have been put forward. Yet the Maastricht goals are broadly in tune with the policy consensus of the late 1980s and early 1990s not only in Germany but also in most other

European economies: 'There is wide agreement in Europe . . . on the importance of price stability, the need to dedicate monetary policy to that aim, and the need to insulate central banks from political interference with the pursuit of price stability' (Kenen 1995: 13).

Indeed, it is probably no accident that EMU really only became conceivable once France abandoned in the mid-1980s its earlier policies of relative accommodation and switched to a German-inspired macroeconomic stance. Without this conversion, it is highly unlikely that the EMU project would have been launched when it was.

AN ADDITIONAL CRITERION?

The previous section has suggested that EMU may make sense for countries that have a similar set of policy preferences. If these countries, in addition, are relatively open and share a number of structural similarities which make the use of exchange rates redundant (or of limited efficacy), then the case for union is obviously strengthened. But problems could arise if different preferences were to clash with asymmetric shocks or responses, or with longer-run unfavourable trends.[7] In such a case, EMU membership could severely constrain countries' ability to attain national goals.

Partly in order to resolve this potential dispute, it may be useful to examine more carefully the policy preference criterion implied by the Maastricht Treaty. This would seem to rest on the acceptance by all countries of a set of fairly strong hypotheses as to how economies work. In particular, policy makers would have to concur in the orthodox assumptions that the main role for macroeconomic policy is to control inflation, and that most unemployment is of a structural rather than of a cyclical nature, against which demand management policy is powerless. This in turn presumably implies that future Union members would refrain from using the European Central Bank (ECB) to stimulate demand so as to reduce unemployment. Disequilibria in labour markets would have to be corrected through hypothetical credibility effects, changes in regulations or reforms in trade union structures. Should these fail, or take an inordinately long time, high unemployment would have to be accepted as inevitable.

Such views, however, are far from being shared by all. First, countries behave in different ways and transmission mechanisms that may be appropriate in one context may not be in another. Second, there are strong disagreements among economists on whether most of today's unemployment is indeed non-cyclical. Estimates of structural unemployment (the so-called NAIRU) have proven to be fickle, often just rising in step with what was happening to actual unemployment. Indeed, in a number of EU countries the late 1980s saw falls in unemployment, in the wake of a boom in aggregate demand, to rates often below what were at the time thought to be 'natural' levels. Yet despite such declines and despite a concomitant acceleration in consumer price inflation, wage inflation remained virtually unchanged (Table 10.1), suggesting the presence of a substantial cyclical component among the jobless.

If disagreements exist among economists about how economies behave, they are likely to surface among policy makers as well. The lip service that is being paid to achieving the Maastricht criteria today may largely reflect political considerations – in particular the fear of being left behind in the next step of European construction. Such virtual unanimity cannot always be taken for granted, notably in periods of economic slowdown. To take a pertinent example, the EMS 'barely survived its first recession in the early 1980s. It did not endure the second one' (De Grauwe 1994: 158).

It is true that 'stability-oriented' policies have served Germany well over the last twenty years, but not all the European countries which are now embracing German-like policies have the microeconomic structures (and notably the labour market and the industrial relations system) that Germany has, nor have their central banks acquired the credibility of the Bundesbank.[8] In the absence of such features, the adoption of German-style macroeconomic policies could generate much inferior outcomes, or even fail (Boltho 1996). If this happens,

Table 10.1 Changes in unemployment and inflation, 1986–91 (percentage points)

	Changes in unemployment rate 1986–90	Changes in wage inflation[a] 1986–7 to 1990–1	Changes in consumer price inflation 1986–7 to 1990–1
United Kingdom	-5.1	0.9	3.9
Spain	-4.7	-0.8	-0.7
Portugal	-3.9	-0.8	1.8
Ireland	-3.8	-2.2	-0.2
Belgium	-2.9	2.4	1.9
Netherlands	-2.4	1.8	3.5
Germany	-1.5	1.2	3.0
France	-1.5	-1.6	0.4
Finland	-1.5	1.5	1.6
Average[b]	-3.0	0.3	1.7

Sources: IMF, *International Financial Statistics*; OECD, *Economic Outlook*, no. 58, December 1995.
Notes
a The coverage of the wage indicator differs across countries as follows: monthly earnings for Spain and the UK; weekly earnings for Ireland; hourly earnings for Belgium, Finland and Germany; hourly rates for the Netherlands; daily earnings in manufacturing for Portugal; total labour costs for France.
b Unweighted.

what appears as a consensus on policy preferences today may give way to differences of opinion once a union has been established. Countries with much higher levels of unemployment than others may feel that some compromise with inflation might be warranted after all. Since decisions by the ECB's board are to be taken by majority, this possibility opens the way for conflicts.

An obvious solution to this potential problem would be to enlarge the Maastricht criteria so as to incorporate some rule about acceptable unemployment divergencies which would parallel the rule about inflation convergence. If performance in both these areas is similar, there should be little risk of future tension. Conversely, if upon entry unemployment (or for that matter inflation) diverged massively, the whole project could be endangered and individual countries would in all likelihood be unable to attain their desired aims.

Indeed, the likely presence in 1997–8 (when decisions on membership will have to be taken) of persistent unemployment divergencies, following several years during which policies had been set so as to fulfil the Maastricht criteria, would be proof that such policies had differential impacts in different countries. In some, low unemployment would indicate that, thanks to labour market flexibility, austerity had had relatively small effects on the real economy. In others, conversely, high unemployment would provide evidence that, be it because of rigidities or other impediments, tight policies had been very costly. Union would make sense for the former group of countries, since these clearly share a common *modus operandi* and could therefore also share a common economic policy. It would, however, be much more dangerous for the latter group of countries, unless these were able to bend the ECB's policies towards greater accommodation.

It is true that in some of Europe's economies (e.g. Italy or Spain) high unemployment reflects, at least in part, structural problems. In such circumstances, it could be argued that application of the new criterion would be a mistake. Yet there could still be some rationale for maintaining the rule. Orthodox economic theory suggests that economic integration is bound to be beneficial to all participating countries/regions. But an alternative view holds that such results are not guaranteed. Indeed, the opposite could occur and relatively backward countries/regions could be left behind as richer ones monopolised the best resources and exploited dynamic economies of scale (Kaldor 1970).

The empirical evidence on this issue is mixed and knowledge as to what makes for successful integration is as yet limited (Krugman 1993). Given this, uniting more backward areas such as those of southern Italy or southern Spain with the more advanced parts of north-western Europe could be risky. Hence, even if the high unemployment rates of such regions had little to do with cyclical factors and restrictive policies, they would be symptomatic of structural differences which could make successful integration in a monetary union very difficult.

Some unemployment criteria would thus seem to be justified even in those cases in which more than just cyclical factors were at work. Setting a target for a particular year is clearly arbitrary. Yet a simple rule of thumb (as those which were, after all, applied by the Maastricht Treaty when deciding on the 'appropriate' levels of inflation or of interest rates) might be that entry into the union should be conditional on the unemployment rate not being more than one standard deviation above the average of the best three performers. In 1994–5 this would have set the target at 9.5 per cent (Table 10.2).

Application of this criterion would make union membership highly unlikely for a number of countries, including France (whose unemployment is expected to lie between 10.5 and 11 per cent). This would deal a virtual death blow to the whole EMU project. Yet a monetary union between two partners, one of whom suffers from much higher unemployment than the other, is fraught with dangers. This is so in no small part because France's conversion to German macroeconomic orthodoxy is as yet fragile (particularly in view of the country's industrial relations system). Use of an unemployment criterion may thus actually help in preventing a union that could prove to be undesirable on economic grounds, and thereby maintain a degree of policy autonomy for individual countries that they could find both welcome and necessary.

Table 10.2 Unemployment rates in the European Union (in per cent of the labour force)

| | | *1997 Projections* | |
	1994–5	*EEC*	*OECD*
France	11.9	10.6	11.0
Germany	8.3	7.4	8.0
Italy	11.6	10.9	11.2
United Kingdom	9.0	8.1	8.3
Spain	23.3	21.0	21.2
Austria	4.5	4.4	4.5
Belgium	10.1	9.8	9.7
Denmark	7.5	5.7	6.1
Finland	17.8	13.9	15.1
Greece	8.9	8.8	9.5
Ireland	15.0	14.0	13.3
Luxembourg	3.7	3.6	3.5
Netherlands	6.8	6.0	6.0
Portugal	7.1	6.3	6.8
Sweden	9.4	8.2	8.7
EU	11.0	9.9	10.3
Standard deviation	4.95	4.32	4.35
Average of 3 lowest countries	4.6	4.6	4.7
'Unemployment criterion'	9.6	8.9	9.1

Sources: EC, *European Economy*, Supplement A, no. 12, December 1995; OECD, *Economic Outlook*, no. 58, December 1995.

CONCLUSIONS

This chapter has argued that the Maastricht Treaty's criteria for EMU (even if arbitrary in their selection of precise numerical targets) may be both necessary and sufficient for eventual membership, provided two sets of crucial assumptions are fulfilled. First, economies must work along certain lines. In particular, neither demand management policies nor exchange rate changes should be expected to have much effect on real variables other than in the short run. Adjustment to shocks would have to come primarily from flexible microeconomic responses. Monetary union, by providing a credible commitment to 'sound finance' and to 'stability-oriented policies', would enhance such flexible responses, notably on labour markets. In such circumstances, the costs of transition and of life under a non-accommodating monetary regime would be likely to be small and temporary, while the gains from unification could be large and permanent. Second, countries should share a given set of policy preferences which reflect this interpretation of how economies work. Hence policy makers would want to stick to the goals of reducing deficits and inflation, since these are seen as the primary (indeed, virtually sole) aims of macroeconomic policy.

But neither of these two assumptions necessarily corresponds to the reality of all EU member countries. Economists are divided on whether economies are as self-equilibrating as orthodox theory assumes (with some countries approaching this model much more than others), and the empirical evidence, particularly on the speed of labour market adjustment, suggests that, far from being transitory, some shocks can have permanently unfavourable effects on unemployment. The impact of credibility and announcements, on the other hand, has, so far at least, been muted. Similarly, country preferences may not as yet have unanimously embraced a unique model. It is true that there has been a good deal of convergence on the aim of controlling rapid inflation in Europe in the 1980s, but there is less unanimity as to whether the much more moderate levels of inflation seen so far in the 1990s should be squeezed out altogether.

If this is the case, bringing together countries that have different economic structures, behave in different ways and may still harbour different preferences could be unwise. Should exogenous or policy shocks generate asymmetric outcomes (in the form of rising unemployment in some economies and rising inflation in others), countries may well wish to follow policies that are appropriate only for themselves (e.g. by trying to push the ECB into the direction of more accommodation). No monetary union of sovereign states could long survive such major disagreements on the goals of monetary policy. To try and forestall such possible dangers, the Maastricht Treaty should have widened its criteria by the introduction of one important additional indicator of potential tensions, namely unemployment. If unemployment is much above average in a particular country, unfavourable shocks and/or restrictive policies would worsen the position further. This in turn would put pressures on the cohesion of the Union and may even threaten its credibility.

The more eclectic approach advocated in this chapter would stress not one but three sets of criteria: similarities in policy preferences (as proxied by the present rules), similarity in economic structures (the presence or absence of which is suggested by a number of more technical studies) and similarity in unemployment rates. On this basis, a small 'hard core' of countries would probably be ready to join a monetary union at the end of this century or at the beginning of the next. Most of 'non-German' Europe would, however, be well advised to stay out and this both for its own sake and that of the stability of whatever EMU may emerge.

NOTES

1   The author is grateful to Chris Allsopp, Wendy Carlin and Andrew Glyn who, by disagreeing with much of what is said here, greatly improved the final product.

2   As is well known, membership of EMU in 1999 is conditional on countries recording in 1997 inflation rates and long-term interest rates no more than 1.5 and 2 percentage points respectively above the average of the three lowest inflation and interest rate countries, budget deficits and gross public debt levels no higher than 3 and 60 per cent of GDP, and broad stability in exchange rates over the previous two years. Since the 1993 enlargement of the European Monetary System's (EMS) fluctuation margins to 15 per cent, the last condition would seem to have lost much of its force.

3   That the public debt criterion, in particular, would seem unnecessary for the formation of a monetary union is underlined by the contrasting experiences of Belgium and Luxembourg. In 1995 these two countries had, respectively, the highest and lowest public debt-to-GDP ratios in the European Union, yet they were successfully sharing a common currency and had done so for decades (*The Economist*, 23 September 1995).

4   The United States accepted the discipline of the Gold Standard in the years preceding 1913 and had a fixed exchange rate in the days of Bretton Woods. Otherwise, however, the dollar floated. Luxembourg, on the other hand, not only shared those two fixed exchange rate experiences, but also tied its exchange rate to Belgium already in 1922 and, bar a revaluation *vis-à-vis* the Belgian franc in 1935 (Meade *et al.* 1962), remained in an economic and monetary union throughout.

5   Thus most of the competitive advantage gained by Belgium at the time of its 1982 EMS realignment had still not been lost by 1995, according to the IMF's estimates of the country's real exchange rate.

6   In 1993, for instance, less than 30 per cent of private sector debt in Britain (and Italy) had been contracted at predominantly fixed long-term interest rates, as against figures ranging from nearly 60 per cent in France, Germany or Spain to 70 per cent or more in Austria and the Netherlands (BIS, *65th Annual Report*, 1995).

7   The latter point has been little stressed by the EMU literature which has concentrated its attention on the likelihood of shocks. Yet it is well known that in some countries at least, external competitiveness at unchanged exchange rates seems to decline over time, a phenomenon usually attributed to the importance of non-price factors in international trade (Thirlwall 1986; Carlin *et al.* 1997). For such economies, in other words, external equilibrium would require some continuing form of real depreciation. In a monetary union this could only come via downward pressures on real wages, which might in turn require large increases in unemployment.

8   It could also be argued that some of Germany's past successes, particularly in combining fiscal policy consolidation with satisfactory levels of activity, were a function not so much of 'psychological crowding-in' (Fels and Froehlich 1987) but of an ability to switch resources into exports, thus relying on foreign demand for stabilisation.

BIBLIOGRAPHY

Artus, J. R. (1975) 'The 1967 devaluation of the pound sterling', *IMF Staff Papers*, 22, 3: 595–640.

Bayoumi, T. and Eichengreen, B. (1993) 'Shocking aspects of European monetary integration', in F. Torres and F. Giavazzi (eds) *Adjustment and Growth in the European Monetary Union*, Cambridge: Cambridge University Press.

Blanchard, O. J. (1984) 'The Lucas critique and the Volcker deflation', *American Economic Review*, 74, 2: 211–15.

——(1992) 'Le rôle de la politique budgétaire dans l'Union économique et monétaire', in Groupe international de politique economique de l'OFCE, *La désinflation compétitive, le mark et les politiques budgétaires en Europe*, Paris: Seuil.

Boltho, A. (1996), 'Has France converged on Germany? Policies and institutions since 1958', in S. Berger and R. Dore (eds) *Convergence or Diversity?*, Ithaca NY: Cornell University Press.

Buiter, W. H. and Miller, M. (1981) 'The Thatcher experiment: the first two years', *Brookings Papers on Economic Activity*, 2: 315–79.

Buiter, W., Corsetti, G. and Roubini, N. (1993) 'Excessive deficits: sense and nonsense in the Treaty of Maastricht', *Economic Policy*, 16: 57–100.

Calmfors, L. and Driffill, J. (1988) 'Centralisation of wage bargaining', *Economic Policy*, 6: 13–61.

Carlin, W., Glyn, A. and van Reenen, J. (1997) 'Quantifying a dangerous obsession? Competitiveness and export performance in an OECD panel of industries', *CEPR Discussion Paper*, No. 1628.

Centre for Economic Policy Research (1992) *Monitoring European Integration*, 3, CEPR, London.

Commission of the European Communities (1990) 'One market, one money', *European Economy*, 44 (October).

De Grauwe, P. (1992) *The Economics of Monetary Integration*, Oxford: Oxford University Press.

——(1994) 'Towards European Monetary Union without the EMS', *Economic Policy*, 18: 147–85.

Dornbusch, R. (1996) 'The effectiveness of exchange-rate changes', *Oxford Review of Economic Policy*, 12, 3: 26–38.

Egebo, T. and Englander, A. S. (1992) 'Institutional commitments and policy credibility: a critical survey and empirical evidence from the ERM', *OECD Economic Studies*, 18: 45–84.

Fels, G. and Froehlich, H. P. (1987) 'Germany and the world economy: a German view', *Economic Policy*, 4: 177–206.

Ishiyama, Y. (1975) 'The theory of optimum currency areas: a survey', *IMF Staff Papers*, 22, 2: 344–83.

Kaldor, N. (1970) 'The case for regional policy', *Scottish Journal of Political Economy*, 17, 3: 337–48.

Kenen, P. B. (1969) 'The theory of optimum currency areas: an eclectic view', in R. A. Mundell and A. K. Swoboda (eds) *Monetary Problems of the International Economy*, Chicago IL: University of Chicago Press.

——(1995) *Economic and Monetary Union in Europe*, Cambridge: Cambridge University Press.

Krugman, P. (1990) 'Policy problems of a monetary union', in P. De Grauwe and L. Papademos (eds) *The European Monetary System in the 1990s*, Harlow: Longman.

——(1993) 'Lessons of Massachusetts for EMU', in F. Torres and F. Giavazzi (eds) *Adjustment and Growth in the European Monetary Union*, Cambridge: Cambridge University Press.

McKinnon, R. I. (1963) 'Optimum currency areas', *American Economic Review*, 53, 4: 717–25.

Meade, J. E., Liesner, H. H. and Wells, S. J. (1962) *Case Studies in European Economic Union*, London: Oxford University Press.

Mistral, J. (1975) 'Vingt ans de redéploiement du commerce extérieur', *Economie et statistique*, 71: 23–40.

Mundell, R. A. (1961) 'A theory of optimum currency areas', *American Economic Review*, 51, 4: 657–64.

Soskice, D. (1990) 'Wage determination: the changing role of institutions in advanced industrialised countries', *Oxford Review of Economic Policy*, 6, 4: 36–61.

Thirlwall, A. P. (1986) *Balance-of-Payments Theory and the United Kingdom Experience*, 3rd ed., London: Macmillan.

Willett, T. D. and Tower, E. (1970) 'The concept of optimum currency areas and the choice between fixed and flexible exchange rates', in G. N. Halm (ed.) *Approaches to Greater Flexibility of Exchange Rates*, Princeton NJ: Princeton University Press.

11

FISCAL POLICY AND EUROPEAN INTEGRATION

Christopher Allsopp

INTRODUCTION

This paper is concerned with fiscal policy in the European Union. At the time of writing, most EU countries are in the process of trying to meet the Maastricht fiscal convergence criteria in order to qualify for European Monetary Union (EMU). The fiscal criteria (60 per cent of GDP for public debt-to-GDP ratios and 3 per cent of GDP for budget deficits) turned out, in part because of slow European growth, to be much harder to meet than expected. In 1995 and 1996, for example, no EU country (except Luxembourg) met both criteria. And in 1996 OECD projections suggested that no major EU country (not even France or Germany) would, without 'fudges', meet the deficit criterion for 1997, despite serious attempts at 'fiscal consolidation'. Moreover, the 'Stability Pact', demanded by Germany, suggested even tighter criteria on a continuing basis for any countries joining EMU.

Whilst the proximate cause of the rush to meet the Maastricht fiscal criteria was the timetable for countries to qualify for entry into the proposed EMU, moves towards fiscal consolidation would, it may be argued, have occurred anyway. By the mid-1990s, it was apparent that most European countries were facing a fiscal crisis. The government debt-to-GDP ratio had been trending sharply upwards since the mid-1970s, with only a brief interruption in the boom period of the late 1980s. OECD figures indicate that the gross debt-to-GDP ratio for the fifteen European Union countries combined rose from about 40 per cent in the 1980s to nearly double that figure (78 per cent) in 1996. Moreover, budget deficits in many countries had risen in the recession to unacceptably high levels – 6.5 per cent of GDP on average for EU countries in 1993, a major cause for concern quite apart from the Maastricht criteria.

At the same time, European countries were facing an unemployment crisis – the level of unemployment rose above 11 per cent in 1993 (and was on some calculations higher than in the interwar recession years). Moves to curtail deficits and debt appeared to risk worsening the unemployment crisis. The Maastricht timetable meant that, in effect, priority was given to rapid fiscal consolidation, despite the threat to growth and employment.

Whilst the problems of medium-term fiscal control have dominated the political agenda, this is not the only, perhaps not even the main, issue about fiscal policy raised by moves towards further European integration (and specifically by proposals for monetary union). Under EMU, or for that matter under a tight ERM-type system, countries would give up independent control over monetary and exchange rate policy. It is widely agreed that fiscal policy would need to play a larger part in macroeconomic stabilisation, compensating for the loss of the monetary instrument. Fiscal stabilisation would be especially important, it is argued, in offsetting country-specific (or asymmetric) shocks.

The two aspects of fiscal policy – the need for medium-term consolidation and the need for active fiscal stabilisation within countries – interact in a most unfavourable way. There is a clear danger that continuing medium-term problems, and Maastricht-type criteria embodied in the Stability Pact for Stage III and beyond, could make the desirable use of fiscal policy for stabilisation in a future monetary union impossible. Yet the issue of fiscal stabilisation and how it should be coordinated hardly features on the EU agenda.

The discussion below is organised as follows. The following section analyses the role of fiscal policy under EMU, arguing that fiscal stabilisation can and should be decentralised – though it would need to be coordinated at the EU level. The subsequent section draws out some of the lessons for fiscal policy of the breakdown of the precursor to EMU, the Exchange Rate Mechanism (ERM) of the EMS, suggesting that a more active use of fiscal policy could have offset some of the major tensions that led to breakdown. The next section considers the difficult coordination problems that arise from the need to combine short-term fiscal activism with medium-term fiscal restraint. The final section concludes, suggesting that a more intelligent framework for fiscal policy is a necessary condition for further European integration and that it would be essential under EMU.

FISCAL STABILISATION, ASYMMETRIC SHOCKS AND EMU

Groups of countries within a currency union, or regions within a country, have effectively no freedom to use monetary policy for stabilisation or to offset asymmetric shocks.[1] Nevertheless, regions or countries will often feel the need for differential policies since it is highly unlikely that a monetary policy will, however well designed for the group, be appropriate for individual countries or regions. Within countries, such as the UK or France, some of the potential problems may be offset by cultural concern with the whole, by automatic stabilisers through the tax and benefit system, or by discretionary action. Nevertheless, considerable concern does sometimes arise, as for example over the north–south 'divide' during the late 1980s boom in the UK. Modern treatments of the 'optimum currency area' tend to focus on the likelihood and expected magnitude of differential shocks, the extent of automatic mechanisms of adjustment (e.g. labour and capital mobility; wage flexibility) and the size of automatic or discretionary offsets (e.g. through the fiscal system).

Turning to the EU, the basic point is that it does not look like an optimum or even a viable currency area. Labour mobility is relatively low (e.g. Boltho 1989). As far as the automatic stabilisers are concerned, the MacDougall Report (CEC 1977) suggested that the within-country stabilisers were extremely substantial: they 'reckoned that one-half to two-thirds of a loss of income in a region due to a fall in its external sales was automatically offset' (MacDougall 1992), whereas stabilisation between countries from the Brussels budget was minimal. An influential study by Sala-i-Martin and Sachs (1992) comes up with an estimated offset through the federal system in the US of 40 per cent (34 points through tax and 6 points through expenditures). The comparable figure for inter-country offsets within the EU (via the Brussels budget) is tiny – they suggest about 0.5 per cent for the tax component. Thus the stylised facts are as follows: within-country stabilisers are high in Europe (considerably higher than in the US), but inter-country stabilisers are extremely small, and very much smaller than the automatic stabilisation provided by the federal system in the US.

There is, of course, no intention of expanding the EU budget so that it becomes comparable with the US federal system. Although an increase of the regional funds is widely regarded as an important concomitant of further EU integration, their scale is likely to be limited and the idea of strengthening automatic inter-country fiscal flows as an aid to stabilisation is not even on the agenda. On the face of it, stability problems for individual countries within the EU, if there were a common currency, would be expected to be substantially greater than US or within-country experience of regional fluctuations would suggest. Not surprisingly, the lack of inter-country fiscal stabilisers is frequently put forward as a powerful reason for regarding EMU as undesirable or infeasible, and there are many who regard the institution of a federal system on the US model as a necessary condition for Europe to be a viable common currency area.

Arguments of this type seem to depend, however, upon several propositions. The first is, fairly obviously, that differential regional or country shocks are likely to arise – or at least that the system has to be able to cope with them. The second is that, in the absence of monetary or exchange rate offsets, they can indeed be mitigated sufficiently by automatic intercountry (or inter-regional) fiscal flows (and that they are in federal systems such as the US) to make the common currency regime feasible. The third is that there are no alternative policy instruments available to offset differential shocks, the use of which could also make the regime feasible (and, indeed, which might be better than automatic transfers from a centralised budget).

There is no problem with the first of these propositions, though it is worth noting that in the 1980s, when the ERM was operating to constrain national monetary and exchange rate freedom, EC countries were lucky not to face large shocks. But the next two are both contentious. Inter-country fiscal transfers may be an appropriate response to some shocks but not to others. In the Sala-i-Martin and Sachs study, some of their discussion seems to assume the traditional shock, associated with the optimum currency area literature, of a required (permanent) change in real competitiveness, for which a federal fiscal offset is not obviously appropriate. It could be seen as delaying needed adjustments and as raising moral hazard problems. Even where a fiscal offset is desirable (in the case of domestic demand shocks), the mechanism under discussion shares with other automatic stabilisers the problem that there is no reason to suppose that the degree of offset is optimal.

The final proposition – the lack of alternatives – is the key issue in this area of debate. The natural candidate for an alternative policy is decentralised fiscal policy. Could domestic fiscal policy, under the control of national governments, be used to offset differential shocks in much the same way as the operation of automatic intercountry transfers from the centre?

It is argued here that, if the focus is on the need for short-term stabilisation, the differences between decentralised domestic (or regional) fiscal stabilisation and automatic stabilisation through some centralised budget are considerably less than frequently supposed. Indeed, on a number of counts, the argument is in favour of decentralisation.

To illuminate the issues, consider the case where a single country (or region) fluctuates relative to the rest (e.g. relative to the rest of the EU). Even without any fiscal transfers, there would be some offsetting stabilisation due to flow and financial wealth effects through the country's external links. In a downswing, the balance of payments would move to surplus: in an upswing the balance of payments would move to deficit. In other words there is always some relative stabilisation which will be greater the greater the proportion of exports and imports. A very small open region would need little additional stabilisation via fiscal policy (Allsopp et al. 1995).

Now consider the effects of a centralised fiscal system. The fluctuating country or region is additionally stabilised by automatic net transfers from the central budget – positive in the downswing and negative in the upswing. It is this fiscal stabilisation that is often regarded as a necessary condition for a common currency to be viable.

But could the fiscal stabilisation be decentralised? The only difference if the fiscal system is decentralised, is that the stabilising fiscal transfers arise from the domestic tax and expenditure system rather than the centralised one. And of course it is the domestic budget that fluctuates as a counterpart rather than the centralised one. The question is whether this makes any difference. So long as we are concerned with stabilisation of fluctuations which average out over time to zero, it should make no difference at all. In the centralised system, economic agents within the country or region receive a positive transfer when in recession which is paid back in the boom. In the decentralised system the same is true. As far as private sector agents are concerned, it makes no difference whether the transfers are received from and paid back to the centre or whether they are received from and paid back to their own national or regional government. A given degree of stabilisation could be provided either way.

Of course, the fluctuations in the domestic budget position would have to be financed: but this would be done under a future EMU by using the Europe-wide capital market.[2] One objection which has force in many situations is that there is a difference between 'grants' from abroad, and loans, which imply future tax payments, which would be anticipated by the private sector agents.[3] This is not a valid argument here, since the cumulative effect on debt and the cumulative grant or transfer are both zero.

Thus, in principle, fiscal policy could be centralised or decentralised. In practice, quite a number of arguments point to the advantages of decentralisation.

1   Politically, a decentralised fiscal system appears much more likely to be acceptable in Europe than fiscal federalism.
2   The automatic stabilisers within Europe which deliver the stabilisation (so long as budgets are allowed to fluctuate) are higher than the stabilisers provided by the federal system in the US. More generally, discretionary policy could increase or reduce the impact to whatever degree seemed desirable.
3   National systems are less likely to lead to arbitrary inter-country transfers on a longer-term basis and hence to the associated moral hazard problems.
4   No-bail-out provisions are likely to be more credible if the powers of taxation are left in national hands (a point stressed by Eichengreen 1996).
5   National or regional authorities are more likely to be able to distinguish between reversible demand shocks, which should be offset by allowing the budget to fluctuate, and shocks such as supply shocks or changes in competitiveness, which should not.

Some of the disadvantages are the obverse of the advantages above. Thus a decentralised system would not operate to provide long-term support to declining or uncompetitive regions. However, whilst few would doubt that an enhanced, centralised, system of grants and transfers may be needed (as with the structural and regional funds), it is not at all clear that longer-term transfers and grants should be provided in an arbitrary way through the tax and benefit system.

The main disadvantage of a decentralised fiscal system is that it is uncoordinated. One problem that this leads to and which was stressed by the Delors Report (EC 1989) is that fiscal policy for the wider grouping – the EU, for example – is left to individual, national decisions, and, without coordination, might be inappropriate for the EU as a whole. What role should be assigned to fiscal policy, and how it should be coordinated with monetary policy, is left however, rather unclear. The main tension, then as now, is between the need for medium-term fiscal restraint and the need for fiscal stabilisation – for individual countries or for the EU as a whole. This issue is further discussed below.

The above suggests that, as far as stabilisation is concerned, fiscal policy could, and indeed should, be decentralised within a future EMU. There would be coordination problems that would need to be solved. (A centralised system can be seen as one way of coordinating fiscal policy for the union – but it is not the only possibility.) With the automatic stabilisers operating in each country (and with possible discretionary actions as well), one of the main losses of economic sovereignty – the loss of the potential use of monetary policy for demand management – would be much mitigated, since there is an alternative instrument. Another loss due to monetary union – the loss of the freedom to devalue which is also associated with loss of decentralised monetary freedom – would remain. Arguably, however, countries are less concerned with this since the devaluation option is seen as inimical to inflation control.[4]

The use of fiscal policy for economic stabilisation would, however, require a large change in policy attitudes, since fiscal issues have typically been seen as medium-term, with monetary policy assigned to shorter-term stabilisation. The difficulties with this assignment cannot be observed directly, since the EU has not had a common currency. They can, however, be seen indirectly as lying behind the pressures that led to the break-up of the ERM. With an objective of increasingly fixed exchange rates, an unwillingness to use fiscal policy rather than monetary policy for stabilisation put intolerable strains on the system, threatening its credibility.

THE BREAKDOWN OF THE ERM

Any system of fixed but adjustable exchange rates is threatened by two sets of forces. The first is divergent trends in underlying competitiveness, which appear to require an exchange rate change as an aid to adjustment. This may be credibly resisted if the government of the country is seen to be committed to the priority of moderating inflation, and if a devaluation is seen as inconsistent with that commitment. The second is if relative conjunctural or cyclical positions get out of line and if it is anticipated that monetary policy will have to change – implying also a change in the exchange rate. In the early 1990s, the ERM came under strain for both reasons. It is argued here that more active fiscal policy responses to the differential shocks could have mitigated the tensions.

The most important shock of the 1990s was German reunification. Essentially, this involved a major 'fiscal' impact – the political imperative of large transfers, through the budget, to the eastern Länder, together with the claim on real resources as these transfers were translated into demand for western German goods and services. The response, however, was monetary (higher interest rates) and many argued that the exchange rate also needed to rise in real terms. Clearly, to state the obvious, such a monetary response would have been ruled out under EMU. Under EMU, other policies, especially adjustment of fiscal policy, would have had to be used to help manage the transition.

This was not the only shock to the system at the time. Other European countries were moving into or in recession, a classic problem of differential 'regional' developments. The extreme case was the UK, where successive items of news about the depth and likely persistence of the recession constituted the shocks to the system. As German interest rates moved up, the UK's situation looked increasingly untenable. But a further fiscal response was extremely unlikely given prevailing UK policy attitudes and worries over deficits and debt. For the lack of plausible alternatives, it became a good bet that interest rates and the exchange rate would have to change. And it is notable that, in contrast to France, the moment exit from the ERM was forced, policy did indeed change very markedly towards the use of interest rate and exchange rate policy to generate recovery.

The basic point, looking at these two countries, is that interest rate responses to their respective difficulties could be anticipated and that such responses were simply incompatible with the maintenance of fixed parity bands. Two questions arise: The first is whether other policies could have released the tensions – in particular whether fiscal policy could have played a much stronger role – allowing the maintenance of credibility. The second is whether, in any case, an exchange rate realignment was necessary and could be anticipated. These issues will be briefly discussed in the context of the individual countries, starting with the UK as the more straightforward case.

The United Kingdom

Ever since the inception of the Medium-Term Financial Strategy in 1980 the UK has typically used monetary policy (with exchange rate consequences) to manage demand when necessary. In the period of shadowing the D-mark in 1987–8, this could not of course be done. When financial liberalisation and rising real estate prices stimulated an excessive consumer boom and marked reduction in savings, the policy had to be abandoned: interest rates were raised and the exchange rate allowed to appreciate. Even when the UK entered the ERM in 1990, one influential argument was that this would allow, via credibility effects and international arbitrage, lower interest rates which had by then become appropriate from the point of view of the domestic economy (surely about the worst possible reason for entering a medium-term exchange rate system!). After leaving the ERM, policy quickly reverted to type, with interest rates being used to manage demand.

I have argued elsewhere (Allsopp 1993) that a fiscal offset to the credit boom would have been more appropriate than the policies actually followed – which were monetary. Broadly, the argument is this. Financial liberalisation and other changes led to a marked fall in savings which (in stock terms) can also be seen as a fall in the (net) demand for financial assets by the private sector.[5] A tighter fiscal policy would have offset the change in savings and, via budget surpluses, lowered the supply of public sector financial instruments (thus mitigating the overall excess supply). A direct, fiscal offset to a marked change in the private sector's desire for savings/wealth would have been more appropriate than an attempt to deal with it by changing interest rates (an intertemporal price) or the exchange rate (an international price). When the shock reversed – which was always likely – budgetary policy could also reverse.

The private sector boom did lead to an improvement in the public sector deficit as tax revenues rose and social security expenditure fell (the budget went briefly into surplus). Thus, in practice the MTFS framework (which contained targets, or more strictly, 'consistent projections' for public borrowing), was over-ruled to the extent that the automatic stabilisers were allowed to operate. The budget went into surplus not because of fiscal 'consolidation' but because of the private sector's debt splurge. To slow the boom without resort to monetary policy (e.g. if the policy of D-mark-shadowing had been maintained or if the UK had been a member of the ERM) would have required much more draconian fiscal action – substantial discretionary tax rises or expenditure cuts, implying even larger budget surpluses – to offset the extremely large impact emanating from the private sector (the savings ratio fell from about 11 per cent in the mid-1980s to 6 per cent in 1988 before rising again to about 12 per cent in 1992). Such a policy would, of course, have meant that there was much more room for fiscal manoeuvre in the early 1990s when the savings impact was reversed.

More interesting, perhaps is the question of whether a fiscal response to emerging difficulties in the second half of 1992 would have been feasible (assuming attitudes to debt and public borrowing had somehow been different). Here simulations can give an indication of what might have been required. A simulation using the Oxford Economic Forecasting model suggested that, with no change in the exchange rate, and with interest rates tied (in line with previous experience) to German rates, the necessary fiscal adjustment to match the recovery path actually achieved would have been relatively small. Subject to the usual qualifications, the simulation suggested that an increase in public borrowing (in the PSBR) of about £4 billion in 1993, declining in 1994 and 1995, would have been needed. These magnitudes are relatively small compared with the scale of the public borrowing 'problem' in the UK, which was of the order of £50 billion in 1993. A similar picture is provided in a National Institute study which includes a simulation of the effects of a smaller realignment than actually occurred plus a fiscal boost (Barrell *et al.* 1994). The longer-term issue of public borrowing in the UK and elsewhere is further discussed below.

The issue of whether the UK exchange rate needed to change in any case, for fundamental reasons of competitiveness, remains highly contentious. On the one hand, devaluation was clearly not desired by the authorities at the time of 'Black Wednesday', and to be forced into it involved the removal of an important nominal anchor against inflation in the medium term (thus the U-turn on policy left the government with a largely unresolved problem of what to put in its place;

see Artis and Lewis 1993). On the other, there are many who argue that the exchange rate was out of line. If it was out of line, and seen to be out of line by financial markets, this itself constitutes an alternative explanation of the crisis.

In the case of the UK, longer-term estimates of the level of the 'equilibrium' exchange rate are not very helpful. Estimates based on concepts of medium-term internal and external balance tended to suggest the need for devaluation, especially *vis-à-vis* Germany, as they were more or less bound to (for the late 1980s at least) since the UK had a large balance of payments deficit, and Germany a large surplus. Purchasing power parity (PPP) estimates gave a different picture, suggesting that the UK was not seriously out of line and that Germany was overvalued. Perhaps the most telling statistic in looking at the UK relative to West Germany is the cost of an hour's labour in manufacturing (including social costs). These figures suggest that prior to leaving the ERM the UK wage level was about 60 per cent of the German; after the devaluation it was about 50 per cent. (At the time, East German wages were, according to the OECD, about 70 per cent of those in the West, so as a 'region' within the EU, Britain had substantially lower wages than the former GDR.) Since devaluation is effectively an attempt to lower real wages, the question is whether Britain really needed to increase the already large differential to balance relatively poor productivity. The view put forward here is that the need for devaluation was largely to stimulate demand rather than being called for to improve supply-side competitiveness.

It can be further argued that the actual debacle of Black Wednesday owed more to the inconsistency of macroeconomic policy than the perception that exchange rates *per se* were out of line and needed to change. There was little new in the government's policy, and the balance of payments issue was certainly not to the fore. The 'news' that, in stages, seemed to trigger the crisis, was about recession; and the perception grew that the UK would need to change policy in order to reflate. With only one instrument plausibly available (i.e. interest rates) the exchange rate was bound to weaken. Moreover, in the circumstances, a large interest rate rise in the short term (to quell speculation) looked politically and economically impossible, so that there was little risk for those betting against sterling.

It can of course never be known whether a different framework of policy, involving a more active role for fiscal policy in offsetting private sector savings shocks, would have defused the speculative pressure that developed over the sterling exchange rate in 1992. But the thought-experiment is highly relevant for those contemplating a possible future EMU. If the UK had been a member of a common currency area in the late 1980s, then fiscal policy rather than monetary policy would have had to be used to slow the boom. Budget surpluses would have been larger, and the scope for fiscal deficits to support recovery in the 1990s would have been greater. Opinions differ on whether an exchange rate change would still have been necessary. What should not be in doubt is that, if the UK had had no freedom to change interest rates or exchange rates (as under EMU), the shocks affecting the UK economy would have led to an even greater boom followed by an even greater 'bust' unless offset by a substantially more active fiscal policy.

Germany

The German situation is complicated by policy views within Germany which are not necessarily shared by outside observers. Germany grew rapidly in the late 1980s, joining the European boom late. At the same time the budget, which had been in substantial deficit, moved to a small surplus by 1989. Sometimes fiscal 'consolidation' is given the credit for stimulating the German economy. This hardly fits the facts. Germany was dragged into the world upswing by exports and a widening balance of payments surplus, which reached 4.8 per cent of GDP in 1989. (In fact, the German private sector, ever since the first oil crisis in 1973, typically runs a large surplus (savings exceed investment); a surplus which can be balanced, as a matter of accounting by either a budget deficit or an external surplus.) In the late 1980s it was balanced by an external surplus. The late 1980s boom, which had a strong investment component, was particularly favourable to German manufactured exports. The mechanism by which buoyant export demand affected the public sector was, of course, partly the operation of the automatic stabilisers (especially tax revenues) and partly 'fiscal consolidation'.

The fiscal stimulus of reunification came at the top of the boom. Combined with the (short-lived) effects of the monetary overhang in the eastern Länder, this undoubtedly led to excess demand in 1990 and inflationary pressure. Taxes were raised, but with the unfortunate effect of generating wage pressure. As noted, however, most of the response was monetary, with the well known adverse consequences for other countries in the ERM who were going into recession. A revaluation of the D-mark, which could have mitigated the tensions, was not possible given resistance by France. Under EMU, or if Germany had not occupied a hegemonic position within the ERM, a fiscal response would have been effectively the only option.

The question of whether some of the difficulties posed for the ERM by German Economic and Monetary Union (GEMU) could have been offset by a different set of policy responses, is much more complex than the equivalent question about the reversible savings shock in the UK. The conventional wisdom is that, given the expansionary fiscal shock (which was about 4 per cent of West German GDP) Germany faced the simple choice of offsetting it with fiscal policy or with monetary policy and chose the latter. This is far too simple an account.

One factor that is often neglected is that Germany, at the time of reunification, had a huge external current account surplus – 4.8 per cent of GDP in 1989. What this means is that, in principle, resources could be diverted from net exports to the eastern Länder without imposing any additional burden on the West German economy. With such a switch, if it could be engineered, the external current account balance would fall and the internal budget deficit

165

would rise in line with the transfer of resources to the east. And the West German private sector, instead of accumulating foreign assets, would be accumulating domestic government bonds (which, to the extent that the resources were used for investment, can be thought of as an indirect claim on the capacity of the eastern economy). To all intents and purposes, such a policy would be the same as a policy of financing the resource flow to the east by government borrowing in the international capital market.

The problem with such a policy is that, in order to divert resources from net exports to the east and to prevent excess demand, the real exchange rate would need to rise (to reduce net exports by 4 per cent of GDP). This account puts the main emphasis on the need for a real exchange rate change following reunification.[6] Since the authorities were not prepared to see this happen via domestic inflation, and since a revaluation was ruled out, interest rates were raised and other ERM countries were faced with inappropriately high interest rates and exchange rates, or were forced to devalue.

This account has a superficial fit with the facts of experience. The difficulty, however, is that it fails in a crucial respect: it does not explain why, soon after the 'boost' from reunification, Germany suffered from weak output growth, and a major recession in 1993.

Much of the puzzle can be resolved by looking at the context. Treated in isolation, there is nothing wrong with the conventional analysis. But there was another shock operating at the same time – the ending of the European and world investment boom. The effects of this can be seen as a shift down in export demand. At the same time there was a shift up in imports from the rest of the world into the eastern Länder. These impacts from net trade can also be seen as 'fiscal' impacts, in this case negative. The external impact was, it may be argued, except for a couple of quarters in 1990, larger than the internal stimulus. The net effect on West Germany of the two shocks was not stimulatory but contractionary.[7] And if this was the case, there was no need for the real exchange rate to rise either.

A crude way of looking at the joint impact is to consider the sectoral balances. The impact on the private sector is equal to the sum of the swing to surplus of the balance of payments and the swing to deficit of the budget. In practice, the external swing was from 4.8 per cent of GDP in 1990 to -1.1 per cent in 1991 – an indication of contractionary impulse of nearly 6 per cent of GDP. The internal swing in the budgetary position from 1989 was only about 3–3.5 per cent. The net effect seems strongly negative.

Crude as they are, these numbers suggest that Germany may need larger rather than smaller budget deficits in the future, whilst reunification expenditure continues. Past experience suggests that the excess of West German savings over investment is typically 3 or 4 per cent of GDP which can be balanced either by a current account surplus or an internal budget deficit. With no balance of payments surplus, the figures suggest an equilibrium internal budget deficit of the order of 3–4 per cent of GDP.

The suggestion that Germany 'should' have a budget deficit of 3–4 per cent of GDP would horrify most German policy makers. The reason, however, is that before reunification Germany was in the fortunate position of having a large savings surplus and hence had potential to finance the transfers to the east without difficulty and without tax rises. To be sure, it would be even better if the private sector would raise its investment in the eastern Länder, tapping domestic German savings, to the required extent (3–4 per cent of GDP). That will not happen, given wages in the eastern Länder, for a long time. Until then, budgetary involvement in the transfer is inevitable and desirable.

As far as Germany's exchange rate is concerned, the worry in the first half of the 1990s was that it was uncompetitive, not that it needed to rise relative to other European countries.[8] In fact, the data suggest that the main period when Germany lost competitiveness was in the second half of the 1980s, before reunification. The late 1980s, with an extremely favourable composition of demand for German exports, looks like the exceptional period, leading to huge payments surpluses despite underlying competitiveness problems.

Some implications

The main conclusion of this section is that, even when considering the extreme cases of the UK and Germany and the shocks experienced in the early 1990s, there were policy alternatives which could have helped to offset them and which could have been more consistent with a continuation of the pre-existing relative exchange rates. This is important in contemplating problems that might arise in a future monetary union – though it is to be hoped that shocks on the scale of those discussed would not arise.

But what is clear from both examples is that underlying policy attitudes, especially to fiscal policy, would have to change rather a lot if independent monetary and fiscal policies were not available. The UK example illustrates that fiscal policy would have had to be used much more actively, in an offsetting way, in response to large swings in consumer behaviour. In the case of Germany, the messages are rather more mixed. On the positive side it has been suggested that, given Germany's large savings surplus and balance of payments surplus before reunification, there was no need from a medium-term point of view to tighten fiscal policy to 'make room' for the transfer of resources to the east. And if Germany's extremely high level of exports in the late 1980s is regarded as exceptional, then there was no medium-term reason for a change in the real exchange rate either. From this rather extreme point of view, German policy makers overdid it on interest rates, on the exchange rate and on fiscal tightening.[9]

But the most important question that arises in the German case is over medium-term fiscal objectives. The high West German private sector savings potential has normally led in the past (since about the mid-1970s) to either a budget deficit or an external surplus. In the mid-1990s, the budget deficit is the counterpart to the transfer to the east, but it would be wrong to see it as caused by this. Unless savings behaviour changes markedly, it is hard to see the budget position coming in line with German policy objectives unless either there is a return to a large balance of payments surplus, or there is a large increase in the scale of private investment (ideally, it might be argued, in the form of investment in the eastern Länder).

Paradoxically, the European country that may in the medium term find it most difficult to meet the Maastricht criteria and the requirements of the Stability Pact, is Germany.

COORDINATION PROBLEMS

It has been suggested in the previous sections that fiscal policy would need to play a more active role in stabilisation in a future EMU. It has also been suggested that fiscal policy could be decentralised. At the same time, most European countries are faced with the medium-term need to get deficits and debt ratios under control – it is this problem that the Maastricht fiscal convergence criteria are intended to address. This combination of objectives for fiscal policy raises potentially serious difficulties for policy design and coordination.

The most obvious difficulty is the potential conflict between the medium-term need for fiscal 'consolidation' and the need for short-term fiscal activism to offset shocks – either within countries or at the level of the centre. The Maastricht fiscal convergence criteria and the Stability Pact are directed towards the medium-term problem, and conflict with shorter-term objectives of supporting recovery or cutting unemployment. Even without this, however, there is the other problem about how fiscal policy should be coordinated between countries so as to be appropriate for a future union as a whole.

Coordination between countries

This paper has suggested that that fiscal stabilisation could and should be decentralised. But would this lead to sensible fiscal policies for the group of countries taken together?

One argument goes as follows. For reversible shocks (where stabilisation is appropriate) and especially for reversible domestic demand shocks (cf. the discussion of the UK above) it could be argued that if each individual country were to offset to an optimal or acceptable degree, then this would deliver optimal (or acceptable) fiscal stabilisation for the group as a whole. Fiscal policy could be subject to the principle of subsidiarity. Asymmetric shocks would be dealt with country-by-country and the response to common shocks would cumulate to produce fiscal stabilisation for the group (see Allsopp et al. 1995). This is in fact a good starting point in considering the coordination of decentralised stabilisation – but there are several difficulties.

The first, which arises out of the discussion of the prevailing framework of fiscal policy above, is that countries would have to want to do this. Any prevailing view that fiscal policy was an inappropriate or ineffective instrument would threaten the neat solution. Second, and more importantly, however, there is a serious potential free-rider problem (Lamfalussy 1989: Allsopp and Vines 1996). This is clearest in the case of common shocks. Each decentralised fiscal authority, assuming that it saw costs (e.g. from changing taxes or expenditure) would be tempted to stabilise too little, and rely instead on the stabilisation provided by others. Generalised, the result would be too little stabilisation and too much reliance on monetary policy for the Union as a whole.[10] This appears a much more serious problem than the prevalent idea that 'irresponsible' governments would do too much (the above discussion of the breakdown of the ERM illustrates the reluctance of some EU governments to use fiscal policy actively and their preference for monetary policy).

A centralised system of automatic fiscal offsets from the central budget (fiscal federalism) can be seen as one way of breaking this dilemma. Short of that, active encouragement of fiscal stabilisation and coordination of responses would be necessary.

The encouragement of fiscal activism, however, runs into several difficulties. The first concerns shocks that should not be offset (permanent supply shocks or permanent changes in competitiveness). It has been suggested, above, that here the balance of argument is in favour of decentralisation: more localised authorities would be in a better position to identify the type of shock that was being faced, and, so long as the 'no-bail-out' policy was credible, decentralisation would reduce the moral hazard problems.

The second is that fiscal policy cannot be seen in isolation from monetary policy. There is, for example, a large difference between a situation in which EU-wide monetary policy is used actively for stabilisation and growth objectives and one in which the central bank targets, for example, exclusively inflation. Quite generally, the roles of monetary and fiscal policy need to be clarified and coordinated.

But the most obvious problem, the dominant problem in the mid-1990s, is the difficult interaction between the need for decentralised fiscal action and the Maastricht fiscal convergence criteria.

The longer-term problem of deficits and debt

Most European countries have experienced rising debt levels over time, and it is a perfectly reasonable objective to stabilise or reduce debt levels.[11] But how should this be done? A direct attack risks producing perverse effects.

The basic point is that a concern with the position of the public sector *per se* is seldom justified (there are, no doubt, cases where the public sector simply perturbs an otherwise well functioning economy, especially in high-inflation developing countries; but this is not the case in most of Europe). The position of the public sector is connected by identity to the position of the private sector (and, in an open economy, to the balance of payments as well). It is a peculiarity of policy making that fiscal policy is seen as something to do with the public sector. It is equally something to do with the private sector. In fact, since we are concerned with the behaviour of the private sector, the emphasis should normally be on the private sector, and with the influence of public policy on the private sector.

Thus the rising debt trend in Europe is, by identity, a rising trend of public sector financial asset holdings by the private sector. It reflects, in more simple language, an excess of private savings over private investment expenditures. There is no way, short of a large balance of payments surplus for Europe as a whole (which might well not be feasible in the international economy), of changing the debt trend unless either European private sector savings decrease or investment increases. The latter is generally regarded as the more desirable. Thus a cure for the problem must involve a revival of productive investment by the private sector. That is where the policy emphasis needs to be.

The point can be put very simply. In order to solve Europe's twin problems of very high unemployment and rising debt, the growth of the European countries needs to rise, on a sustained basis, by at least one percentage point per annum. Such an increase in growth would 'go with' a rise, in the medium term, of the investment/GDP ratio by about 2.5–3 per cent of GDP, and this would be the counterpart to the medium-term improvement of public deficits and the debt trend.

Since most policy makers would share the objective of increasing investment and growth and reducing public borrowing, the key question is how to bring this about. In the mid-1990s the dominant view appeared to be that fiscal tightening together with 'supply side' measures, such as increased labour market 'flexibility' as well as (perhaps) the effects of monetary union itself, would lower long-term interest rates and improve confidence sufficiently to support the required revival of investment spending. Since the short-term effects of fiscal tightening are negative, such a strategy depends to a dangerous extent on favourable, longer-term expectational effects. Without recovery, a revival of investment and a sustained increase in its share, the strategy would fail.

In fact, in the mid-1990s, there was a widespread tendency amongst European policy makers to underestimate the difficulties of fiscal consolidation within a group of countries as large as Europe (Allsopp and Vines 1996). For an individual country, a strategy of large-scale fiscal adjustment frequently involves lower interest rates, a lower exchange rate and a swing to surplus in the balance of payments. The exchange rate objectives of the Maastricht process rule out this strategy for individual countries – which would be regarded as beggar-thy-neighbour. The Maastricht process has, however, succeeded in generating a coordinated fiscal policy of restraint. With limited possibilities of 'solving' the counterpart problem by running a large Europe-wide balance of payments surplus – both because of the size this would have to be and because Europe as a whole is a relatively 'closed' economy – the missing part of the strategy is any credible way of bringing about the required adjustment of investment.

There is an important issue of the sequencing of policy moves. A far less dangerous strategy would be to lead the way with monetary stimulation, postponing tax increases until growth and investment revived. A concerted move to lower interest rates would help to support a revival of investment spending. More important than the direct effects would be the signal it would give, throughout the EU, that governments were committed to a revival of European growth, without which the needed investment response would be unlikely to appear.

CONCLUSION

This paper has argued that fiscal policy will need to play a larger part as European integration proceeds and that a more active role for fiscal policy would be essential under a future EMU. Fiscal policy would need to be used more actively for stabilisation, within an environment of medium-term fiscal restraint. The potential conflicts are not at all easy to solve.

It has been argued that fiscal stabilisation could and should be left with individual governments, but that it would need to be coordinated. Europe starts from a good position, in that the fiscal stabilisers, within countries, are already high. But without coordination fiscal activism would tend to be too little rather than too much, and inappropriate for the Union as a whole. EU governments need to cooperate to ensure that the automatic stabilisers are in practice allowed to operate, and beyond this will need to encourage discretionary fiscal offsets against short-term shocks.

Concentration on the Maastricht fiscal criteria and the proposed Stability Pact to the exclusion of thinking about the role of fiscal policy within a future economic and monetary union, is extraordinarily dangerous. The role of fiscal stabilisation in a future EMU needs to be high on the political agenda. But the debt and deficit aims of EU governments are more dangerous than that. As objectives they are entirely reasonable – Europe cannot go on accumulating debt at the rate experienced over the past fifteen years. But a change in the public sector position must involve a reciprocal change in the private sector. In practice this means that investment and growth in the EU needs to rise. Given the scale of the fiscal change being attempted, this means, as a rough order of magnitude, that the European growth trend needs to rise by at least 1 per cent per annum on a sustained basis. There is no credible strategy to achieve this. But, if the needed higher investment is not achieved, this does not just mean a slightly lower growth, but a continuing tendency to recession and unemployment combined with a failure to bring public borrowing and debt under control.

NOTES

1 There may still be some scope for differentiated monetary policies, such as subsidised loans for particular purposes or for activities within a particular area. But the amounts involved are small and can be disregarded here.

2 The amount of financing needed would not depend on whether the system was decentralised or centralised. Clearly, the relative impact would depend on the degree of centralisation. Obviously the budgetary authority (the national or regional government) would need to be large enough not to run into financing difficulties. The main justification for the fiscal offset in the first place is that the government is less liquidity-constrained and has better access to markets than individual agents acting on their own account – otherwise the offsets could be left to the individuals.

3 Sala-i-Martin and Sachs argue that federal transfers are not subject to the Ricardian objection in that the future taxes would be paid by someone else in other regions.

4 The loss of the freedom to adjust the exchange rate as an aid to the adjustment of competitiveness is no loss if it just leads over time to wage and price inflation. Though this appears to be the view of many EU governments, the loss of sovereignty could under certain circumstances be great.

5 In terms of the standard approach of the economics textbooks, this was an I-S impact (a shift in the I-S curve) not a monetary (or L-M) impact, as is often assumed.

6 Refinements can be added. Thus, in many forward looking dynamic models, the initial rise in the real exchange rate gives way in the longer term to a fall as foreign borrowing (for Germany, this equals reduced accumulation of foreign assets) during adjustment leads to a lower equilibrium real exchange rate (debt hysteresis).

7 The treatment of the internal and external shocks as independent is a simplification. Clearly, German policy responses in the early 1990s were one of the reasons for recession elsewhere in Europe, so that part of the negative external impact can be seen as due to German monetary policy. The initial slowdown in the UK, however, was due to internal policy. More generally, the world boom was slowing and a fall-off in West German exports would probably have occurred anyway.

8 OECD figures suggest that in the mid-1990s wages in the eastern Länder are about 70 per cent of those in the western Länder.

9 The problem is that, at least for a short period, there was excess demand and there was a rise in inflation. Without the possibility of an independent interest rate and exchange rate policy (as in a future EMU), fiscal tightening would presumably have had to be greater, even if only temporarily. But the response of wage inflation to the fiscal tightening that did occur in the early 1990s was extremely unfavourable.

10 The tendency for under-provision of fiscal stabilisation would be greater, the smaller (and therefore, the more decentralised) were the fiscal authorities.

11 Before looking at this, why should high debt levels be regarded as dangerous? There are two reasons, which can for example be analysed within a life-cycle or overlapping generations framework. Within such a framework the asset stock is functional in inter-generational transfers (e.g. between the young who are saving and the old who are dissaving at a moment of time). National debt is an asset for the private sector to hold. An excessive national debt could lead to crowding out of the capital stock or, if total assets are excessive in relation to the desire to hold them, to excess demand and inflation. Which of these would result in practice would depend on policy: an excessive asset stock balanced by high interest rates would conventionally lead to capital crowding out: otherwise inflation would result (in the latter case it would be appropriate for the government to run a budget surplus to restore equilibrium without inflation).

BIBLIOGRAPHY

Allsopp, C. J. (1993) 'Strategic policy dilemmas for the 1990s', *Oxford Review of Economic Policy*, 9, 3.

Allsopp, C. J., Davies, G. and Vines. D. (1995) 'Regional macroeconomic policy, fiscal federalism and European integration', *Oxford Review of Economic Policy*, 11, 2.

Allsopp, C. J. and Vines, D. (1996) 'Fiscal policy and EMU', *National Institute Economic Review*, 158.

Artis, M. J. and Lewis, M. K. (1993) 'Après le Déluge: monetary and exchange rate policy in Britain and Europe', *Oxford Review of Economic Policy*, 9, 3.

Barrell, R., Britton, A. and Pain, N. (1994) 'When the time was right? The UK experience of the ERM', in D. Cobham (ed.) *European Monetary Upheavals*, Manchester: Manchester University Press.

Boltho, A. (1989) 'European and United States regional differentials: a note', *Oxford Review of Economic Policy*, 5, 2.

CEC (1977) *Report of the Study Group on the Role of Public Finance in European Integration*, Brussels: Commission of the European Economic Communities.

EC (1989) *Report on Economic and Monetary Union in the European Community*, Luxembourg: Office for Official Publications of the European Communities.

Eichengreen, B. (1997) 'Saving Europe's stabilisers', *National Institute Economic Review*, 159.

Lamfalussy, A. (1989) 'Macro-coordination of fiscal policies in an economic and monetary union in Europe', in EC (1989) *Report on Economic and Monetary Union in the European Community*, Luxembourg.

MacDougall, D. (1992) 'Economic and monetary union and the European Community budget', *National Institute Economic Review*, May.

Sala-i-Martin, X. and Sachs, G. (1992) 'Fiscal federalism and optimum currency areas: evidence for Europe from the United States', in M. Canzeroni, V. Grilli and R. Masson (eds) *Establishing a Central Bank: Issues in Europe and Lessons from the United States*, Cambridge: Cambridge University Press.

12

CONCLUSION

States, the European Union and macroeconomic policy

Anand Menon and James Forder

The aim of this book has been to examine the impact of the European Union on national macroeconomic policy. In keeping with the overall approach of the series, our emphasis has been on detailed empirical examination of the relationship between the state and the EU. However, given the nature of the sector and the fact that much of the current debate concerning macroeconomic policy in Europe concerns the future implications of EU involvement in this sector, certain of the contributors were also asked to consider the possible future implications of increased European-level competence over monetary policy for policy and policy making at the national level.

This concluding chapter mirrors these twin aims. The first section looks at the findings of the empirical chapters concerning the past impact of the EU on national macroeconomic policy, highlighting the different ways in which EU pressures have been manifest and the role of the EU in relation to other factors acting on the autonomy of the state in this sector. The second goes on to consider the possible future relationship between the EU and its member states in the context of a monetary union. A final section attempts to explain the varying levels of impact exerted by the EU.

EXPLORING EU IMPACT

EU impact: an overview

The scope of EC and subsequently EU action in the macroeconomic domain has, as Harrop so vividly illustrates, expanded markedly since the early days of the Common Market. The Treaty of Rome called for member states to coordinate their economic policies and for cooperation between national administrations and central banks, as well as establishing a monetary committee (Article 105). It also emphasised the importance of national balance of payments

174

equilibria and established that the exchange rate should be treated as 'a matter of common concern' (Article 107). Yet for all this, and apart from introducing the possibility of mutual assistance in the case of a member state suffering serious balance of payments problems (Article 108), immediate progress towards creating institutional means – beyond those already existing in the form of the Bretton Woods System – to achieve these policy goals was negligible.

When, at the Hague summit of 1969, the member states first seemed willing to take practical steps towards creating such European-level institutional competencies, they were constrained by a clear difference of economic outlook as to the priority to be given to the convergence of inflation prior to monetary union. Nevertheless, in 1971 the ECOFIN accepted the Werner Report's stated objective of achieving monetary union by 1980. Whilst aspects of that plan were in certain respects more far-reaching than even the Maastricht Treaty,[1] its principal achievement was the establishment of the 'Snake in the tunnel'. In the turbulent period following the collapse of Bretton Woods, the divergent policies pursued by the major European countries soon reduced the Snake, stripped of its dollar 'tunnel', to a D-mark zone for West Germany and the smaller countries: Britain, France and Italy all withdrew as it became impossible to defend their parities. The incentives for policy coordination, exchange rate stability and European integration did not prove strong enough, at least amongst the larger countries, for the system to be maintained, and the Werner plan therefore came to nothing.

The turning point came only after the 1978 decision to replace the rump of the Snake with the European Monetary System.[2] To see this decision, as some have, as an attempt to constrain the policy of particular countries (Dyson 1994: 178–9; Tsoukalis 1977: 38) is, as Oppenheimer makes clear, much less than the whole story. Initially, it was primarily a collective venture aimed at establishing exchange rate stability, not at imposing a certain monetary policy, or promoting policy coordination. Nevertheless, the evolution of the system towards a West German-led, low inflation area soon began. As demonstrated by Forder and Oppenheimer (1996) and Oppenheimer in this volume, the explanations of this evolution were only partly European in origin. Be this as it may, it entailed a significant European influence over policy in the member states.

The preceding chapters have pointed to numerous instances of European-level involvement in macroeconomic policy affecting national policy and policy making. In the first place, and most obviously, the Exchange Rate Mechanism, with its relatively tight fluctuation bands, limited exchange rate flexibility – though relatively regular parity realignments introduced a degree of flexibility into the system. These realignments, however, as Gregory and Weiserbs point out, generally did not fully accommodate prior inflation differentials, so that an anti-inflationary bias was introduced to the policy of the devaluing country.

Cameron (1995: 44) argues that the resulting loss of competitiveness of the high-inflation countries led to trade surpluses with EC partners for their low-inflation partners, with deficits for themselves. In the first decade of the system, the German cumulative surplus was in the order of $200 billion in intra-EC

175

trade, whilst that of the Netherlands exceeded $100 billion. In contrast, the deficit figures for Italy, France and the United Kingdom exceeded $40 billion, $75 billion and $100 billion respectively.

Yet the degree to which the EMS represents a constraint on the autonomy of the member states should not be exaggerated. Several factors indicate that the loss of autonomy suffered was not as great as may perhaps appear at first sight. In the first place, a unilateral exit from the 'constraints' of the system was and is always available. Indeed, the option has been exercised, most publicly in the crises of 1992–3, but also of course in early realignments where on some occasions countries appear to have effectively determined their new parity themselves.[3] Indeed, the fact that this possibility exists clearly motivates the school of thought that feels monetary union to be urgent in order to prevent 'competitive devaluations' since, *ipso facto*, any such competitive devaluation demonstrates the extent to which national autonomy has been maintained.[4]

The power to ultimately opt out of course exists in many – if not all – policy areas, but perhaps not with the same technical ease, or with the same kind of legal legitimacy. EMS parities are achieved through domestic economic, and most of the time specifically monetary, policy. Intervention in the currency markets may occur, but members seek to avoid putting themselves in a position where it will become large-scale or prolonged simply because this is then taken as a sign of a likely realignment. But this means that the tools by which EMS obligations are met remain exclusively in national hands.

Granted that technical control over the levers of policy remains in national hands – unlike, for example, in the case of agricultural price supports, where the very instruments of policy have been taken away from the member states – it is noticeable that in the monetary case, the levers of policy have remained legally in national hands as well. The most that can be said is that participants undertook a commitment to achieve certain exchange rate outcomes. It was never the case that Community institutions acquired legal rights over, say, national interest rates. Thus the EMS also stands in contrast to those areas where, although the technical control over policy has remained in national hands, member states are legally bound to carry through certain policy actions, such as under some of the provisions of the Social Chapter, whereby states are legally obliged to provide certain rights to workers.

Thus from the practical and legal perspectives, the loss of autonomy in the monetary field seems relatively slight in comparison with other areas. Not only – as is the norm – did the members opt in to monetary integration, making it essentially voluntary, but they also retain an eminently practical opportunity to opt out again, should they so wish. This is unusual, as in many areas there are considerable technical or legal obstructions to opting out – it is difficult to imagine a state unilaterally opting out of the CAP, for instance. Moreover, both the practical ability to carry out policy and the legal right to do so in any way they choose have been maintained at the national level.

There is an irony about this argument, as a certain school of economic thought, associated with Giavazzi and Pagano (1988) suggests that (for non-Germans) it is precisely the loss of autonomy associated with joining the EMS that is the source of the benefit: it is supposed to be helpful to 'tie one's hands' by committing to a policy. What the economic theory says about this (in contrast to many politicians, journalists and indeed economists) is that such an action – for example, committing oneself to maintaining a particular D-mark exchange rate – affects private sector economic agents' expectations and thereby changes their behaviour. This change in their behaviour may make the policy committed to easier to achieve in a purely technical, economic sense; or it may make it possible to achieve it at lower cost, but again in a technical, economic way.[5] Taking all that for granted would require several leaps of faith, and indeed such effects, if they exist, have proven hard to identify. Dornbusch (1989) for example, did not find such a benefit from EMS membership. Much more extensive testing by Posen (1998) has failed to find it in relation to central bank independence either, although that is now an even more popular proposal for 'improving credibility'.

In this way again the EMS stands in contrast to other policy areas: whatever the benefits of the CAP may be, it has never to our knowledge been claimed that their source is the loss of autonomy that membership entails. Yet with the EMS, the gain in 'credibility' associated with the adoption of a D-mark peg supposedly arises precisely because policy makers in the peripheral countries have put themselves in the position of following the lead of the Bundesbank. Their autonomy is, in the world of credibility theory, a curse. It brings only temptations to inflate at long-run cost. Nor is this line of thinking limited to economic theorists – far from it. Chapters in this volume by Reland and by Vaciago have both made clear the significance of such arguments as this in conditioning policy in both France and Italy. Although such ideas held sway for a shorter period in the UK,[6] Artis makes clear that it was present and indeed it is explicit in Lawson (1992).

It is, we presume, the combination of the relative ease of opting out of the EMS and it being thought undesirable that this option exist, which has led governments to seek to constrain themselves within the System more tightly than the System did itself. To a large extent they have attempted to do this by public pronouncements to the effect that they would maintain their parity. In so far as such a pledge, once made, is electorally sensitive, it creates a constraint. Thus an element of constraint – and loss of autonomy – comes into the system which was not there in its design. It is a self-imposed constraint and operates not legally or technically, but politically. It is the political necessity of avoiding embarrassment as a result of failing to do what one has publicly promised that creates the constraint on policy. Moreover, this loss of autonomy is not easily revocable: governments might mould public opinion slowly in favour of fixed exchange rates, but they cannot remould it quickly in another direction to accommodate a new policy.

There exists, moreover, a second irony related to some of the economic arguments put forward concerning the effects of the EMS. Not only are the constraints not as binding as many have portrayed them, but the claimed

benefits of EMS membership – notably that it consistently helped reduce inflation to a significant degree through its economic effects – are impossible to
prove. Such a link has been claimed many times. For instance, the apparent coincidence between EMS-inspired currency stability and broad convergence of
interest and inflation rates in the late 1980s led both academics and politicians to
claim that the former was somehow causally responsible for the latter. Hence
some have suggested that participation in an established system of pegged
exchange rates can enhance the possibility of achieving the goal of controlling
inflation, not least through the harnessing of the credibility of the system.

Yet in the first place, it was not the ERM that converted European states to a
belief in the centrality of low inflation to economic success. The willingness on
the part of France and Italy to treat the exchange rate as a constraint is
explained by the simple fact that national policy preferences had altered.
Currency depreciation had not significantly enhanced competitiveness and
export performance; inflation itself undermined attempts to achieve increased
international competitiveness.

Second, it can be argued that, even once states joined the exchange rate
mechanism, it was not the latter which was responsible for the fall in inflation
that they experienced. There exists no real evidence that EMS membership
causes low inflation, since inflation in countries that did not participate in the
ERM followed a similar trend to that in those that did.[7] The early period of the
EMS was a period of falling inflation all round the world. Indeed, in terms of
speed and extent of inflation reduction, Thatcherite Britain represented a
striking success story, with inflation falling from over 20 per cent in 1980 to less
than 4 per cent by 1983.[8]

In contrast to the absence of compelling evidence to indicate an economic
effect of the EMS, national political leaders have found ways to enhance their
autonomy through a political effect. The corollary of political leaders' investment in committing themselves to maintaining the parity of their currency, is
that there is public support for the European project in many countries. It is this
combination which permits the strategies of scapegoating and legitimisation of
policy by reference to European objectives. Here it is not that the commitment at
European level makes a policy target technically easier to achieve, but that it
makes it politically easier to pursue: national political leaders blame policy
choices at the European level for, or use pro-European arguments to legitimise,
policies which are unpopular at home. They may in fact have been instrumental
in forming the European policy, or that policy may in fact not be ultimately
binding. Nevertheless, such tactics serve to make more palatable a policy which
would otherwise be difficult to implement and hence have the effect of
enhancing the autonomy of the national executives concerned.

Thus, we feel, membership of the EMS brings no detectable credibility
benefit, nor does it in itself reduce inflation substantially in any other way.[9] Nor
does it in fact offer much of a constraint on policy. What it does do is offer
politicians an opportunity to stake political capital on maintaining the parity.

And having encouraged a broadly Europhile public to think of the parity as representative of a commitment to Europe, it facilitates the pursuit of policy objectives which (it is hoped) make the maintenance of the parity possible.

Such an approach has been particularly apparent in the case of Italy. Dyson and Featherstone (1996) show that the Italian government throughout the 1980s used the constraints imposed by the European level as a way of justifying their anti-inflationary crusade. Moreover, the Maastricht criteria are being used in a similar way. In the same vein, the introduction of the so-called Euro-tax has been justified as being necessary to keep Italy within the core group of EU members. Along the same lines, Mitterrand in 1983 transformed what could have appeared as a humiliating defeat for the socialist economic policy of Keynesian expansion into a triumph achieved in the name of Europe. Indeed, throughout the 1980s, as Reland points out, Europe provided a justification for unpopular economic policies. Moreover, the firm support for Europe displayed by the Socialist administration not only earned the tacit support of many UDF members, but also rallied business and administrative elites to the President's cause. Clearly, such an approach depends on a substantial degree of public support for Europe. Similar attempts by the Conservative government in Britain to justify VAT on domestic fuel did little to endear it to the British people!

Another tactic employed by national political leaders to increase their autonomy has been to use integration as a way of disguising the nature of, and insulating policy from, the domestic audience. Artis argues that EMS membership represented a useful indirect method of targeting inflation at a time when to do so in a more direct and explicit way would have been politically very difficult: the battle against inflation was thus made less controversial than it would otherwise have been. Gregory and Weiserbs show that one of the welcome side-effects of the early period of the ERM was to render exchange rate realignments routine and purely technical episodes, and hence insulate them from sectional strife at home. This of course required a prior commitment to the maintenance of the system, even at the cost of accepting occasional mildly embarrassing devaluations.[10] Europe thus briefly worked in such a way as to de-politicise and render purely technical certain aspects of macroeconomic management, thereby partly removing them from the realm of domestic political debate.

However, events over the last few years have clearly illustrated the limits of the ability of national officials to use Europe as a means of overcoming domestic pressures. One effect of EU macroeconomic policy has been to foster political resistance to it in several of the member states and even, in some cases, to partially reshape the political landscape, as evidenced by the divisions within the British Conservative Party (and its Labour counterpart); by the departure of the Communists from the Government majority in Italy and by the creation of the D-mark Party in Germany. Increased political and public ambivalence in the face of EU macroeconomic initiatives have in turn limited the degree to which states can use Europe to legitimise policies. There has, for instance, been a marked tendency on the part of the French government to claim that the painful

179

fiscal retrenchment measures currently being taken would be necessary even in the absence of the convergence criteria.[11]

Turning to fiscal policy, the EMS arrangements still left national governments with substantial room for manoeuvre. At a microeconomic level, fiscal harmonisation was usually treated as a separate issue from monetary integration. This created the opportunity, as described by Gregory and Weiserbs, for the Belgian government to attempt an 'ersatz devaluation' – the so-called 'Maribel operation' – based on the same principals as the 'ersatz revaluation' of the D-mark in 1968 (Emminger 1977) although of course not explicitly based on taxing trade. Such creative use of domestic taxation policy to mimic exchange rate realignment has of course become much harder because of subsequent alterations to the regulations governing VAT. In the future it seems likely that the single market and consequent removal of restrictions on intra-EU trade, as much as explicit legislation, will increasingly constrain national fiscal policy. Harrop, for instance, expresses doubts as to whether the United Kingdom can maintain higher excise duties on beer, wine and spirits given the ability of consumers to purchase these goods more cheaply abroad.

A direct impact on the macroeconomic side of fiscal policy awaited the Maastricht Treaty, at which point significant effects are quickly observed. The desire to meet the convergence criteria has led some countries to adopt drastic measures, the 'Euro-tax' in Italy being perhaps the clearest example, but the remarkable German dispute over gold valuations in May 1997 illustrated that no state was immune. Italy in fact has been forced to confront one of the side-effects of the battle against inflation waged in the 1980s – the grave debt imbalances of the Italian state. Similarly, the scale of French austerity plans cannot be explained without reference to the perceived need to form part of the first group of states to enter EMU. The increased impact of EU strictures was in part due to a change in European-level strategy for ensuring policy convergence. As Harrop points out, the Maastricht criteria insist not simply on a convergence of economic policies but also of economic performance, with emphasis on ex-ante surveillance.[12]

Finally, it should be recognised that the effects of integration did not spring solely from the monetary elements of EU policies. Hence, as Harrop points out, the expansion of trade which has accompanied the development of integration has enhanced economic interdependence between the member states, rendering national macroeconomic policy less effective. Similarly, as Artis argues, the shifting direction of British trade patterns increased the attraction of tying the pound to a D-mark rather than a dollar 'pole'.

Nor is it only the convergence criteria that are pressuring states to reform their fiscal policies. As Harrop also points out, the receipt of financial support from Cohesion funds is conditional on the recipient state pursuing a programme of economic convergence so as to prepare for EMU. Transfers from the fund are made only on condition that the budget deficit of the state in question remains within acceptable bounds, and cease if it is felt to have taken insufficient measures to eliminate an excessive deficit.

The EU has also had an impact on aspects of the policy-making process within member states – for example, the workings of the Common External Tariff have diluted the influence of national protectionist groups. Perhaps the most obvious of these kinds of effects is the enhanced role of central banks, which is at least in part an outcome of European integration. The most profound change stemmed from the Maastricht Treaty's requirement of central bank independence, which has certainly influenced developments in France and Italy and perhaps also the UK. Reland makes the importance of this clear when discussing the assertive line taken by the newly independent Banque de France.

Whilst the terms of the Treaty certainly affected policy making in this way, it should be remembered that states enjoyed leeway in transposing Treaty stipulations into national arrangements. For instance, whilst the central aim of the European Central Bank is, unequivocally, the pursuit of price stability (Maastricht Treaty, Article 105), the statute granting independence to the Banque de France stipulates that this institution must, certainly, aim to ensure price stability, but only 'within the framework of the general economic policy of the Government' (Taylor 1995: 113–15). It is not the case, moreover, that European-level arrangements have consistently placed pressure on member states to allow more independence to their central banks. As Artis points out in his chapter, British membership of the ERM was seen as contributing to effective maintenance of low inflation by means of the credibility effects of association with a stable currency zone – thereby mitigating the need to confer greater independence on the Bank of England, which according to the view in question, might have represented another possible way of increasing policy credibility.

Finally, there are other ways in which the relative influence of actors within the state and their ability to influence state policies and preferences can be altered. Reland points out that the reforms of the French financial market carried out during the 1980s increased the need for rapid and knowledgeable interventions in the financial markets and for adjustments of interest rates, hence empowering the Banque de France and transferring more policy autonomy to it at the expense of the political authorities.

National variations

Whilst the foregoing reveals some areas in which the EU has directly limited national autonomy, what is perhaps most striking about the findings is the limited number of such cases. It is doubtless tempting to believe the rhetoric utilised by politicians either to criticise the unhappy effects of EU constraints, or to hide behind such supposed constraints in order to justify unpopular policies. This is so not least because on the surface there appears to be a broad convergence of national macroeconomic policies in western Europe around the orthodoxy adopted by the Union in the early 1990s. Yet such appearances can be deceptive.

A perusal of the chapters in this volume reveals that in many cases EU impact was neither as far-reaching nor as uniform as might at first appear.

The clear picture to emerge from the chapters in this book is that EU impact varies greatly between the member states. Germany, for instance, stands out as a country which has ultimately sacrificed relatively little in the way of autonomy. Indeed, although the Bundesbank initially feared that an obligation to intervene in foreign exchange markets in support of weak currencies would limit its ability to achieve price stability at home, it is arguable that German autonomy has been increased by the development of the EMS. Insofar as it led to the adoption of German policy preferences by the other countries, the EMS has meant that they have resisted devaluation, thereby partially protecting German industry from the loss of competitiveness that follows from a rising D-mark. On the other hand, it could be argued that the reluctance of the others to permit an upward revaluation of the D-mark after German unification limited the Bundesbank's ability to control inflation through appreciation of the currency.

In the British case, as Artis points out, EU institutions and policies had very little impact on national policy. Indeed, close attention to this case shows that one must be careful to distinguish EU-inspired convergence from alternative explanations of national policy. Whilst the United Kingdom did in fact adopt policies such as the liberalisation of capital movements, the centrality of the fight against inflation, and a supply-side ideology very much in keeping with the economic rationale behind EMU, it did so for its own reasons. In contrast to Germany and the United Kingdom, EC/EU action has certainly affected both French and Italian Governments. Whether or not it is the case that budget deficits need to be brought down in the face of global financial markets and their contemporary power, it is incontestable that the determination with which these countries have attempted to bring this about is only explicable in terms of the desire to qualify for stage three of EMU.

However, one should be careful, despite appearances, not to exaggerate this impact. There is now a widespread belief that the high level of intra-EU trade makes the control of inflation a priority, and controlling debt is increasingly a goal shared by governments, irrespective of the Maastricht constraint. According to Reland, the development of the *franc fort* policy stemmed from a desperate desire to maintain credibility and preserve long-term interest rates at manageable levels, rather than simply from the constraints of ERM. It is this, not the constraints of the system, that led France to turn down the German offer of a realignment prior to the currency speculation of 1992–3, and also later not to allow the franc permanently to depreciate once rules of the EMS permitted this, with the widening of the bands of fluctuation in August 1993.

FUTURE POSSIBILITIES: THE IMPLICATIONS OF
EMU

Clearly, prediction is a hazardous exercise. In the case of the possible effects of EMU on the EU member states, it is particularly so for two reasons. First, great uncertainty exists as to which countries will participate in the first stage of EMU. Certain of the criteria – notably the conditions concerning a deficit and debt-to-GDP ratios – may be interpreted flexibly, implying that countries whose economies have not reached the levels of convergence which the negotiators at Maastricht felt to be appropriate could still join the Monetary Union. Even Theo Waigel, Germany's Finance Minister, has retreated from his previously rigid stance that countries that hope to qualify must reach the public deficit target prior to doing so (*Financial Times*, 7 April 1997). Notwithstanding doubts about the rationale of the criteria, allowing non-convergent economies to participate brings risks of its own. It raises the possibility of conflict over policy within EMU and creates a danger of the positions of the overindebted becoming unsustainable. The inclusion of any such countries may also raise the spectre of jeopardising investor confidence, leading to an unpredictable response by a credibility-hungry European Central Bank.

The prospect of an EMU from which certain states are either excluded or choose to exclude themselves, raises questions concerning the relationship between participants and non-participants. There has been much conjecture about this, though little is clear. What can be said is that the issue has raised fears among probable non-members of the first round of participants – notably Britain – concerning the implications of exclusion for inward investment. On the other hand, probable participants have already started to voice their concern lest those states outside the single currency will be in a position to use competitive devaluation to achieve competitive advantage, presumably attracting additional inward investment. All that can be said with any degree of certainty is that it is striking, given the amount of time and effort devoted to other aspects of the EMU project, and the huge amount of detail in the Treaty concerning precise levels of inflation and so on necessary to qualify, that so little attention appears to have been devoted to this crucial issue.[13]

The second area of uncertainty concerns the commitment (or lack thereof) of prospective EMU participant countries to the economic orthodoxy espoused in the Maastricht Treaty. It is clear that most, if not all member states have taken steps to try to ensure compliance with the convergence criteria (even if some such measures are clearly one-off steps to improve immediate fiscal positions). However, once states have qualified there is a possibility that they will attempt to rewrite the rule book, undermining the strong commitment of the arrangements to price stability and perhaps also to the independence of the European Central Bank. It is not difficult, for instance, to find officials in the French Finance Ministry who, off the record, will support this course of action. Tensions within EMU, and growing dissatisfaction with the economic philosophy underpinning it, in fact appear probable. Perhaps surprisingly, given the notorious difficulty of finding common positions between economists, the contributors to this volume who were asked to deal with the likely effects of EMU seem agreed that these could well be negative.[14]

In the first place, it is far from clear that the criteria will suffice to indicate convergence. Boltho makes explicit the case for a measure of unemployment as an additional criterion. The benefit of this is that it might identify the countries which are at a similar cyclical point, thus allowing the Monetary Union at least to begin with common policy interests. In a sense, the budget deficit criterion might have done this, if meeting the criteria had not become an end in itself, since an enlarged budget deficit would normally be a sign of recession. But of course, it is clear that countries are now engaged in pursuing fiscal policies largely unrelated to their cyclical position.

These doubts can only be enlarged by the criticisms of the contributors to the effect that the provisions of the Treaty create a deflationary bias and thereby threaten calamitous consequences for employment. Boltho, arguing that much of Europe's unemployment today could be eliminated by appropriately expansionary fiscal policy; Gregory and Weiserbs' concerns that the so-called 'Growth and Stability Pact' could create serious problems in the event of recession; and Allsopp's analysis of the private sector behaviour accompanying the poor fiscal position all point in the same direction.

If Europe starts with high levels of unemployment, which are then worsened by unforeseen events, so that a state already close to its borrowing ceiling is forced to take deflationary fiscal action, it will exacerbate income reduction and hence deepen recession. Political tensions will arise as deflationary pressures are felt most severely in countries close to their debt ceilings. As Gregory and Weiserbs point out, this, at the least, contravenes Article 1 of the Treaty aimed at raising community-wide living standards. It also runs the risk of fatally undermining the notion that a popular commitment to Europe can be encouraged by functional integration – in this case the reverse is more likely.

Indeed, one can take this further. The 'Growth and Stability Pact', as agreed at Noordwijk in April 1997, calls for fines on states that continue to run excessive deficits. These sums will, after a certain time period, be transferred to those states which remain within the deficit parameters laid down in the Pact, providing a fiscal stimulus for the latter whilst exacerbating the problems of the former. Although the budgetary difficulties likely to be encountered by a state faced with financing a fine when already overborrowing have been noted, a less noted problem is that the transfer from one country to the rest ultimately requires an improvement in the fined country's current account of the balance of payments. In so far as this is achieved through an increase in exports, that requires an improvement in competitiveness. Since that cannot be achieved through devaluation, it is likely to require a fall in the wage relative to other countries. Clearly, this means the problems of the fined country go well beyond politically unpopular fiscal measures. The stringencies of the stability pact do nothing to correct the fundamental causes of the European fiscal deterioration. As Allsopp argues, that would require an increase in investment. Yet it hardly seems that increasing unemployment and fines on the most recessionary countries represent a move in that direction.

One escape route could be to think in terms of a European-level fiscal policy that would remove from the members the need for fiscal stabilisation. The logic here is that European-level problems clearly require European-level solutions. This has been advocated, for example by Reboud (1995) among others. Allsopp, on the other hand, argues that a decentralised policy, properly conducted and coordinated, would be preferable to a centralised one, but still, if that is now barred by the Stability Pact, a centralised one is better than nothing, as is clearly the message of Gregory and Weiserbs.

However, at present those instruments that can provide fiscal support to states, such as the European Investment Bank and the New Community Instrument, provide only relatively small sums. Moreover, the way the EU budget works is inherently pro-cyclical – as it cannot run deficits and its spending ceilings are expressed as percentage of Community GDP. It is not clear how this problem will be resolved.

In another direction, many of the advocates of EMU claim that a European single currency will help to increase the autonomy of the European states by allowing them collectively to do what individually they cannot. The chapters on both Germany and France claim that size of the internal European financial market and the significance of the Euro relative to individual national currencies in world markets will give Europeans increased weight in international economic dealings. In particular (and this is a common argument in France), many feel that the Euro will compete with the dollar for the place as the world's leading currency for investors. As a result, some claim Europe will benefit from enhanced prestige and political power in international relations, allowing Europeans to combat the expanding influence of American-style capitalism. In so far as the Euro displaces the dollar as a reserve currency there is a tangible gain in seigniorage as well.

It is hard to find compelling evidence either way on the likely significance of such factors. However, two notes of caution should be sounded. First, we should again bear in mind the fact that the effects of EMU will not be the same for all states. Germany already possesses a highly respected international currency. Second, it is not at all clear that EMU will, as many seem to hope, increase the ability of Europe to defend what some choose to call a 'European social model'. Recent bitter arguments concerning the phenomenon known as 'social dumping' have cast into sharp relief the constraints upon west European states hoping to impose costs on businesses to fund their welfare states.[15] One possible impact of a single currency will be to make such business relocations less costly, by removing currency transfer charges – a fear that has been widely expressed following the decision taken by Renault in 1997 to lay off several thousand workers in Belgium.

EXPLAINING EU IMPACT

What lessons can we draw about ways the EU influences state autonomy? Perhaps the first and clearest is that this volume has (as have the two before it) pointed to the dangers of attempting to generalise about EU impact. This has varied over time, between countries and between different aspects of macroeconomic policy. State autonomy has been increased, decreased and left unaffected. The EU has nullified the effect of other pressures, has reinforced them, or has failed to have an effect on them. Such other factors – the ideological preferences of governments, the pressures of internationalised capital markets and so on – themselves partially explain why EU impact has been so patchy. Policy making has been affected more in some states than in others. The reactions of private actors have changed, but to differing degrees in different states.

National differences

How then can we account for these differences? One important explanation is the differences between the member states themselves. Boltho points to three which appear particularly important: the relative openness of their economies, their economic structures and their economic preferences. The relative openness of the economies of the member states is important in that the more open an economy is, the less the loss of the exchange rate instrument will be felt. However, there is a wide degree of divergence between the extremes of, for instance Luxembourg on the one hand, and more closed economies on the other, implying varying degrees of impact associated with the renunciation of exchange rates as a tool of macroeconomic management.

Member-state preferences have both converged and diverged in the years since the creation of the Common Market. During the 1950s and 1960s, a broad consensus existed over the role of macroeconomic policy. All member states could agree with Article 2 of the Rome Treaty, which defined the goal of the EEC as being to bring about 'a harmonious development of economic activities, a continuous and balanced expansion, an increase in stability and accelerated raising of the standard of living'. The crisis of the 1970s led to increasing divergences. By the mid-1980s and most explicitly in the Maastricht Treaty, a new orthodoxy was apparent at the European level.

However, this new economic philosophy was not adopted by all states to the same extent, and the degree of divergence from the philosophy of the Treaty (and indeed of the principles underpinning the ERM) represented a crucial determinant of their impact at national level. Hence, EC/EU impact on Germany was limited, whilst France and Italy found traditional policy preferences under pressure, with the French Socialist government's early commitment to the fight against unemployment being particularly constrained within the confines of the anti-inflationary ERM. British priorities coincided to a large extent with European-level choices: exchange controls were removed prior to the

EC decision to do so; Britain has also, ironically, of its own volition, adopted most of the assumptions of the EMU project, including especially the primacy of monetary policy over fiscal policy in economic management.

It should be clear that national policy preferences are not immutable. The move from strategies targeting growth and full employment to the price stability fetishism of contemporary EU policy is a case in point. Nor is there any particular reason to expect preferences not to change again. Those who now preach the doctrine of price stability and supply-side economics as a panacea would do well to remember that at the end of the 1960s, economists were, in a very similar way, announcing that Keynesianism represented a recipe for continued growth and prosperity. It is not inconceivable that, given the steady rise of unemployment in contemporary western Europe, even the economic preferences of states committed to the fight against inflation, such as Germany, will begin to alter under the political pressure of an increasing number of jobless.

Finally, Boltho points to divergent economic structures in the member states as the third national-level variable that can explain differential EU impact. Such differences need not be macroeconomic. For instance, the relative effectiveness of national labour markets will condition the impact of European macroeconomic arrangements on unemployment. Other important differences between states are more macroeconomic in character. The absence of sizeable French pension funds entails a high dependence on foreign capital, and creates difficulties for the French firms in raising capital. This increases the constraint implied by stable parities and capital liberalisation, increasing the impact of Europe on state autonomy. Thus French governments have been forced to maintain high interest rate levels in order to attract and to keep foreign capital. Interest rates themselves are of differing importance across the member states. In France, long-term rates are of crucial importance, as a result of the scale of public borrowing (see Boltho, this volume, note 5). In contrast, as the majority of French mortgages are fixed-rate, short-term interest rates do not have the same political and economic significance as they do, for instance, in Britain. Such differences will probably persist, at least in the medium term, reinforcing the arguments presented in the second part of the book concerning the possibility of asymmetric reactions to economic shocks.[16]

Finally, of course, there have been differences in the extent to which it has been useful to governments to present policies as being necessitated by European decisions. This has hardly been possible in Britain, but has been common in Italy – with the difference easily accounted for by the different public attitudes to integration. Together with this, there have been differences in the degree to which governments – and indeed individual politicians – have found it tactically useful to tie their own hands by making public commitments to particular exchange rates. We tend to view this as a contingent matter depending on the way that policy happened to evolve in different countries. In this case, perhaps the single clearest example was the British government's attempt to assure the foreign exchange markets that there would be no devaluation by constantly referring to the ERM as the centrepiece of policy.

European-level factors

The second broad area of explanation concerns the European level. One striking aspect of European macroeconomic policy is that membership has not been, and will not be, inclusive. Not all the member states participated in either the Snake or the ERM for their entire lives. Britain and Denmark negotiated opt-outs to the EMU sections of the EU, Britain during the Maastricht IGC itself, Denmark at the Edinburgh summit of 1992. Thus EU impact is differentiated across the member states because the EU provisions that apply to each member state are themselves different. Moreover, it is important to remember that non-participation can happen in one of two ways: either through choice, or through non-qualification. In the former case, states may suffer no consequences in terms of autonomy if they choose simply to ignore EU provisions that do not formally affect them.[17] In the latter, states may willingly alter their policies to try to comply with the convergence criteria but, in failing to meet them, ultimately fail to reap the rewards in terms of increased control over European-level policy.

A second factor relates to decision making at the European level. Given the fact that the effects of recent EU policy have been (and promise to continue to be) so asymmetrically distributed amongst the member states, this raises the question of why the member states agreed to the Maastricht provisions on EMU. The answer perhaps lies in the unequal influence wielded by the member states during the IGC negotiations that culminated in the signing of the Treaty. Certainly, Treaty revisions within the EU must be approved unanimously, which provides member states with a large amount of bargaining leverage should they simply refuse to agree to a provision. Yet despite this, some states have more ability to shape negotiating outcomes, especially if they can use a credible threat of non-agreement (Moravcsik 1993: 499–500).

It is hard to imagine a more clear-cut case of this phenomenon than macroeconomic cooperation. For Germany, the ERM, as it turned out, provided the advantages of stable exchange rates along with the continued ability of the Bundesbank to determine policy in accordance with Germany's own interests. As for its partners, they were placed in a position of tying their currencies to the D-mark whilst enjoying no control over the broad parameters of policy laid down by the Bundesbank. Faced with the asymmetries of the ERM, France and Italy in particular had attempted, during the course of the 1980s, to reform the system. That monetary union represented a way of counteracting what was perceived as undue German influence within the ERM became clear after the Basle-Nyborg agreement of 1987 when French Finance Minister Edouard Balladur called, to all intents and purpose, for EMU. He was supported in this by his Italian counterpart, Amato. As one observer has phrased it, for Amato 'the political cost of an "agreed loss of sovereignty" . . . was preferable to the unilateral loss of autonomy to Germany that existed in the EMS and the economic costs suffered in that system' (Cameron 1995: 46).

A German refusal to agree to EMU therefore represented a serious threat. As a result, the Maastricht negotiations over EMU represented a clear case where Germany enjoyed more bargaining leverage than its partners. As Tsoukalis has neatly put it:

> A monetary union without Germany makes no sense; and Germany will not have a monetary union unless it is on its own terms. Until now this has been the bottom line; and it has been recognised as such by the other countries.
>
> (Tsoukalis 1997: 171)

Germany thus managed to dominate the negotiations and to achieve agreement on a monetary Union that conformed to its own policy preferences (*Financial Times*, 30 October 1991). And, as Tsoukalis further argues, Germany's position of power continued to be in evidence even after the completion of the IGC, in decisions concerning, for instance, the choice of Frankfurt as location for the European Monetary Institute (precursor of the ECB) and the timetable for the introduction of a single currency, as well as the name of that currency.[18] Germany, of course, did not simply impose its own conditions on its partners; in particular it is clear that there was a widespread acceptance of much of the 'German model' of monetary policy. Nevertheless, it is clear that certain states enjoy more influence than others over European policy developments, allowing them to shape these according to their own policy preferences.

It is important, however, not to over-emphasise the notion of rational governments using and shaping integration in the pursuit of well defined ends. One reason why some governments have struggled to control the impact of integration is that they have not been the only actors involved in the process of shaping it. Hence former British Chancellor Nigel Lawson claimed that it was because of pressure from Delors and against the wishes of Britain and Germany that the Luxembourg Presidency put references to EMU in the Single European Act (Lawson 1992: 890–4). Equally it is clear that central bankers have generally been happy to take the opportunities offered by the monetary integration process to promote technocratic solutions to monetary problems, and thereby also their own status.

A further explanation of EU impact concerns unintended consequences: member states may sometimes fail to control the outcome of integration. The EMS is a case in point. As Artis points out, its statutes provided for 'elaborately symmetrical arrangements' and indeed the system was based on the assumption that adjustment burdens would be evenly shared between all participating states. Asymmetry, however, soon came to be one of the defining features of the system. Moreover, as pointed out above, weaker currency economies increasingly came to suffer from spiralling balance of trade deficits with EC partners. The Maastricht convergence criteria were presumably intended by Germany to ensure that states whose economic situations might threaten the stability of a future single currency would not join a monetary union. The fact that, at the time of writing, Germany may fail to qualify, whilst Spain and even Italy may do so, is illustrative of German inability to control the process, despite having dominated that of drawing up the rules of the game.

A related weakness of a rational actor approach is that it can often fail to look beyond narrow economic cost-benefit calculations to other reasons that explain the willingness of states to accept costs or constraints imposed at European level. In the 1970s, both France and Italy pulled out of the Snake when the policy priorities of European arrangements conflicted with their own. How, then, do we explain why member states were willing to put up with the far greater constraints implied by convergence and a putative EMU? Partly, as mentioned above, the explanation lies in a desire on the part of Germany's partners to gain a degree of control, via a European central bank, over monetary policy. Yet this does not answer the question as to why withdrawal was chosen in the 1970s but not the 1990s.

The fact is that, in certain instances, states accept integration, even if this involves certain costs in terms of autonomy, simply in order to further integration. That is to say, integration does not simply alter the ability of governments to put into practice their policy preferences, but can become such a preference in itself. Thus drastic Italian fiscal retrenchment reflects a desire on the part of that country to be involved in the process of monetary union. The French have demonstrated something akin to a desperation, since the end of the Cold War, to limit German autonomy, often through ambitious integrative schemes. In the German case, it appears on the surface as if it has little to gain by sharing control over macroeconomic policy within a possible monetary union, when the asymmetry of the ERM appears to have served it well. Here again a purely economic, rational cost-benefit analysis would be of little help. It is clear that, for Germany's present Chancellor at least, Economic and Monetary Union is necessary as a way of furthering integration, a matter, as he put it, of 'war and peace in the 21st century' (*Financial Times*, 19 October 1995). One reason why Germany has decided to pursue EMU is because of a desire to promote integration. In some instances, therefore, European effects on national policy are accepted in order to ensure the continued progress of integration.

CONCLUSIONS

The patchy picture painted in this volume of EU impact on national policy and policy making shows the difficulty of generalisation. It was pointed out in the conclusion to the volume on industrial policy that the nature of the policy sector involved is one of the crucial determinants of the scope and scale of impact of the European Union on member states. What this book has shown is the fact that the characteristics of a policy sector can vary. In some instances, macroeconomic policy comes across as highly technical; European involvement has, on occasion, served the task of rendering it even more so, insulating it from domestic pressures. On the other hand, EMU represents a very different case, in that although 'a highly technical issue and therefore understood by few, [it] was to go on to provide the highest political drama' (Dyson 1994: 1). European involvement in this case has dramatically and very publicly interacted with national policies and engendered heated public and political debate and often serious additional constraints, imposed by a divided political class or a public opinion increasingly attentive to European issues, on national executives.

What the findings of this volume have underlined is the fact that the impact of European integration is a crucial aspect not only of the study of integration but also of national economic policy. The economic fates of many countries in western Europe are tied to the EMU project. Similarly, it is no exaggeration to claim that the short- and medium-term future of European integration will rest on the progress or otherwise of monetary union. The future of European initiatives in this sector will in turn be determined by the scope and nature of its impact on its member states.

One thing which is clear is that one must be careful with the notions of autonomy and constraint. An essential characteristic of monetary integration is that states have opted into arrangements by which they are 'constrained' by the obligation to play by the rules. No technical limitation is created for their autonomy and legal impediments to their sovereignty have been less than complete. Nevertheless, having opted in, they have chosen to play by the rules, even if, as in the case of the French and Italian adherence to the EMS before 1983, playing by the letter of the rules was all they did – it is hard to see that either of these countries' economic policies was greatly affected by their membership of the EMS in that period. This has the appearance of integration for integration's sake. Noticeably, the British, also pursuing their own policy, opted not to be formally bound by an agreement to coordinate policy. Yet later, the governments of those same states – France and Italy – are presenting the rules of the EMS as delimiting the boundaries of acceptable economic policy within the country. Clearly, there was neither a formal nor a technical constraint after 1983 which was not already present before. So these governments first opted for a formal, but not meaningful loss of autonomy which they could have avoided; they then subsequently presented themselves as having relinquished more than they had. Later still, with the removal of capital controls (insofar as they were previously effective, at least) a degree of autonomy is genuinely sacrificed. But again, the claim that EMU will restore 'pooled' autonomy must be set against the voluntarism of the sacrifice of autonomy in the first place.

Thus when considering constraints on autonomy we need to make two distinctions. First, between the different kinds of constraint that the EU can impose, ranging from: those imposed against the wishes of one or more member states (for instance legislation adopted under Qualified Majority Voting) to those freely entered into by all participants (the EMS); from arrangements from which exit remains a serious possibility (again, the EMS comes to mind) to those where withdrawal would be far more problematic; from the removal of policy instruments from the national level, to the stipulation that certain laws must be enacted or policies implemented at that level, to simple agreements to coordinate policies. Whatever the political rhetoric that accompanies them, different arrangements impose different levels of actual constraint. Second, we must distinguish between the limits created by the rules themselves – actual constraints imposed by European-level rules or procedures – and those created by the interpretation members place on them – not necessarily, as one might suppose, to grant themselves extra freedoms, but rather in order further to limit themselves. These can be very much self-imposed constraints, although they are portrayed as emanating from the European level. In the macroeconomic sphere at least, these distinctions between the differing kinds of constraint Europe can impose, and between actual and rhetorically constructed constraints is of crucial importance. Correspondingly, the autonomy of states within the EU is not only dependent on the impact of Europe and the various tools at the disposal of the European level, but must also be understood in part as the autonomy they choose to grant themselves – individually – even once the 'rules of the game' have been determined.

NOTES

1 For example, it envisaged Community control over national budgets. See Tsoukalis 1977; or Gros and Thygesen (1992: 13).
2 The EMS and the ECU were only legally incorporated as part of the EC system with the ratification of the Single European Act.
3 See Gros and Thygesen (1992: 73–5). Their brief discussion is interesting in part for presenting the smaller countries as sometimes being happy with the terms of realignments proposed by the larger ones, but resenting their being presented as a *fait accompli*. Thus they evidently believed that they maintained sufficient autonomy to participate in the making of such decisions.
4 Padoa-Schioppa (1994) is one. His view has been criticised by Forder (1995).
5 For example, agents expect lower inflation so they agree lower wage increases. Inflation either falls as a direct consequence (a Keynesian story) or it lowers the unemployment cost of using monetary policy to reduce it (a monetarist one). There are many other possible such 'credibility effects', some of them harmful, but this one is popular in Europe.
6 Being overtaken in the mind of Chancellor Lamont by the realisation that the true way to improve credibility is to target inflation directly, shortly after September 1992.
7 See for example Gros and Thygesen (1992: Chapter 4) or Dornbusch 1989.
8 Data from Artis and Lewis (1991: 74). No wholly convincing argument is likely to be available since one cannot control for other factors which affect inflation in order to identify the impact of the ERM. There are no unambiguously correct measures of the tightness of monetary or fiscal policy, or of the militancy of unions. Even measuring the sensitivity of various countries – in and out of the ERM – to cost-push impulses from abroad represents a formidable challenge. The basic point is that the period when ERM inflation rates fell is a period when world inflation rates fell.
9 To the extent that it restrains the fall of the currencies of the higher-inflation countries, it promotes disinflation there, but of course, it is pro-inflationary in the other countries where currencies have had their rise constrained. Even in the high-inflation

countries this effect must be set against the possibility that, absent the EMS, those countries would pursue a determined enough policy to cause an appreciation, as occurred in Britain in the early Thatcher period.

10 Only mild, because at that stage the politicians did not choose to stake political capital on their maintenance.

11 'Let's first of all take on board the fact that it isn't Europe which is imposing constraints on our economic policy. With or without the single currency, France has to fight the deficits' (Chirac 1996).

12 Indeed, one could go one step further. Recent doubts among the northern states concerning the desirability of Italian entry into the first stage of EMU reveal that not only is performance being measured, but so too are preferences, given the emphasis currently being placed on 'sustainable convergence' (*European Voice*, 10–16 April 1997). The issue of changing national preferences and the existence or absence of broad convergence of these preferences around the economic philosophy of the TEU is a subject we will return to later.

13 Although there are, of course, other equally puzzling gaps.

14 Alternatively, this may be what is technically known as a sample selection bias.

15 Clearly, decisions by companies as to where to locate take into account more than simply issues of government-imposed costs.

16 The structure and openness of economies affect policy preferences, and vice versa. Hence, whilst small and open economies are suited to certain economic policy choices such as low and stable inflation, larger, more closed economies may not be. The crucial point here is that a European-level economy may well be more like the latter than the former, raising the question as to whether the policy choices that have proved effective for countries with one kind of economic structure and open economies will necessarily prove appropriate to a regional, European economy. It seems clear that within a relatively closed economy such as a possible European one, the argument that low inflation is a prerequisite for external competitiveness loses much of its force given the relative unimportance of such external trade.

17 Ironically, as already pointed out, British policy would probably not have to alter too much even if Britain decides to participate in EMU.

18 As Thiel and Schroeder point out, the German Government did not want the new currency to have the name of ECU as this was associated in Germany with a weak currency.

BIBLIOGRAPHY

Artis, M. J. and Lewis, M. K. (1991) *Money in Britain*, Hemel Hempstead: Philip Allan.

Barro, R. and Gordon, D. (1983) 'Rules, discretion and reputation in a model of monetary policy', *Journal of Monetary Economics*, 21, 1.

Cameron, D. (1995) 'Transnational relations and the development of European economic and monetary union', in T. Risse-Kappen (ed.) *Bringing Transnational Relations Back in: Non-State Actors, Domestic Structures and International Institutions*, Cambridge: Cambridge University Press.

Chirac, J. (1996) 'For a European social model', *Libération*, 25 March 1996.

Dornbusch, R. (1989) 'Credibility, debt and unemployment: Ireland's failed stabilisation', *Economic Policy*, 8.

Dyson, K. (1994) *Elusive Union: The Process of Economic and Monetary Union in Europe*, London: Longman.

Dyson, K. and Featherstone, K. (1996) 'Italy and EMU as a "Vincolo Esterno" ': empowering the technocrats, transforming the state', *South European Society and Politics*, 1, 2, autumn 1996: 272–99.

Emminger, O. (1977) 'The DM in the conflict between internal and external equilibrium, 1948–75', *Princeton Essays in International Finance*, no. 122, Princeton NJ: Princeton University Press.

Forder, J. (1995) 'Is Europe ready for monetary union?', *Oxford International Review*, summer, 16–20.

Forder, J. and Oppenheimer, P. (1996) 'The fluctuating rationale of monetary union', in J. Hayward (ed) *Elitism, Populism and European Politics*, Oxford: Oxford University Press.

Giavazzi, F. and Pagano, M. (1988) 'The advantage of tying one's hands', *European Economic Review*, 32: 1055–82.

Goodman, J. B. and Pauly, L. W. (1993) 'The obsolescence of capital controls? Economic management in an age of global markets', *World Politics*, 46, 1, October, 50–82.

Gros, D. and Thygesen, N. (1992) *European Monetary Integration*, London: Longman.

Keynes, J. M. (1929) 'The German transfer problem', *Economic Journal*, 39, 1–7.

Lawson, N. (1992) *The View from No. 11*, London: Bantam.

Moravcsik, A. (1993) 'Preferences and power in the European Community: a liberal intergovernmentalist approach', *Journal of Common Market Studies*, 31, 4 December, 473–523.

Padoa-Schioppa, T. (1994) *The Road to Monetary Union*, Oxford: Oxford University Press.

Posen, A. (1998) 'Central bank independence and disinflationary credibility: a missing link?', *Oxford Economic Papers*, forthcoming.

Reboud, L. (1995) 'Politiques budgétaires et relance conjoncturelle?', in Y. Mény, P. Muller and J.-L. Quermonne (eds) *Politiques Publiques en Europe*, Paris: l'Harmattan.

Taylor, C. (1995) *EMU 2000? Prospects for European Monetary Union*, London: Royal Institute of International Affairs.

Tsoukalis, L. (1977) *The Politics and Economics of European Monetary Integration*, London: Allen & Unwin.

——(1997) *The New European Economy Revisited*, Oxford: Oxford University Press.

INDEX

accountability 20
acquisitions 95
added value 90
aggregates: credit 76; financial 72; money 76
agriculture 12, 22; additional revenue to finance 21; EU budgetary expenditure has revolved around 20; large numbers of workers moving from 47; levies 16; national aids to 14; share of output 61; *see also* CAP
aid 20
Allsopp, C. 6, 40, 184
Amato, Giuliano 127, 188
American Can 95
American-style capitalism 185
Andreotti, Giulio 63
appreciation 33–4, 64, 65, 67, 71; limited ability to control of inflation through 182; real 61, 74
arbitrage 162
Artis, M. J. 6, 134, 180, 189
assets 99; financial 163, 170; foreign 166; riskiness of 35
austerity 71, 85, 87, 88, 150, 180
Australia 52
Austria 20, 23, 77, 146, 147
automatic stabilisers 72, 157–60 *passim* 63, 165
autonomy 6, 28–44, 58, 89, 106, 186, 188, 190; budget 113; central bank 124; competing pressures on 2–4; constraints on 124; fiscal 52; governmental 85, 86, 93; increased 182; limited 181; loss of 176, 177, 188; nature of, in the monetary realm 105–7; policy 12, 63, 70, 85, 86, 88, 97, 109, 151;

possibilities for EU to enhance 4, 5; surrendered 107

backward regions 21, 150
balance of payments 11, 31, 78; crises 33; deficit 76, 164; deterioration 32; equilibria 175; help in the case of difficulties 23; large current deficit 74; protection of 32; strong 62; surplus 159, 164–8 *passim*, 170; weak 63
balance of power 128
Balkans 21
Balladur, Edouard 86, 99, 100, 101, 188
Baltic Republics 21
Bank of England 130, 181
Bank of Italy 63, 120, 124
Banking Act (France 1984) 91
banking sector 72, 90;
    compartmentalisation and specialisation 91; intermediation 92; need to maintain competitiveness 92; subjected to encadrement du crédit 93; *see also* central banks; commercial banks
Banque de France 90; CPM (Monetary Policy Council) 101, 102; independence 86, 100–2, 116, 181; more influence in monetary policy making 93; strengthened role 94
Barber, Sir Anthony 72
bargaining 13, 188, 189
Barre, Raymond 62, 71, 87, 90, 95
Barro, R 133
Basle-Nyborg Agreement (1987) 70, 188
Bayne, N. 33
'beggar-thy-neighbour' strategy 54
Belgium 23, 54, 77, 145, 185;
    exports/imports 13; fiscal policy 51;

113, 116; borrowing in own 39; crises 97; different, assets denominated in 35; fixed 77; floating 30, 77; hard 135; highly respected 185; international reserve 4; international substitution 135; key 107; misalignments 70; optimum 55, 144–8, 158, 159; overvalued 108; parallel 113; strong(er) 61, 66, 89, 109, 111, 115; weak(er) 61, 76, 107, 108, 110–11; *see also* appreciation; common currency; convertibility; depreciation; devaluation; EMS; EMU; pegs; revaluation; 'Snake'; single currency; stabilisation; stability; *also under various national currency units*
current account: deterioration 30, 31; equilibrium 32; excessive deficit on 38; external balance 166; surplus 166; Treasury bills 93
customs union 14
Czech Republic 76

De Boissieu, C. 92
debt 39, 51, 168, 169–71; attitudes and worries over 162; cumulative effect on 160; imbalances 123; international crisis 76; long-dated 99; new range of instruments 92; outstanding 52; ratio to GDP 53, 119, 125, 156, 183; reducing levels of 147; repayment 40, 99; stabilisation 125; structural transformation of 93; sustainability 40; third-world crisis 67
decentralisation 159–60, 169
decision-making 86, 188; ECB Council 107; independent 55; monetary 109; politicisation and bureaucratisation of 70
defence: common 20; policy 2
deflation 52, 59, 66, 71, 184; bias towards 53, 70; CPI 123; impact on unemployment 54; policies 12, 88; wage and price 54
De la Rosière (Banque de France governor) 101
Delors, Jacques 88, 189
'Delors Act' (1983) 91
Delors Committee Report (1989) 39, 49, 66, 75, 109, 111
demand: adverse 53; aggregate 148; contraction in 54; country-specific

change in 52; credit 72; domestic, increase in 97; excess 166; exogenous 53; export 165, 166, 167; fall in 31, 163; import 89; market 120; microeconomic shifts in 145; obligation to expand 32; stimulating 148, 164; *see also under following headings prefixed* 'demand'
demand management 162; Keynesian 45; potential use of monetary policy for 161; repudiation of 50
demand shocks 53, 54, 146–7, 159, 160; reversible 168
demand-side 69; policy instruments 56
Denmark 23, 146, 188; accession to EC membership 59; budgetary deficit 18; centralised labour markets 146; excise duties on beer, wine and spirits 16; indirect and direct taxes 15; inflation 25; Maastricht referendum 76–7, 123
depreciation 38, 59, 74, 78, 178, 182; asset 99; frequent 109
depressed regions 22
deregulation 50, 56; financial 90–5, 97
deutschmark 36, 59, 64, 70, 135, 136, 175; adverse effects of a rise in 24; anchor currency 49, 133; appreciation 65, 67, 71; complete domination by 97; dampening upvaluations of 61, 71; EMS dominated by 86; franc and 108; giving up 115; haven for capital flight 106; key currency 107; lira and 108, 123; lobbying against strength of 60; loss of competitiveness from rise in 182; nominal interest rate differentials and 78; pegging 1, 37, 64, 65, 72–3, 107, 133, 177; real appreciation of franc relative to 61; revaluation 23, 75, 76, 165, 182; reward to Germany for giving up 25; rival to the dollar 129, 130–1; 'shadowing' 72, 73, 162, 163; strongest currency within ERM 49; tying currencies to 180, 188; upward pressure 77; way to limit the power of 96
devaluation 23, 24, 25, 71, 88, 94, 184, 187; 'competitive' 38, 39, 54; 'ersatz' 180; frequent recourse to 87; monthly targets 74; need for 164; not desired 163; periodic 48; prospective candidates for 123; using fiscal policy to 'mimic' 51

INDEX

Trade) Uruguay Round 13; *see also*
WTO
Gaullists (France) 103
GDP (gross domestic product) 15, 20, 21,
170, 185; ceiling for deficit 114;
combined, member states 52; debt ratio
to 18, 53, 119, 125, 126, 156, 183;
exports and imports as percentage of
13; intra-EU trade in 144; M2 ratio to
120; national spending 19; per capita
23; real 75; *see also* France; Germany;
Italy
GDR *see* East Germany (former)
GEMU (German Economic and Monetary
Union) 165
Genscher, Hans-Dietrich 109
German inflation 30, 61, 95, 166, 187;
difficult to control 106; France's
differential with 89; low(er) 36, 48–9,
67, 97–8, 175; other participants'
economies and 70; rise on the eve of
unification 71; traditional concern 19
German unification 11, 76, 96, 135, 165,
182; boom following 45, 52; 'boost'
from 166; cost of 97; disruption to
development of EMS 54; fiscal impact
161; income transfers 23; prolonged
and intensified economic upswing 75;
resources needed for 24
Germany 87, 88, 96, 100, 147, 164;
balanced budgets 19; budgetary deficit
18, 39; countries increasingly
dependent on the economy 11;
cumulative surplus 176; currency
stability 95; current payments surplus
60; deflationary policy 12, 66, 71; D-
mark Party 115, 179; eastern Länder
19, 22, 76, 165–8 *passim*; EC/EU
impact limited 186; EMS 24, 30, 54,
86, 105–11 *passim*, 116; EMU 71, 105,
106, 107, 110, 111, 112–17, 188–9,
190; ERM 24, 98, 107, 165, 188; fiscal
policy 165–8; fiscal stimulus 32; French
monetary link with 24, 62; GDP 75,
165, 166, 167; gross debt-to-GDP ratio
18; interest rates 97, 99, 162, 163, 167;
monetary policy 6, 75, 89, 97, 105–18,
189; partnership between France and
60, 71, 110; policy preferences 189;
price stability 59, 63, 69, 107–10 *passim*,
113–15 *passim*; production costs
differential with France 94; production

structures 146; protectionism 12;
reflation 60, 65; shocks 167;
unemployment 75; VAT 15; war
reparations 41; *see also* Bundesbank;
deutschmark; East Germany (former);
GEMU; Genscher; German inflation;
German unification; Kohl; Schmidt;
Waigel
Giavazzi, F. 1, 49, 72, 177
Giovannini, A. 1
Giscard d'Estaing, Valéry 62, 71, 107
globalisation 97; side-effect 3–4
GNP (gross national product) 16;
budgetary expenditure rises more
slowly than 18; OPEC countries 59
gold 30, 66
Gold Standard 30
Goldstein, M. 40
goods: capital 89; collective 17;
domestically produced 40, 51; durable
51; manufactured 89; merit 20;
movement across borders 52; public 20;
tradeable 59, 121; traded 51
goods and services 74, 161
Gordon, D. 133
government spending 17
grants: cumulative 160; outright 19
Gray, J. 34
Greece 22, 48, 65, 146, 147; indirect taxes
15; monetary financing 17; no excise
duty on wine 16; VAT 15
Green Rate 61
Gregory, M. 5, 179, 180, 184
Group of Five 87, 135; *see also* France;
Germany; Japan; United Kingdom;
United States
Group of Seven 60, 135; *see also* Canada;
France; Germany; Italy; Japan; United
Kingdom; United States
Group of Three 135; *see also* Germany;
Japan; United States
growth 33, 59, 71, 89, 114, 121, 170;
aggregate 90; continued 187; credit 90;
employment-creating 87; Fordist model
87; good rates 23; lasting, strategy
aimed at 67; medium-term 98;
monetary 120; money supply 72;
output 166; projections 45; real wage
51; revived 171; slow 156; stimulating
12, 93, 145; threat to 157; trade a
major engine of 47; Treasury notes 93
'Growth and Stability Pact' 184

202

205

71; fiscal policy 51; intra-EU trade in GDP 144; protectionism 12
New Community Instrument (Ortoli Facility) 19, 185
Noordwijk 184
Nordlinger, E. 2
Norway 23, 76, 77, 124
NTBs (non-tariff barriers) 14, 15
numeraire 65

OATs (long-term treasury bonds, France) 93, 99
Objectives (EU structural funding) 22
OECD (Organisation for Economic Cooperation and Development) 60, 90, 92, 156, 164
Ohmae, K. 3
oil 69, 165; price increase 23, 45, 60, 88; shocks 32, 33, 36, 58, 67, 124; unspent revenues 59
OPEC countries 59, 69, 88
openness 144–5, 186
Oppenheimer, P. M. 30, 175
opt-outs 25, 176, 188
output 11, 17, 46, 47, 51; agricultural 61; increasing 37; lost 122, 133; oil, restrictions on 69; recovery of 76; reducing 34; share of international transactions in 144; threat to 59; weak growth 166
outsiders 13, 26
Oxford Economic Forecasting model 163

Padoan, P.-C. 63
Padoa-Schioppa, T. 38, 39
Pagano, M. 1, 49, 72, 177
Paris 92, 93, 98
parity 61, 63, 86, 94, 108, 177; defence of 175; D-mark, rather than ECU 73; EMS 176; ERM 71, 90; fixed 30, 48, 49, 162; high 72; maintaining 99, 179; multilateral 49; readjustment of 97; realignments 70, 75; small changes 77; stable 99; widening of bands 46; see also PPP
PAYE (pay as you earn) 15
Péchiney 95
pegs 23, 30, 47, 59, 61, 69, 133, 135; adjustable 77; Bundesbank hostility to 60; commitment to 134; D-mark 1, 37, 64, 65, 72–3, 107, 177; ECU 76; fixed

74; hard or soft 132; maintaining 77, 131; nominal 132; optimal 129; real 132; stationary 74; undeclared 72
pension funds 98, 187
performance see economic performance
Plaza Agreement (1985) 37
Poland 76
policy coordination: incentives for 175; international 5, 60; macroeconomic 1, 29–36, 96; monetary 25, 55
policy making 94, 101, 146, 186; constraints on 11, 124–8; European, politics of 29; government's autonomy in 93; joint 63; national 1, 4, 45–57
policy preferences 3, 147–52, 182, 190; national 2, 11, 186, 187, 189
political union 11
politics 29, 72, 109–11, 124, 127; 'domestic' 4
pollution 17
poor(er) states/regions 21, 22
Portugal 22, 48, 65, 147; devaluation 77; indirect taxes 15; inflation 74, 75; monetary financing 17; no excise duty on wine 16; VAT 15
pound (UK) see sterling
PPP (purchasing power parity) 164
price stability 30, 72, 107, 108, 110, 115, 187; commitment to 69; defending 114; early importation of 63; ECB aim 25, 181; obstructing the pursuit of 60; primacy of 113; restoration of 59; wide agreement on the importance of 148; worthwhile goal 109
prices 70, 73, 75, 87, 89; agricultural 61; asset 35; commodity 58, 69; consumer 123, 148; domestic 54, 74; greater flexibility 55–6; import 33, 49; intertemporal 163; less than perfectly flexible 52–3; movements 30; oil 23, 45, 60, 67, 88; pressures 121; producer 123; real estate 162; relative 51, 54; rising 74, 162; spiralling 124; sticky 53; three-month freeze 71; see also CPI; price stability
privatisation 20
procurement policies 14, 20
Prodi, Romano 127
production: changing patterns 47; distorting effect on 15; location of 52; structures 145, 146
productivity 94, 95, 123; gains 75;